YOU, INC.

YOU, INC.

A detailed escape route to being your own boss

PETER WEAVER

Dolphin Books
DOUBLEDAY & COMPANY, INC.,
Garden City, New York

ISBN 0-385-09895-2

Dolphin Edition: 1975. Originally published by Doubleday & Company, Inc., in 1973

DEDICATION

My father, Robert A. Weaver, once wrote a little book called *Up from Muttontown*. It told of his family's struggles with poverty in the early Pennsylvania oil field days. His mother and father always wanted to run a little wayside inn. And they did. When customers were scarce and the money ran out, they would work for somebody, temporarily, until they had enough funds to start another inn.

My father describes his father's philosophy of work this way:

"He told me once never to work for anyone else. If you're no good, he said, you'll be fired anyway. If you *are* good, your boss is making a profit on your work. Run a peanut stand if you have to, but whatever it is you're doing, be captain of your own boat."

I didn't pay attention to my father's advice when I started out to work. No good, red-blooded American boy pays much attention to his father's advice. Well, in the long run, he was right. It's to him, and my grandfather's spirit of freedom, that I dedicate this book.

P.W.

CONTENTS

INTRODUCTION   1

PART I   A LIFEBOAT

1   Why Leave?   9
2   Fears and Excuses   15
3   Out, Not Up   21
4   Finding Money   28
5   Finding Fringes   39
6   Your Own Corner   52

PART II   WHAT TO DO?

7   Creative Moonlighting   69
8   Ideas That Work   80
9   Patent Poker   96
10 Franchising: Instant Businesses   107

PART III   AGES AND STAGES

11 Free from Parents—Then What?   121
12 The Mangled Middle   137

13 Housewife Horrors   157
14 Senior Shock   175

PART IV THE FINAL BREAK

15 The Family Lawyer   195
16 Accountants, Bankers and Other
    Professional Help   210
17 Getting Started   224
18 Keeping Going   237

EPILOGUE: CAPITALIST COMMUNES
           VS. THE ESTABLISHMENT   259

CHECKLIST: SELECTED READING AND
            SOURCES OF HELP   285

INDEX   291

INTRODUCTION

A few years ago, I left a good-paying job with a national magazine to venture out into business for myself. Several friends thought I was "crazy." Even my family was nervous. But I had to do it.

After working for the establishment for more than twenty years I'd had it right up to here. I felt my ideas weren't getting out. I was being squelched. The series of bosses I had with three different companies weren't evil people. They were just doing their job, as they would always tell you each time another personal freedom was snipped away.

I began to think about the fact that other people in the company, the organization, the establishment—whatever you want to call it—were making decisions about my life and I didn't have much to say about it. I was told when I could go on vacation. When I could not. Which of my ideas were acceptable. Which were not.

I needn't go further into why I was restless, why I resented so many bosses telling me what to do. You've probably been through the same thing. If you haven't yet, you've probably heard the grim tale from friends or acquaintances.

For a while, I felt guilty. Maybe something was wrong with

me. I was getting good pay. I worked for a prestigious company. Others (poor fools) envied me. And, as I looked back, I realized I had eventually become restless and discontented in each of the previous companies where I had worked.

Nobody likes to admit that they're crazy or a malcontent, so I began to probe into my career to find the happiest moments. Without fail, the "highs" were the times when I had achieved something on my own, won an award or written something outside of the organization.

Early in my career, when I was particularly teed off with the way I was being bossed, I started up a little news column of my own. I was granted permission to do it since there was no conflict; I was going to write about Latin America, where I had once lived and worked and my boss wasn't interested in the place.

So it started. I called my little moonlighting business *Weaver Reports.* I opened a bank account to cover expenses and, hopefully, to receive checks from subscribers. I got several papers to buy the column, which I mailed out every two weeks or so. One chain of twenty-two newspapers bought the column and my name began to appear in a number of cities.

I didn't make much money, because the audience was limited. The general public wasn't all that interested in Latin America, Fidel Castro notwithstanding. Even so, my little bank account grew. But the main thing—more than the money—was the fact that my sanity was spared. I now had hope. I *could* do something on my own. Some day. My little business, *Weaver Reports,* carried me through rough times in the company where I worked.

Then I got another job. Salvation at last, I thought. I was given more freedom at first and learned a lot about setting up an office. I was in Washington. My bosses were in New York. Unfortunately, the relative freedom lasted only a couple of years and then I began to get sat on, little by little.

It really can't be helped, I guess, if you continue to work for somebody, to stay in the establishment and be bound tighter and tighter in the organizational mold. You get the comforts of being in the organization—steady pay, medical insurance, pension plan and all that. But, for these comforts, you have to give the organization most of your waking hours and, eventually, your life.

My wife, Vida, and I talked about it late one night after the children were in bed. We talked about all the bosses, all the crap. As we sat there, cross-legged on the bed, she recalled how happy I was, how happy we both were, when I was doing my sideline newspaper columns. I had let the little moonlighting business slide when I became taken up with my new job. I looked at an old checkbook with the bold (now, ironically pretentious) title on the checks: WEAVER REPORTS.

That's what I wanted. If only I could do something else on my own again with no bosses scowling over my shoulder. From that time on I plotted and planned. What would I do?

My work had taken me more and more into the problems companies were having with consumers and, of course, the problems consumers were having with companies. I had written about the mess in the repair business and the mess in medicine. I began to learn what manufacturers and others were doing to their customers and what the customers could do to defend themselves.

Maybe it would work, I thought. A consumer column for the general public. The time seemed ripe. Ralph Nader had publicly flayed General Motors, got away with it and was on his way. I started bouncing the idea off friends in the newspaper business. It took a year or so in the plotting stage (I even thought of a TV series). Finally, I mustered up enough funds and, more importantly, enough courage, to make the break.

I broke and ran. Escape beckoned and I ran without looking back for fear I would trip. The economy was beginning to stumble back into one of its periodic recessions. It wasn't the "right" time to go out on one's own. No time is "right." I ran scared and my family suffered. We cut expenses to the bone. I did part time magazine assignments to keep money coming in while my business was slowly building. I'm still running, and I'll never go back. I've made a lot of mistakes, but they're *my* mistakes, not some other dummy's mistakes. I've learned a lot and, if I could only do it over again, I think I could avoid some of the dumb moves I made.

In spite of the mistakes and the initial bad business conditions, I'm making it. My little business, Weaver Communications, Incorporated, aside from the nationally syndicated newspaper column, now supplies my own tapes for a syndicated radio show, produces a magazine column and provides a base for lecturing and teaching special journalism courses at a local university.

After seeing all this develop, some friends who were still struggling inside the walls of the establishment sidled up and began to ask questions. How did I do it? Some had fledgling ideas of their own and wondered what I thought about them. Could *they* make it too?

Readers of my syndicated consumer column also wrote in and asked questions about starting their own business. I had to field all kinds of questions from patents on through franchising. I dug out the answers. While teaching a journalism course at George Washington University, I had my eyes opened. A number of students desperately wanted to do something on their own, something "meaningful." I told them they needed to get "portable skills" so they could eventually do the work they wanted without depending on any single organization too much, or too long.

I found myself giving more and more advice on "how to break out." Someone suggested I do a book. "Put it all down like an escape plan," one student said. An "escape plan"? Maybe I could do it.

With the help of a student researcher, I combed the Library of Congress to see what had been written on getting out, on setting up your own business. There were a number of books. But mostly they were puerile, "gee whizz" sort of things with titles like *How You Can Make It Rich with Your Own Business.*

The advice often came out as jargonistic nonsense and the emphasis was all wrong. The concentration was on "making big money." Money isn't the point. You probably won't "make big money" if you go out on your own. But, you can make enough to live a good life. Actually, you probably *shouldn't* make big money. Because, if you do, you risk becoming engulfed again in an organization—your own organization.

So here it is. My "escape plan." I had lots of help from what seems to be a growing "brotherhood" of others who have escaped, who have started their own business. I'm going to mention them by name wherever possible. They helped me overcome my fear. Maybe I can help you overcome yours.

I purposely put the chapter on "Fears and Excuses" near the front of the book. Fear of the unknown, fear of failure, fear of facing up to the fact that your life is wasting away—these are the things that really keep most men and women from breaking out. It isn't the money. That's often just an excuse.

After the fears and how to handle them, I've marked out several turns on the escape plan that might help answer the question: What to do? Some successful ideas. Some sources. Then, later on, there are the special "Ages and Stages" people find themselves locked into. The young, the mangled middle-agers, the retired, the housewives.

Finally, on the escape plan, there's a break-off point when you have your own little office and you actually start running the place. You're the boss. If you ever get out and fly on your own, maybe we can get together some day and compare notes. Who knows? Maybe we can pull the burgeoning "brotherhood" of self-bossers into something more permanent, where we can share ideas, help others escape and even share some common expenses (legal, tax advice, group insurance). Until then, keep after it and—good luck.

Part I
A LIFEBOAT

1
WHY LEAVE?

Why should anyone shun the security of working inside an organization—company or government—for the insecurity of trying to make it alone on the outside?

It's usually the first question that those who still work for the establishment ask. Usually, they're trying to rationalize their own vague feelings of restlessness or unhappiness with the fact that they "know where the next paycheck is coming from" and they get all those "fringe benefits." They're taken care of from cradle to grave by the establishment. It may not be the greatest, they say, "but it's secure."

Is it secure? Today, maybe. But tomorrow? Ask some of those aerospace engineers and others who lost their jobs what it's like to be lulled into a false sense of security by all the money flowing from government contracts. Now you see it, now you don't. The government giveth, and the government taketh away. The flow stops and, suddenly, you're out on the street blinking in bewilderment.

If it isn't cutbacks in government spending, it's another recession or a merger. "Sorry, you know how it is . . . but we're phasing out your department." Yeah, you know how it is. You know that now you're out of a job and all those fancy medical plans, sick leaves and pensions don't mean a damn.

Then there's the problem of "human obsolescence." You may be plugging away at your job and suddenly realize "they're phasing me out." Why? Because the stuff they taught you back in high school or college is old hat. New techniques are needed and those young squirts they recently hired seem to know all the angles. Can't happen to me, you say? Hah! Listen to what Dr. James Schulz, Brandeis University economist, has to say:

"Technology is moving at a faster clip. They're now talking about engineers who become obsolete at age thirty-five. They say engineers burn out. Their education becomes outmoded by new technology. Some are shifted off into dead ends or, like burnt-out light bulbs, they're unscrewed and thrown out."

Dr. Schulz isn't the only one who speaks out against the dangers of getting unscrewed ("screwed" seems like a better word). Dr. Harry Levinson, industrial psychologist at Harvard and Boston University, says:

"It's dangerous to cling to an organization too long. Reductions in forces are happening every day. There's a built-in manipulation to make people obsolete. Some employees are automatically down-graded as they grow older to attract new talent at the front end."

Then, says Levinson, "there's the new-broom syndrome." By this he means a new boss who comes in, doesn't like the way you part your hair, and you're swept out.

The "security" of an established job, of working for an organization, is not all that secure. You've got to prepare yourself to be able to leave before the "unscrewing" begins. You've got to start making more of the decisions about your life and stop having them made for you by a series of bosses who always seem to say, "You know how it is," when they give you the shaft.

Says Levinson in his book *Executive Stress:*

"Mentally healthy people use their resources in their own behalf and in behalf of others . . . They are in charge of their activities, the activities are not in charge of them . . . If a man does not manage his own life, then it will be managed inadvertently by others . . . Your life is yours. You have to take charge of it, manage it, assume responsibility for it."

So far, we've talked primarily about the economic and technological reasons why you should, at least, seriously consider leaving an established job to head out on your own. There are even more important reasons for shunning the organizational way of life. A scientist might describe these reasons as "psychological." A humanist would describe them as "soul."

Every time they turn down one of your ideas without really considering it. Every time you're told what to do, what not to do and when to do it—your soul gets scarred and shrivels a little. Your intellectual growth withers. You can't even make your own mistakes. They make them for you.

This is what really got me. Without giving too much thought to it, people above me would dismiss a series of suggestions with a wave of the hand and would tell me "this isn't for us . . . you know how it is."

Peter Nagan, who now runs his own successful company, Newsletter Services, Inc. (which writes and publishes business newsletters), can sympathize. The same thing happened to him before he got out to start his own business. He says:

"When I was working for a big corporation, my immediate supervisor was a fellow who was competent enough but I felt he didn't have any God-given right to order my life. I'd present a carefully thought-out, deeply felt idea and—with a shrug—he'd just mow me down."

I guess what we're all grumbling about is our lack of freedom. For the somewhat dubious security the establishment offers, we have to give up much of our intellectual freedom. Humans —even animals—don't like giving up their freedom, so, in order to get you to do a lot of things you'd rather not do, organizations bribe you and keep raising the ante whenever you or your colleagues get uppity and threaten to leave. These bribes are sometimes labeled "raises," or "expense accounts," or even "free parking space."

So you stay on and wonder why you get an ulcer, growl at your family and friends or can't sleep nights. You don't like yourself. Nobody does when they have to accept a bribe. If this makes you unhappy, you've got lots of company. Listen to how labor expert Sam Zagoria, author of *Public Workers and Public Unions,* analyzes the current job scene:

"American workers—male and female, black and white, manual, clerical, technical and managerial, old and young— are being infected by a malaise . . . Some employers, jarred by lower productivity, higher absenteeism, occasional in-plant vandalism and even drug addiction, recognize that just below the surface is the fact that a growing number of employees see themselves engaged in joyless, dehumanizing chores."

Changing from one establishment job to another usually doesn't work. The bribe may be bigger. Working conditions may be easier to take at first. But, after a while, many of those "joyless, dehumanizing chores" seem to keep crawling back into your work week.

Sometimes you're lucky. You hit a really good job. You get a relatively free hand to do what you want. The boss is a prince and things look bright. "What, me worry?" you say. "I've got a deal . . . they're paying me to do what I like best." I hate to be a bore but things might not always be coming up roses. Remember those economic disasters? Whole industries, whole cities have been ravaged by the whims of government spending or some flip-flop in technology.

Even if you're in a job you love and the odds are against any economic upheaval, you should still consider making a side bet on a little business of your own that takes only part of your time.

"Starting a venture on the side," says Professor Richard Beckhard, Sloan School of Management, M.I.T., "will make you a better person where you're working." Beckhard ought to know. He started his own sideline consulting business and says it makes him a better teacher, helps him keep more in touch with the real world. He encourages self-satisfied management to become involved in outside projects to sharpen their skills, get a better perspective.

There's a great deal of satisfaction to be had in working on your own project outside the organization. It's like planting a seed, watering it and watching it grow. This relevancy of one's creative efforts often becomes blurred inside a large organization. Also, when you have your own project going and it's a success—not necessarily a big success—you gain confidence in yourself. This confidence is reflected in your work inside an organization. I know, I did better work after I started up my first sideline news columns. I was cooler. I was less dependent on the organization and a little more relaxed.

According to Dr. Levinson, "people need a wider variety of sources of gratification. You can't afford to have all your eggs in one basket. If you drop the basket, then you've got scrambled eggs."

A young man who's still on the inside working for a major corporation, cites his own experience:

"I found that I had more guts in meetings. When something was wrong, I would say so even if I knew it wasn't what my superiors wanted to hear." In a very real sense, this man's company is benefiting from the confidence he gained by starting up a little business outside its walls. Any organization benefits when it hears the truth and not just what some boss wants to hear.

Before we leave the "whys" of starting up your own little business, let's not forget that final blow everyone in all organizations must face. I call it the "final firing." They call it "retirement." You may be sublimely happy with your job. The days go by. Pretty soon the years go by and then they give you a nice little luncheon, a little gift, maybe, and wish you well in your new "leisure." Zapp! They cut you off. For many, this cutoff comes as an economic disaster. When you feverishly open up your Social Security and pension package, you find very little in it. For most employees retirement means a sudden, brutal drop in annual income.

Any good doctor will also tell you when a man or woman stops working, they often start going to pieces. Their children no longer depend on them. Now their organization no longer needs them. Somehow, little aches and pains seem to grow into serious illness.

If you have had something going for you on the outside, when you retire you can devote more time to it and make it grow. Your little business needs you. People who buy your product or services need you as do those who may be working for you.

So, if you're happy with the job you now have, look at a sideline business as sort of a "lifeboat." Even though the seas are calm and a captain has a big and powerful ship underneath him, he never sets sail unless he knows he has enough lifeboats and they're all in working order. He even conducts lifeboat "drills" to make sure that, if disaster strikes, he'll be ready for it.

You should do the same thing. Build a little business, a little lifeboat. Outfit it. Conduct periodic drills to make sure it will work right when, and if, you ever need it. You may even find it's more fun being in charge of your own lifeboat than it is being just another member of the ship's crew.

2

FEARS AND EXCUSES

Everybody has secret dreams about being his own boss. When you're trapped in your work, fantasies begin to form. You picture yourself running a restaurant, selling handmade toys or even writing a best seller that becomes a movie.

But the dreams usually fade along with the effect of those three martinis. There are always "reasons," usually excuses, why you can't think about breaking out on your own. Not now, anyway. You just moved into a new place and you need that steady income to make the payments. Then, there's the new car. And what about the kids' college fund and the medical insurance? You sink back. The trap closes again.

If only I had some extra money, you say, then I'd show 'em. Money, or lack of it, is your excuse. What about saving money? What about investing? What about working on some moonlighting deals to make extra money?

All this takes time, you say, somewhat defensively. Spending all day at the grind, the rat race, takes all of your time, all your energy. How can you expect anybody to even think about outside work, let alone do it?

Time and money. The classic excuses. What's really holding you back is the fact that you are afraid. You may not like the work you're doing but you know what it is. Going out on your own. That's scary. That's the unknown. What if it doesn't work? What if it fails?

Fear of failure, fear of the unknown. We all suffer from it. I suffered. Did I ever. The trouble was, I had become too dependent on organizations to take care of me and my family. I hadn't learned to face these fears and be able to conquer them. The excuses were always there, easy to grab. I didn't have enough time, or I didn't have enough money.

Everybody has to be dependent. No man is an island, and all that. But the degree of dependency is what is important. If we become overdependent for too long, we are weakened. When they rip the security blanket away, we're lost. We don't know what to do. Somebody has always done it for us.

In his book *Executive Stress,* Dr. Levinson says it's hard to give up dependency on an organization "just as it is hard for the adolescent to give up the pleasure of being dependent on his parents. The adolescent has to fight his way out of his adolescence." You have to fight your way out of being dependent on any one organization too long, just the way the adolescent has to fight his or her way out of the family nest.

Dr. David S. Viscott, a psychiatrist at Boston University Medical School and president of his own little company, Sensitivity Games, Inc., states this problem of interdependence quite bluntly in his book *Feel Free:*

"When society suckled you, it suckled you on the milk of interdependence, the milk of compromise. When it weaned you, it did so only after you were too bloated, too groggy with the surfeit of being taken care of. You got used to that over the years. You learned to accept it as good, to see independence (freedom) as uncertainty. Interdependence became your goal because it was taught to be your goal."

You have to face up to the fact of what you're doing with your life. It's not easy. But there are some ways you can start building up that flabby little spirit of independence which has grown weak because, as Dr. Viscott says, you've probably become "too bloated, too groggy with the surfeit of being taken care of."

You've got to realize that it's quite normal and natural for you to be afraid of venturing out on your own. If you aren't afraid, you just don't understand the problem. It *is* dangerous to cut off steady income. It *is* dangerous to attempt something you've never tried before. These fears can be faced just as a pilot momentarily faces dark clouds overhead and rises up and into the sunshine. You pass through and beyond.

You can minimize the dangers by sticking with your organization, your base, until you've built up a series of minor successes. What you need is the confidence that comes from planning something of your own, putting it into action and making it work. You've got to start up a little venture. Something your organization, your boss, your parents, your husband, your wife, nobody else, controls.

Chances are, the first time out on your own, your little side venture will fail or just run out of steam. Expect this. It happened to me. My first sideline business, *Weaver Reports,* went only so far and could go no further. Not enough newspapers wanted information on Latin America. It was too limited in scope. I could never live off the money it was making. Officially, then, my project "failed."

Unofficially, it was a success. I was happy, I made some extra money to put into my growing "go-to-hell" savings fund. And I learned something about marketing a product or a service. I learned you can never break out—and stay out—unless you've tested what you're going to sell and found enough people who want to buy it. I also gained confidence in myself because I discovered I could do something on my own even if it was limited in the money it could make.

Peter Nagan left his company to start up a newsletter and it failed. It wasn't designed right and the price wasn't right. So back he went to the establishment—another company this time —to get more money and more time to redesign his newsletter. Says Nagan:

"I finally found the right formula. I cut it to two pages. It only cost customers a dollar twenty a year per unit instead of ten dollars. Then I began to get buyers. It took a trial and error period to get started." Nagan, by the way, now has several successful newsletters and a profitable printing business to boot.

Your confidence in yourself builds as you move along in this trial and error period. The successes are more frequent. The failures less frequent. Even so, you will still face plenty of anxiety when you make the final leap out of the establishment. Psychologist Levinson says you should "expect isolation and the temporary fear that you won't make it." "You must," he says, "make certain of two things: That you're in charge and that you have reliable guides."

You can find reliable guides all over the place if you know where to look. Start talking to people who have broken away from an organization and are successfully making it on their own. You'll like them. They're usually loquacious and like to talk about their business and how they made it. It's their life and they love it. These self-bossers can advise you on mistakes to avoid and where you can get information and professional help. But, most of all, they'll give you the encouragement and support you'll need to break away. They get a vicarious charge out of helping someone else make it over the wall. As I said before, they form a sort of "brotherhood."

When I finally wanted to make the break, to write my own consumer column, Peter Nagan gave me all sorts of advice and criticism. So did columnists Robert Novak, Art Buchwald and others. Since I've been out on my own, I too have advised others who want to start up their own column, newsletter or whatever. I'm helping a fellow in a nationally known publication right now. Maybe, some day soon, you'll see him out on his own.

When you're out you'll face a new kind of tension. It's different than the tension you suffered inside the organization. Organizational tension comes from manipulation, frustration and helplessness. Outside the organizational shell there are tense moments but you're in charge. You can solve them. When you do, you get tremendous satisfaction.

Dr. Viktor E. Frankl, professor of psychiatry at the University of Vienna and originator of "logotherapy" (which focuses on man's groping for a higher meaning in life) puts it clearly in his book *Man's Search for Meaning:*

"I consider it a dangerous misconception of mental hygiene to assume that what man needs in the first place is equilibrium . . . a tensionless state. What man actually needs is not a tensionless state but rather the striving and struggling for some goal worthy of him. Man does not simply exist, but always decides what his existence will be, what he will become in the next moment." So you need some tension, some rough spots to go through. Happiness, says Roberto Campos, former Brazilian Finance Minister, "sometimes depends on a state of creative chaos." Happiness, then, is not necessarily related with serenity. You can find plenty of serenity in graveyards.

To face these moments of creative chaos and tension it takes a lot of concentration on what you're doing. Some successful self-bossers found they could work on outside projects and temporarily unplug from the tension of work inside the organization. Others found that their organizations consumed too much of their time and energy.

If your job really drains you and it's hard to concentrate on building your outside venture, you might have to seek what I call a "halfway house" on the route to independence. This could be another job that may pay less than you're making but gives you a lot of free time and relatively easy work to handle.

Or it could be a part-time job where you work only so many hours or so many days a week. Either way, you will have a base to operate from and enough time to devote to your project. You may make less money for a while, but that's to be expected. Look at it as an investment in your education. If the halfway house is in the same field as the business you're building, so much the better. You can learn something and make contacts that will help later on when you're on your own.

3

OUT, NOT UP

So you've decided that life inside an organization is not for you. At least, not forever. If you're young, you want to know how to avoid being drawn into some organizational career. If you're older, you want to know how to get out.

The important thing is the decision you've made. You've now decided that you're going to set up some little *ME, IN-CORPORATED,* outside the establishment. When you make this decision, a sort of philosophical "click" goes off inside. You begin to look at your organization and the establishment in a different light. All the organization's manipulative tricks are exposed.

You don't fall for the games bosses play such as the phony competition where they pit one aspiring employee against another to see who gets the promotion. You also begin to see the hollowness of moving up inside the organization.

When you sense that mystical "click," you suddenly realize that your true direction is out, not up. Instead of looking at what the bosses are doing and wishing you were up there, start looking out to try to find what you really want to do with your life.

When you've decided that you're going out instead of up, you can become cooler, more objective, more observant of what's going on inside your organization. Now is the time to make friends with people in the organization who can help you with the business you plan to start, even if you don't know yet exactly what you want to do.

In short, start using the organization instead of letting it use you. The change of direction from up to out can really clear your head. You can begin to pick up new skills which will help you on the outside. If you don't know how to type or write well, maybe they'll pay you to learn. If you feel you might like to learn public speaking, photography, radio and TV skills, accounting, sales, anything that will help later on, get them to teach you.

There's something like $35 billion a year being spent by companies and government organizations in the training of employees. Some of this training is done inside the organization, some is done outside. In some cases, they pay for all of it. In other cases, you pay half.

But remember, you're not going to acquire skills aimed just at helping you climb the organizational ladder. Oh no, you're going to learn things that will help in your new business.

If you're not sure what you want to go into on your own, use different organizational training courses to get ideas. You can also get ideas by talking with, or working with, specialists in your organization. If your new business calls for bookkeeping skills, start fraternizing with your company's accountants. Don't scare them. You don't want their job. Tell them you're helping a friend with a little business.

You can even volunteer for certain jobs in the organization that others may not want. If some seemingly unimportant task takes you outside the organization to call on customers or suppliers, grab it. Those suppliers or customers may be helpful some day in your own business.

Slowly but surely you begin to use the establishment. Regard it as if it were a big wave. You can try to fight it and get crushed, or, like an expert surfer, you can ride it and let its power carry you where you want to go.

It's a waste of time to fight the establishment or the organization you're in. You'll either end up a pathetic figure like Cervantes' Don Quixote, tilting at windmills, or they'll simply kick you out. When some of my students claim they are "anti-establishment," I tell them they're silly. It's like a surfer saying: "I'm anti-ocean." In paraphrasing the liturgical chant: The establishment is now, always was and ever shall be. Amen.

Oh, you can have capitalistic establishments, socialistic establishments, all kinds of establishments. But, fundamentally, they're all the same. They want to use you one way or another.

For a young person starting out, it may be necessary to get a job inside an organization, maybe several organizations over the years, before you have the skills and the finances to break out on your own. Often, a young person has to "shop around" various jobs to see what kind of work is most interesting.

When you're doing this and you've experienced that out-not-up click—you can take an establishment job and use it without it using you. You can find out what you want to do and what you don't want to do. You can pick up some necessary skills. Look at it as a sort of "graduate school" where you're preparing yourself to go out on your own and are getting paid for it. With this attitude, you might shun some of the so-called glamour jobs which promise a rapid rise up the organizational ladder.

I'm not saying you should refuse promotions or more money. Just remember: Rent them your body for a while but never, ever, sell them your soul. While you are renting your body, keep your mind on extracting portable skills or a profession that you can take with you when you make the break into your own business. While building up these skills, you should keep a little file of ideas for your side venture. Also keep a file of names, addresses and phone numbers of people who might be helpful to you.

When you do get an idea of some service or product you might want to sell, start keeping a file of clippings and other information that relate to it. Bounce your ideas off some of the people who are already working in the field you want to enter.

Get your idea down on paper. Spend some money on it. If it's an idea for a service (newspaper column, repair work, delivery service or whatever), get the facts and figures down. Get comments from people who might buy the service. Organize your facts and your thoughts and put them into a bound presentation. Insert costs, prices and other vital figures. Use maps, surveys, charts, even pictures, wherever possible. Get some professional printer to make at least twenty copies of your presentation. Then, use it to start lining up customers and financial support.

If it's a product you've designed (hand puppets, new kind of garden equipment or recreational gadget), put your idea down on paper and get some drawings made by a professional. Get some working models made. Take them around to potential customers. Sell a few if possible. We'll talk about patent protection in another chapter.

Aside from possibly attracting customers, this exercise of getting things down on paper or in model form will organize your thoughts and will help you focus on the direction you want to take. It also builds confidence. When you see your idea in a professionally produced presentation, you'll ask with some pride: "Did I do that?"

As one management consultant told me: "All kinds of people yak about some great new invention or service they're going to offer. So few of them ever do anything but gush for a while and then forget about it." For this reason, most professional people won't even listen to your idea unless you've invested some time and money preparing it. If you put money into it, consider it an investment even if it doesn't work the first time. It's the only way you can really learn how to take the next step.

With something solid to show, you can get good criticism and advice from others who have made it on their own. Don't just talk up your idea with your family and friends. They're easy to sell. Take your idea out to the pros and get their criticism. Get people to agree to buy your product or service. You may find that what you thought was a great idea has a catch to it. It may be too expensive or it may have to be modified to fit the market's needs. You'll find out. They'll tell you.

You may have to go back and learn more about the business you want to start. You may have to go back to the drawing boards or rewrite your presentation. Keep working at it. But don't go too far in the other direction by nit-picking each little detail trying for perfection when enough people already say they want to buy it. You may be slowly succumbing to the old fear of breaking the umbilical cord with the organization.

There will come a time when your idea looks like it will actually make it. Your creation shows signs of taking off. This is great for building the confidence you'll need, but don't get carried away with it. Don't let the exhilaration of your infant enterprise's initial success lead into making an ass of yourself back at the office. You may have a sudden, pent-up urge to pee on the boss's desk and to brag to your fellow employees about how you're finally going to "break out of the place." Resist the urge. Keep cool. Only discuss your project with your immediate family and, maybe, with one or two close friends who do not work in your organization. You can, and should, discuss it with others who have made it out on their own. They'll be with you. They know the importance of keeping it a secret until the right time.

If you whisper about your big project to your fellow workers, you might hear a whole list of reasons why you shouldn't make the leap. They'll try to unnerve you and they might succeed. According to psychiatrist David Viscott in his book *Feel Free:*

"Your compatriots are going to be jealous. Don't expect any of them, except the most open of them, to express feelings of warmth toward you . . . In a flash you will hear all of the arguments you have been struggling with, and they'll be presented to you as if they are absolutes pointing only in one direction, the one opposite your choice . . . Why can't they let you go? The answer is simple. Society fears a free man."

If you let your sudden high with your new project bubble over into bragging or, even worse, snottiness around the office, you might make an enemy of your organization or you might even get fired before you're really ready to move.

While working on your project, make sure you do the best damned job possible in your work for the organization. There are a number of reasons for this. Primarily your conscience should tell you that while they are paying you, you owe them a fair amount of work. And another thing. Don't ever get into a conflict of interest situation with your organization's competitors. Any such spiteful move will eventually hurt you more than the organization you're leaving.

Be a model employee. When it's time to make the break out into your own business, announce it with some humility to your boss. Say you'll miss the place, especially your friends (and you probably will for a while). Try to get your organization's blessing, if not outright help, for your new venture. In some cases an organization can become one of your future customers. When you're out on your own, you don't need any enemies back in the establishment. Even though you might have held some hard feelings for your boss or organization—leave "friends."

A word about your family. If you're not married there's not too much of a problem. If you are married, be careful how you spring your new escape plan on your spouse. You can scare the pants off a mate by marching up glassy-eyed and saying: "Guess what? I'm leaving that damned job and I'm going to be my own boss." Your spouse will think at first that you're either flaky or you've had one too many on the way home from work. When it sinks in, however, your spouse may feel threatened, fearing that you may eventually want to quit the family too.

Announcing a big change like this is a touchy subject, believe me. Handle it carefully. First, you have to level with your spouse and children about the fact that you're not happy with your work. Then tell them you're looking for something more interesting to do.

Then, if possible, get some outside encouragement for your new project. Get some praise from professional people in the field or, better yet, a solid contract or commitment from someone who wants to buy what you're selling. The more evidence of possible success you can show your family, the easier it is for them to adjust to the idea of change.

You should bring your family in on your new project. Get them to help. Let them experience the little successes as you build, but don't hide the risks. Until you make your final move out of the organization, ask your family to keep quiet about your new project. You don't want it blabbed around until the first sale is made, the first contract signed, and you are ready to make your break. At every turn, level with your family about your project. Their support and understanding are absolutely essential.

4
FINDING MONEY

To break out on your own, you have to find the money to buy
time to let your business grow until it can pay for itself. Statis-
tics show that more than half of the small businesses, started by
the likes of you and me, end in failure. Wiped out. The main
reason for this poor showing is the fact most new businesses
don't have enough financial backing to last through the first
crucial years.

I've found that you have to be able to dig up enough money
to make ends meet for at least two years. If you don't, the first
crisis that comes along can upset your shaky boat and send
you packing back to another establishment job.

Find money, you ask? Where can anybody find money these
days with all those bills to pay? There's the kids' education, or
the car. There's the mortgage, or the rent . . . the doctors and
dentists, and all the others. There's money around but you're
probably so near drowning in organizational ooze, you can't
see it.

There are two ways to "find" money for a new project (other
than stealing or inheriting a small fortune). One way is to
earn extra money through investing a certain percentage of
your salary in savings or securities. You can also moonlight

and put all extra earnings into your breakaway fund. The other major way to get your hands on money is to quit spending what you have in such a foolish manner. When you're determined to break out, when you have a goal set for your own business, you'll be surprised how much money you can find by simply going down the family budget with ax in hand.

If you're single, you sweat this out in solitude. If you're married, you and your spouse have to start leveling with each other in order to come up with a hard list of family priorities. Start with the obvious things such as food, shelter, clothing, education, transportation.

Look over your food bills. Can you get good, nutritional meals for less money? If you're an average family you should be able to chop from one third to one fourth off your monthly food bill. Remember, eating out can be a big part of a monthly food bill—and it's expensive.

My wife and I came up with a priority list as part of a self-imposed recession. Unfortunately our self-imposed recession, which started when my new business started, was soon followed by the real thing on a national scale. At least then we had company. A lot of our friends were cutting back too.

In the food column, we quit eating at restaurants unless somebody else paid for it (business acquaintances would occasionally take us out). We quit giving parties except for an occasional potluck dinner exchange with a few close friends. You'll find a lot of money evaporates into entertaining and eating out.

You can save additional money by getting local brand food instead of name brands. In most cases the chain store's own brand is made by one of the name brand manufacturers anyway. When you pay more for a brand name you're mostly paying for their lavish advertising campaigns. This goes not only for food, but for liquor and even such things as cosmetics and panty hose. The big manufacturers often have one line of production for their own brand and another line for various local brands they produce under contract. It's all the same product. You just pay more for the highly advertised name.

After food comes housing. A lot of money goes into the so-called roof over your head. While you are in the anxious period of making a break from an establishment job, you might not want to take on the added burden of moving. But consider it as a possibility, especially if your breakaway deadline is a year or so off. You have to ask yourself, how much does your place mean to you? Could you live somewhere else for less? If you own your home, could you sell it and make a profit that could go into your new business?

When you make the break, you must consider these things. The idea is not to keep up with the Joneses. You have to back away from the Joneses so you can channel the money into your own working capital.

My wife and I love our home. We had it built in the heyday of steady income I got from the establishment job. But, when we went into business on our own, we put the house up on the chopping block as a "possible cut." It's in a nice area and would bring in good rent. We could make a profit on the rent or an outright sale and we could move to a less expensive place near the children's school. Then we could save on housing *and* transportation costs. So far, we haven't had to do this. But we know it's there and we know approximately how much additional money it can bring in if we need money to get over a business crisis.

In going over these cost-cutting exercises, a husband and wife can learn a lot about each other. I always thought my wife would never give up our home except under catastrophic emergency conditions. I was wrong. If a man or a woman is unhappy with their work, she reasoned, then no custom-built house, no shiny car, no parties, no eating out can really bring happiness.

While working for the establishment, we used to take vacations that cost us hundreds of dollars. Money went out clickety-clack through computerized credit card systems to a series of airlines, hotels and restaurants. We felt compelled to do it "to get away from the grind."

During the first year of my business, we all felt we needed a breather but we couldn't afford the airline and hotel route. My two boys looked crestfallen. They loved trips and many of their friends (whose daddies were still with some "paid vacation" establishment job) were talking about the "neat places" they would soon visit.

I asked the boys if they would like to take a long weekend camping trip up into the nearby Maryland mountains. They warmed up to the idea. We bought a little tent on sale for forty dollars. My wife outfitted us with food and drink and we took off. She stayed home and had a marvelous time sleeping in late, puttering around the garden and the kitchen, taking naps and just "catching up" with reading and letters.

For "us boys" it was a trip we'll never forget. The meals we cooked tasted great, even though a few things were a bit burnt. We even caught a couple of fish. It rained one night and we had a minor flood, but it was pure adventure for the boys. We came back refreshed and the whole trip only cost thirty dollars (not including the tent, which we'll use again). After the money started coming into my business, we began to take some longer and more ambitious vacations, but I'll never forget that weekend in the mountains. We were under pressure and the family pulled closer together.

Vacations aren't the only transportation expenditures you can save money on. Another big one can be found in "personal transportation." How many cars do you have? Have you investigated other ways of getting yourself from here to there without owning one or two cars?

The Bureau of Public Roads made a study of the average

car owner's costs and found that it takes $1,200 a year to keep yourself moving in medium-priced "wheels." That's if absolutely nothing goes wrong. But, as you know, things *do* go wrong.

Dig out every expense item that relates to your car. Ask your bank or auto insurance agent to show how much you're paying in true depreciation costs for your car. Depreciation can run from $500 to $1,000 a year. Then add up all the gasoline and service station bills. Don't forget insurance, parking and all those repairs. If anything goes wrong with your car, annual costs can shoot up to $3,000.

Ask yourself: Can I take a bus or even taxis instead of using the car? One friend, Florence, who is a secretary, thought she would like a car to drive to work and to use for occasional weekend trips to the beach or ski slopes. I told her to find out how much a rental car would cost for weekend flings.

To her surprise, she discovered she would pay approximately half as much to use somebody else's wheels for transportation than she would have to buy, insure, maintain and park her own car. And she wouldn't have to worry about the repair hassle or getting insurance renewed after each fender bender. Let them worry about all that junk. It's their car. You're just borrowing it. Maybe you can give up a car, maybe you can't. Think about it. There's a lot of money tied up in a car—more than you ever realized.

We had two cars when I started Weaver Communications, Inc. My wife used one to transport the kids and get the shopping done. I used the other to drive to work. I needed the money, so I sold my car. I took a bus. I hitched rides. I did a lot more walking. I took taxis when necessary and even rented a car now and then. The money I saved was like getting a $1,500 annual dividend check. It was found money. My business is finally doing pretty well and I can afford another car. But I'm not going to get one. It's silly to throw that kind of money away.

If you must buy a new car, set up your own specification list describing the make and model you really need (not some super special). Put down only those accessories that are necessary—no more. Have dealers bid on your specification list. You don't necessarily have to pick the lowest bid. Pick the place that has the best reputation for service.

Investigate the possibility of buying a used car. Most new cars drop thousands of dollars in value during the first two years. You buy a two-year-old car and let the other guy pick up those depreciation costs. Use it for three years or so and then trade it for another two-year-old. Buy your used car from a dealer who sells the same make and model new cars. Or buy your two-year-old car from a company that leases to corporations and professional people. They usually rotate their cars every two years and you can pick up some bargains this way.

After you've gone over your transportation expenses, take a look at what's going into education. Naturally, if your children go to a free public school, there aren't many expenses for the moment. But what about college? "Where are we going to get the college money?" is the usual plaintive cry you hear from those who want to start their own business but are afraid to take the temporary cut in income while things get going.

It's a legitimate worry. Don't get me wrong. I worried about it. I'm still worried about it. You can easily spend $3,500 a year and more to send a boy or girl to college and this doesn't include transportation expenses. If you have two or three padding through the halls of academe at the same time, it can be an economic disaster.

Some suggestions. Investigate every possible channel for scholarships, grants, long-term cheap loans and other forms of assistance. There are several companies that use a computer to find oddball scholarships to fit your child's qualifications. It's estimated that some $75 million to $100 million in special scholarships and grants goes unclaimed every year because par-

ents and students don't know how to find them. A student may
have a background that's tailor-made for a specific scholarship.
Many of these scholarships are not directly related to grades.
For example, one New Jersey student who was getting a few
B's, but mostly C's, got a combination of grants through a
computer search which paid most of his four years' college expenses.

The computer companies not only look for scholarships, they
can help find the right college or university for your child's economic and intellectual needs. There are many little colleges
around the country that offer a good education at relative bargain prices. You fill out a detailed computer form for the
search. Parents and students have to confess themselves, giving
all academic, economic and personal background information.
Then the computer scans some 2,500 colleges and universities
and delves into some 115,000 scholarships and grants. You get
a list of ten colleges and ten scholarships in descending order of
desirability. High school guidance counsellors sometimes have
the names of these computer search outfits. If not, try your
state and local department of education officials and nearby
universities. While you're at it, get a copy of *Financial Aid for
Higher Education* put out by the Department of Health Education and Welfare (in Washington). Another good booklet on
financial aid for college is *Need a Lift,* put out by the American Legion.

Don't overlook some of the community colleges in your area.
Many of these two-year colleges offer an excellent education
for half of what it costs to send your child to a state institution
and a small fraction of what it would cost for a four-year college or university.

Aside from the big saving in money, a community college
can have a distinct educational advantage over the traditional,
four-year institution. Community colleges seem to concentrate
more on the student and less on administrative bureaucracy.

They have work-study programs where the student keeps more in touch with the real world by working at some local, part-time job that's related to a particular line of study. Students seem to be more involved in their work and less involved in drugs and other such sidelines. The community is the important thing, not the campus. Government surveys show that community college graduates do just as well in four-year universities (after they transfer) as do "native" students who started out as freshmen.

These are just some of the family checkbook items where you can squeeze out money to put into your business. You can probably spot several others. When you find out how much money is wasted on what you once thought were "essentials," don't get too carried away with budget chopping. Don't cut out things that may seem frivolous at first but are really necessary for your health or sanity. For example, on our family "chop" list, I put down the expense of a horse I own for weekend riding at a nearby stable. This horse was costing me something like ninety dollars a month and I thought I could pick up well over $1,000 a year by selling him. My wife found she, too, could pick up a bundle by canceling her part-time studies at a nearby university and by canceling the help we hired to give her more free time to study.

I wouldn't let her give up her studies. They were part of a goal. They kept her sanity. She wouldn't let me give up my horse. Riding every weekend and some weekday evenings gets me out of myself. My troubles disappear when I'm with the horse out on the trails. I come back refreshed. My wife says, "That horse keeps the doctors away." She's right. We both agreed to put the horse and the studies way up top on our priority list under "essential health expenses."

You will probably find similar things, like our horse and the studies, that get you out of yourself and keep you sane. If you don't have one of these hobbies, you'd better get one. Maybe it's music, maybe it's collecting coins or taking an art course. Whatever it is, keep it. It's an investment in your health and your ability to recharge your batteries. You'll need all the recharging you can get when you start out on your own.

While we were making decisions as to what to keep, what to throw out, my wife fought to keep things that seemed part of our personalities. "When a plane's in trouble," she said, "you might throw out some seats and some baggage to lighten the load . . . but you don't throw out the pilot and the co-pilot."

We didn't throw out the essentials that helped support the pilot and the co-pilot, but we did chop a lot of frills. We were able to cut monthly expenses almost in half.

So far, I've concentrated on cutting expenses—throwing out excess baggage. Just cutting isn't enough, though. You have to have extra income or cash reserves to draw on. You have to figure, as conservatively as possible, how much your new business can make in the first year. Base this figure on hard facts, not hopes. If you have a contract for your product or service, how much will it bring in—minus all operating expenses? You may have a start-up period of many months before your new business can bring in money over and above all operating expenses.

How much money will you need during this start-up period? You'll need enough to fend off the bill collectors and keep your family going, albeit on a reduced budget. You need enough money to buy time for your venture to develop. I figure two years is the minimum. Of course your new business should bring in more and more net income as it develops. You have to keep figuring approximately how much, and when.

To get the extra funds you'll need until your business salary can pay most of the family bills, you can work a part-time moonlighting job. Your spouse can work part time. All extra money from these jobs should go into the special start-up fund for your business. You can make the fund grow faster by careful investing. The safest, but slowest, investments are found in savings accounts, certificates of deposit and government savings bonds. Faster, but riskier, money-makers can be found in the stock market. That's where I built up most of my reserves but I don't recommend it unless you first build a special "panic button" savings account which can tide you over a financial crisis. You should have "no touch" savings deposits that will keep your family going at least three months if your major job income is cut off.

Once you have this savings base, then you might want to venture into the stock market. Make an investment plan and stick with it. Look up the top five hundred companies in *Fortune* magazine's May issue (most libraries have it). From the top fifty, select four or five companies that have the highest "net income as per cent of stockholders' equity" (listed under a special column heading).

Armed with the names of these few leading earners, you can then select a broker. Pick a brokerage firm that's well known. Ask the broker for more background information on the companies you have selected. He should give you copies of the most recent *Standard & Poor's* stock reports. Pick a company that sounds most promising, one whose product or service you know. It's a good idea to invest a fixed amount a month until you collect around $2,000 worth of shares in any given company. Brokers have "Monthly Investment Plans," where you bring in a fixed amount and they keep buying the stock for you. This way you minimize periodic stock market reverses by "price averaging." If your stock goes down, you can get more shares at a lower price to average out the paper losses you have on shares purchased earlier at a higher price. When the market goes up again, things average out.

To learn more about buying stocks, you might want to join an investment club. Your broker may know of a club or you can write: National Association of Investment Clubs; P. O.

Box 220; Royal Oak, Mich. 48068. They'll tell how to get into a club and will include some "home study" material. This association, for example, warns home studiers never to invest in a broker's "tip" or "sure thing." Get information from the broker, not tips. Do your own selecting. The more you build up your own knowledge of investments, the better chance you have of creating a fund that can eventually be used for the final goal— an investment in your own company.

Be extremely cautious about getting a loan as a means of starting up your new business. Don't commit yourself to any big amounts for a long period of time. The trouble with loans is the fact that they're so inflexible. You have to pay a fixed amount on time and you don't know what will happen to the economy, or local business conditions, over the crucial, start-up years. Business may be good when you start out, but then comes a downturn. If you're tied to a big loan, you're stuck. It doesn't give you the flexibility to retrench. Loans can be useful at certain stages of starting up a business—but watch it. If you have to rely too much on a loan, it may be better to wait another year or so until you have built up more of your own capital.

Make sure your venture capital is clearly set aside, away from the family funds. If you already have some savings that can go into a new business, peel them away from the family account and commit them to a special development fund. Always keep things separate. This way, you can consider it an investment in your company—above the family needs—and you won't have to regard each business expenditure (your salary included) as some sort of agonizing "drain on the family finances."

5
FINDING FRINGES

So you've popped a few pencils figuring how much it will cost to set up your new business and keep going for a minimum of two years. Now what about the unforeseen accident, serious illness or other such catastrophy? Who pays for that? Until now, Big Daddy in the establishment usually paid for it.

It's one of the fringe benefits. If you get sick or have an accident, you still get your pay. If you go to the hospital, your organization's medical insurance plan covers it.

With this security blanket ripped away, who will take care of you if an emergency strikes? These are the questions all of us face when we head out of the organization into our own business. This fear of disaster striking without any organizational protection is enough to keep many a prospective self-bosser firmly stuck in the nine-to-five daily grind.

You don't have to give up all of these "fringe benefits" just because you want to strike out on your own. If you hear somebody warning about losing fringe benefits, it may be propaganda designed to keep you tranquilized and in the fold. There are other organizations all set up just waiting to take care of you and they don't tell you how to run your business or your life. They're called "trade associations." Sometimes they're called clubs, institutes or societies. They're organizations of people who do the same kind of work or who are interested in the same subject.

If you can't find an association, club, institute or society that relates to your new business, you must be working on a pretty weird project. There's an association for every conceivable kind of occupation or interest and most of them offer medical insurance, life insurance and disability insurance to members at relatively cheap, group rates.

When I left my establishment job, my wife and I suddenly found ourselves without medical coverage. We called Blue Cross and Blue Shield to get individual coverage to pick up where our group coverage left off. Oh, they were glad to do it —for a price nearly twice what we had been charged under the group plan. No thanks.

I then remembered that the Overseas Press Club of America offered its members major medical insurance and Blue Cross and Blue Shield at the lower, group rate. When I was a correspondent overseas some years back, I joined this club. When I came home, I dropped my membership. Now I applied for reinstatement. Dues were only thirty-five dollars a year and I immediately signed up for the extra, inexpensive medical insurance. We were covered.

Later, when I began doing my own "Mind Your Money" radio show, I was politely but firmly asked to join AFTRA (American Federation of Television and Radio Artists). I grumbled until I found out that AFTRA has an excellent medical insurance plan for its members. It could give me and my family more coverage than we were getting at the old establishment job. I dropped the Overseas Press Club and picked up on the AFTRA medical plan.

So, you see, I was able to find professional associations which were able to give me new supports, new "fringes," to take up for those I lost when I left my establishment job.

What about you? You say you don't have a clearly defined profession? Listen, whatever kind of work you plan for your new business—service or sales—there's got to be a jolly association somewhere to provide group rates for insurance.

Best place to start looking is in the latest edition of *National Trade and Professional Associations of the United States*. This is must reading for anyone contemplating going into business for themselves (unless you already have an association in mind). You can get a copy for fifteen dollars from: Columbia Books, Inc.; Suite 300; 917-15th St., N.W.; Washington, D.C. Inside you'll find names, addresses, phone numbers, chief officers' names and descriptions of more than 4,600 associations. They're all listed alphabetically and cross-referenced by subject names.

For example, if growing orchids is your bag, look up "flowers and plants" in the book and you'll find The American Orchid Society. For candlemakers, there's the Candle Manufacturers Association and, if you're a gal who has bookkeeping skills, there's the American Woman's Society of Certified Public Accountants. Starting a little art gallery or antique shop? Look up the Art and Antique Dealers League of America, Inc. And, as a bonus, you'll find some associations have rival groups that might offer a better deal on fringe benefits.

Many of these associations include giant corporations as members. You needn't worry, because associations usually welcome micro-members and often make a big show of how democratic they are. "Same fine protection and service for all members, no matter what size, race, creed, etc."

Let's look into a couple of major associations to see what you can get. The Direct Mail Advertising Association has some 1,600 members whose principal business is selling products or services through the mail. Membership dues are $165 a year and you get all sorts of newsletters, bulletins, "how-to" pamphlets and other material that might assist your budding mail-order business. Dues are tax deductible.

Members are offered major medical insurance at low, group rates. Same thing goes for term life insurance and disability insurance. If you're having troubles with your business, you can phone or write in to get personal advice.

The Direct Selling Association is mostly made up of companies that sell products from door to door or through sales parties in homes. Membership includes Avon, Amway, Stanley Home Products and Tupperware, just to name a few. For these big companies, dues are a minimum of $450 a year, but a new kind of "small business" membership is being contemplated. It will cost only around $100 a year and will give those who are starting up their own small sales business the same kind of protection the big boys get, such as technical and legal help, inexpensive major medical and life insurance and other goodies.

The Direct Selling Association also has an offshoot called American Individual Merchants (AIM). This covers all those Avon Ladies, Amway distributors and others working on their own selling products manufactured by DSA members. Membership in AIM is two dollars a year and is quite a bargain.

Here's a good way you can use an AIM membership while you build up your own business. Let's say you are planning to manufacture and sell your own product such as hand puppets, mod clothing or whatever. If you take on the product of one of DSA's members, especially if it's a product related to what you're making at home, you can sell your own product along with the name brand as you make the rounds. You get instant "diversity," you get the prestige of a big name company product and you get the organizational protection of AIM—and you're still your own boss. When your own product really begins to sell, you can drop the big name manufacturer's product or keep it as a "sideline."

Even if you eventually join some association such as AIM,

DMAA or DSA, you have to be careful how much insurance you load yourself up with. Wherever possible, you should insure against the economic catastrophy situation and should not try to protect yourself against relatively minor woes.

John C. Post, a canny fellow in his seventies and a professional money manager for doctors and dentists, has some strong, and I think very wise, views on the "wrong kind of insurance most Americans clutter themselves up with."

John Post thinks most of us should only have major medical insurance with as high deductibles as we can afford. "You pay for all the relatively small stuff," he says, "let them pay when the bill runs into the thousands of dollars."

George Haines, an independent broker who handles much of the casualty insurance coverage for John Post's clients, says you should look at medical insurance the same way you look at car insurance. "You need all the liability coverage you can get," says Haines, "because there's no end to what they can drag out of you with lawsuits." Without collision insurance all you can ever lose is the price of the car. When you buy collision insurance, you save money by getting as high a deductible as possible and you drop the coverage altogether after the car ages.

With medical insurance, Haines says you can apply the same philosophy. You protect yourself against the sky's-the-limit catastrophies and avoid paying high-priced premiums for so-called "first dollar" coverage designed to protect against smaller but more frequent medical expenses.

After reviewing your personal or family needs, you'll probably find that you can save considerable money by getting "major medical" coverage and dropping "minor medical" coverage offered by various insurance companies and Blue Cross, Blue Shield.

By hooking onto a group plan offered by some association, a married couple in their thirties can get major medical coverage for around $100 a year in premiums (that's just a little over $8 a month). Outside a group it costs $175 a year. This kind of coverage has you pay the first $1,000 but absorbs almost all other expenses on up to $25,000 (some policies even cover you up to $100,000). This way, you know that all you'll ever have to pay is $1,000 or so and you can have that amount in your emergency savings fund. If you want to discipline yourself, you can deposit in savings the amount of money you would have had to pay in "minor medical" insurance premiums. Put it in a medical or health fund of your own to help pay minor medical bills.

You can get insurance to cover minor medical bills through many association group plans but it still costs a lot. For example, the same couple in their thirties would have to pay $145 a year on top of their $100 cost for major medical coverage. This jumps your monthly medical plan costs from $8 to more than $20. Outside of a group plan, of course, the cost is almost prohibitive.

By dropping the minor medical coverage, you're not missing too much. Remember, Blue Cross, Blue Shield and the major insurance companies don't include many kinds of medical bills in their contractual fine print. They also have to "approve" every claim and it seems that most of the time they either flatly turn down your claim or drag their feet for months or even years before paying you back.

My wife and I have had to haggle for more than a year to get reimbursed for medical bills we thought were included in the plan. Often, we'd only get a fraction of the amount with no explanation. There were times when the insurer didn't answer claims for many months and then they'd send back some sort of gibberish which required yet another round of correspondence.

To repeat: If you can afford to insure yourself out of savings for the minor bills, just get the major medical coverage with as high a deductible as you can stand financially. You'll be better off and you'll save yourself money and time—both of which can be used in your new business.

So much for the medical bills. What happens if you're laid up and can't work for several months? Who's going to pay the home and family maintenance bills? You might also have some office bills to be paid.

The insurance companies have come up with a series of alluring policies designed to play on your fears about the possibility of sudden loss of income due to illness or accident. They have invented all sorts of names such as "income protection" or "office overhead protection."

"Just think," the ads say, "you can get $1,000 a month to age sixty-five—and it's all tax free to spend any way you like." At first glance it does sound tempting to those of us starting out on our own. At second glance, however, you find out what that nice-sounding security costs.

A thirty-year-old man who wants to get $1,000 a month to age sixty-five (or any age under that when he can start working again), has to pay around $525 a year in premiums. If you're willing to endure a six-month waiting period before collecting any money, you can cut the figure down to $335.

For office overhead protection (rent, employee salary, phone bill, etc.) you have to pay $135 a year in order to get $1,000-a-month coverage for a maximum of twelve months. You have to wait one month before you can start collecting.

Again, I think it's better to self-insure whenever possible. Maybe your kind of business lends itself to building up a backlog which can be sold while you're laid up. Or, better yet, maybe you can arrange a "buddy system" with some other person who is out on their own. Each one handles the other's sales or service whenever any disabling illness or accident occurs.

I have this kind of arrangement with a friend and I also have a talented employee who can help "fake it" for me in case I'm laid up for several months. Maybe a spouse can pitch in or you can do part of the work at home while recuperating. This kind of jerry-built contingency planning might not be as "worry free" as those welfare-type company fringe benefits but, remember, you *were* paying a price for those benefits. It might have been dull work. You might have had an insensitive boss. But mainly you were paying for those benefits by giving up some of your own, personal freedom.

Life insurance is another matter. At certain stages in your life you've got to have it. According to professional money-manager John Post, you should protect dependents with as much term life insurance as you can afford. It's even better if you can get it through a group plan. Straight life or ordinary life insurance that's tied to a savings or investment gimmick is far more expensive and usually leaves you with less overall coverage than you really need. Listen to what Brandeis University economist James Schulz has to say about these expensive policies:

"Straight life or ordinary life policies, as some companies call it, is not really life insurance . . . It's life insurance plus a very mediocre savings certificate. They make you pay in more than is needed to insure your life. They take your money and invest it to get as much as 10 to 15 per cent on it for themselves. They invest in securities that adjust to inflation and then come along and promise to pay you a fixed 4 per cent or so return. Inflation eats up your return. You get nothing back and they make quite a profit."

Term insurance gives your dependents just plain protection in case you die. You pay less for it—much less—so you can afford the overall coverage you need. Your money isn't eaten up in a phony insurance-investment plan. Insurance should be considered as "disaster protection" for family members who are dependent on the main money earner. Single people usually don't need life insurance. Neither do children, wives and others who are not the major money earners.

In the early years of a family's growth, the major money earner needs considerably more coverage to protect the other partner (usually the wife), who has to care for the children and is too tied down to do much work. If both husband and wife work, then the children should be protected by policies on both parents proportionate to their earning capacity. The older the children get, the less insurance you need. You can pare it back as the kids go on into college, when they are able to work and there's far less dependency on the mother to be cook and chauffeur.

Five-year, renewable and convertible term insurance is ideally suited for your need to expand and contract your insurance coverage as your family changes. Unfortunately, my wife and I didn't find out about this until we had been long involved in the costly straight life policies. We did find, however, that we could borrow nearly $10,000 on the "cash value" of our straight life policies and did so forthwith. Interest is usually only 5 per cent a year and you can pay back the money any time you want—or never. You don't get the insurance coverage in case of death but, if the money is well used, you won't need it. We put it into knocking down our house mortgage, on which we had to pay 7 per cent interest. We gained two interest points right there.

Also, we dropped a certain number of policies and replaced them with term insurance. And, at every turn, we resisted sales pitches which were aimed at buying insurance for everybody in the family. "Get your children insured now and they'll be covered for life without the need of a medical exam," the insurance companies say. Children don't have dependents, so why do they need insurance? Same goes for a wife unless she's working and the family depends on the money. The insurance salesman asks: "But, if your wife died, you'd have to hire a full-time housekeeper to watch over the kids and run your house, right?" Wrong. Save the premium money and spend it on your wife's intellectual and physical betterment. She'll love it. There would be a painful period after a wife's death, but you could get by financially. A lump-sum insurance payment won't bring back her love.

If you trim your insurance back like this, then how much basic coverage should you retain? By cutting back on the expensive, less useful types of insurance, you can better afford to get the pure protection you need. Money manager John Post has a very loose rule of thumb: You need half your annual income for the total number of years of heavy dependency. By "heavy dependency" he means the years your spouse would be strapped with the kids. You can figure date of birth to around eighteen years as the heavy financial dependency period for a child, with the amount of dependency decreasing as the child approaches eighteen.

Let's work out an example of Post's rule. Say you make $15,000 a year and your youngest child is twelve. That means six more years of heavy dependency. Half of your annual income is $7,500. So, six times $7,500 comes to $45,000—the amount of basic insurance you should have. This figure of half annual income is calculated, Post says, on the theory that, with the husband gone, there will be less expenses for such things as commuting (and all sorts of other work expenses). You've got to count on cutting back on expenses. You're playing a betting game with the insurance companies. It's a game they usually win. It has a sort of grim, reverse spin. If you die next week, your family wins and collects the insurance money. If you live to a ripe old age, you pay out many thousands of dollars in insurance premiums and "lose." The insurers claim you "win both ways" when you buy straight life because you get paid-up insurance at a certain stage. This means no more premiums need to be paid and when you die somebody will get the money. If you take all the extra money that goes into the premiums for this deluxe insurance and invest it, you'll probably come out money ahead. Better yet, take the extra premium money and buy more coverage with cheaper term insurance during the heavy dependency years.

You can actually lessen the effect of dependency years by investing in what I call "wife insurance." You don't buy a policy on a wife's life, you invest in her education and work ability. The more a wife is able to retain and build up a profession or other specific job skills, the better she will be able to cope with a husband's ill-timed death. My wife is taking courses at American University and some of them will help her eventually get a job or make money on her own as a writer. I'm paying her to help me two or three days a week in my office. As time goes by, I feel more confident that she will be able to bring in money in case anything happens to me. Most wives would much rather have the protection of self-sufficiency than depend solely on some insurance policy. You get immediate benefits and don't have to wait until somebody dies. In a later chapter we'll investigate the possibilities of a wife eventually building up her own business, using the room-and-board security of a home as a base to work from.

That word "security" keeps popping up, doesn't it? You can't get rid of it. You need the security of medical and life insurance coverage. You need the security of some kind of job and income protection—whether it's your own contingency plan or somebody's expensive insurance program. And, finally, you need some kind of security for old age, when you want to slow down or are unable to work. As we've seen, older people can take a real beating in this country. Most pension plans never pay off and Social Security barely supplies enough money to feed yourself.

Organizations always throw that "fine retirement plan" at you as one of the fringe benefits you get for taking their guff through an entire lifetime. Money to "enjoy your old age," they say. Listen, I've been through three pension plans with three

different companies over a span of twenty years and I haven't
one cent to show for it. Nothing. Oh, I got back the money I
contributed, but I was lulled into a false sense of security thinking I would have a nice fat pension some day. No such luck.
When you leave the warm embrace of the organization, your
pension plan is chopped off. You have to stay with most outfits an unconscionable length of time in order to have your
pension money "vested" (where you own it and are assured
payments commencing at age sixty-five). And another thing,
almost no pension plan offered by establishment companies or
government agencies takes care of an employee's widow or
widower. It's entirely possible for you to work for some company for thirty years, retire and then die within the year. If so,
your husband or wife gets nothing. You've worked all your life
for just a couple of months' pension benefits and your spouse is
cut off from the funds when you die.

Under careful examination, you'll find that most of these
highly praised pension plan fringe benefits are fraught with so
many "catch 22" gimmicks, your chances of ever collecting
anything are mighty slim. Even so, a number of people have
told me that leaving a pension plan was a valid reason for not
breaking away to start up a business. Only if you're within a
few years of cashing in on a pension plan is it worth sticking
around. This is particularly true for such as the military, who
start young and get a pretty good, guaranteed pension if they
stick it out twenty years. They can use the monthly checks as a
basis for starting their own business.

If you're quite a way off from ever collecting on a pension
plan, it's best to forget about it. Concentrate your efforts on
getting out and into your own business. As a matter of fact,
you might find that your own business can build up a much
better pension plan, much faster than you ever could working
for somebody else. There are all sorts of pension plan tax loopholes designed to benefit corporate executives and professional

working people. You can cash in on these if you eventually incorporate your business. It's a good idea to work out the details of these ploys with a good tax attorney, but basically the scheme goes like this:

With your own corporation, you can set up a pension plan and/or a profit-sharing plan. Any money you make above your office expense and your salary can be channeled into one of these plans. In some cases, it might even be a good idea to put some of your company earnings into a profit-sharing or pension plan even if it means you can't pay yourself enough of a salary to make ends meet at home. If you have a savings account built up, you can withdraw monthly amounts to help defray living costs and still come out ahead, because you'll actually be building up another type of savings account much faster in your pension or profit-sharing plan. This is because you won't be taxed on earnings that go into these plans.

You can even borrow money out of your pension or profit-sharing plan to pay for such things as the kids' college and other tough family expenses that crop up. Of course, you have to pay the money back at the going interest but you can do this out of future earnings and the interest goes back to you anyway. There are ways you can take funds out of these plans before age sixty-five. A good tax specialist can tailor-make a plan to suit your changing financial needs. This gives you much more flexibility than you could ever get with the typical organizational pension plan. Most of these establishment plans are designed to protect the organization from having to pay in too much. They're not designed to protect the worker.

For those who do not want to incorporate, Congress has provided a self-employed "Keogh" pension system whereby you can channel a limited amount of tax-free income into a retirement fund. It's not as juicy a deal as the corporate plan but it's still better than the house-of-mirror pensions most employers offer.

6

YOUR OWN CORNER

By now, you've got a lot of ideas about what you want to do and what you don't want to do. You've got ideas about where you might get your hands on some money and some ideas about cutting back on monthly living expenses.

But that's all you've got—ideas. Ideas are necessary, don't get me wrong. They're the seed for the eventual growth of your own business. Unfortunately, many a dreamer who wants to break out of a confining job never gets by the idea or dream stage. The main reason why most of us get stuck with our dreams and never move into high gear is we haven't focused on what we want to do. We haven't put it down in writing, we haven't organized it so it can be seen and evaluated by others.

Maybe I should have put what I'm about to tell you right up front in this book. It's so important. I was afraid that this trick, to focus on what you want to do, is so simple it would be dismissed outright or passed over lightly. That's why I wanted to get you first to look into yourself and to consider seriously being on your own some day.

So here goes. Don't laugh. Listen to what I have to say and think about it. Take a hundred dollars or fifty or whatever and open a special checking account at some bank where you do not already have an account. If it's a neighborhood bank or a relatively small bank near the place where you work, so much the better. Before you go in to open up your new account, think of some business name that fits your personality or the idea you want to develop. When I started to moonlight with a series of columns on Latin America, my bank account was called "Weaver Reports." A bright young university student I know, has invented a de-fogging spray for glass and has several other oddball but useful products in the development stage. His little bank account is called "General Eclectics."

Fiddle around with it. Doodle. Think up some names and pick the one that fits your project. I'm kind of a ham and like to see my own name in the title somewhere. Lord knows, I've worked long enough for others who had their own names on the company letterheads. Officially, you can't just say "Me [your name], Incorporated" unless you actually go through the legal steps of incorporation. Some banks are fussy about special names for accounts and might charge fifty dollars or so for the privilege. Shop around. Many will permit any name if it doesn't conflict with another account. Having your own name in the title helps identify your account and is one of the reasons I chose "Weaver Reports" and, later, "Weaver Communications, Inc."

When you open your account, say you're starting up a new business and it's just in the development stage. After you've signed up, ask to see the vice-president or general manager in charge of new accounts. Explain your plans. Bankers love to hear about a new and, hopefully, budding business account. The banker can be an important contact and possible advisor later on.

So why all the fuss about opening a checking account with your new venture's name? Because it's probably the first time you've actually committed some money to your cause and the name of your game is right down on those checks in bold print where everybody can see it. It gives much needed importance to your cause. When you buy supplies or pay for legitimate business expenses, those you're dealing with can see that you have some kind of organization. You're not just working on an out-of-pocket lark.

Even more important, your own checkbook is a real focus point for your business. There it is. You've taken the first big step. It serves as a daily reminder. That little bank account jags your conscience and demands to be fed.

At first, it's best to have your home address for your account. You don't want any correspondence sent to the place where you work. When you use your own address, you've got to find some place in your apartment or house that's "your corner." It may be just that—a corner. You should have a desk, some kind of inexpensive filing cabinet, possibly a typewriter, some shelves for supplies and a bookshelf.

As soon as possible, you should invest in some fairly decent letterheads and envelopes with your venture's name and your address (the phone number can be added to the letterhead). They don't have to be engraved, mind you, but they should be designed and printed by a professional. At first I used green ink but then switched to black.

Again, having your own letterheads is like having your own bank account. It gives your new business some prestige. People you write, whether they're suppliers or prospective customers, are more responsive to a business name with a definite address. Using your own personal letterheads or your employer's letterheads is out. Don't do it. It confuses people and diverts attention away from your project.

By now, you've incurred a few start-up expenses. You've gotten stationery, you've gotten some stamps and if you didn't have a desk, file cabinet, typewriter and whatnot, you've had to buy those. You've paid for these out of your new account, I hope. Don't ever pay for any business expense out of your personal account.

Before you opened your business account, you might conceivably have incurred some "investigative" expenses aimed at starting up a business on your own. Maybe you took taxi rides to discuss possible business ideas with others who have gone out on their own. Maybe you invited an already established self-bosser to lunch to talk about your hopes of going into business for yourself. Think back and note all those preliminary expenses. They're tax deductible and should be down in your books as such.

If you've already incurred an expense before you opened up your new account, put it down on a monthly or quarterly "expense account" and pay yourself back from your business bank account. The Internal Revenue Service likes it this way. IRS agents are much more fussy and apt to call you on the carpet if you try to put these expenses down on your personal tax form as deductions. Later on, we'll talk about getting professional help for your books and your income tax problems. But, for the moment, all you need is a separate account, a separate set of books and a separate tax form at filing time.

Internal Revenue Service offices around the country can provide all sorts of booklets and free advice on how a budding business should be organized to qualify for all the tax deductions. Part of your home suddenly becomes tax deductible because it's part of your new business. Specific use of your car and other equipment you own can be deducted as legitimate business expenses. Just keep notes on what you use and what you spend and put it down on your regular "expense account" for reimbursement from your new business checking account. It might be a good idea to have a separate phone in your home, once your venture gets rolling. At every turn, keep business expenses separate from your regular living expenses. Every paper clip, every stapler, every filing folder, every book you buy for your business—everything—should be noted and duly deducted comes tax time.

It's kind of fun once you find out how many things are tax deductible. You begin to cash in on loopholes and incentives your boss's outfit has been enjoying for years. But be careful. Don't get carried away. Don't just buy all sorts of fancy equipment because it comes as a possible tax deduction. Remember, you don't actually *make* money through deductions—they just reduce the tax you pay on earned income. Keep your home office expenses trimmed down to the essentials and concentrate on getting a contract or selling some samples of whatever you're going to produce. Put any income you make right into the separate account. Make a note of which deposits come from earnings and which deposits come from your own investment capital. If you work on a side, moonlighting job, it's a good idea to invest that income in your new venture. If it is at all related to your venture, you might be able to reduce the tax bite through your list of home business expenses. IRS agents can help you with these questions. Their offices can usually be reached through the Federal Office nearest you (found under U. S. Government in the phone book).

Earlier, I mentioned the need of a filing cabinet. You may think a drawer or a box will do. This won't work. You need something more substantial as part of your attempt to focus attention on your new business. You can start with a one-drawer metal cabinet. You can get them for just a few dollars by checking the classified ads in your paper and by calling office furniture stores. You needn't get a new one. A used cabinet will do.

What do you put in there? Well, you put all your financial statements, canceled checks, deposit slips in under "finances." You put all your correspondence with suppliers in one folder and correspondence with prospective buyers in another folder.

One good chunk of the file drawer should be devoted to "ideas." Start clipping articles and advertisements that relate to

what you might want to do. Maybe there's a course that could
get you started into something new. File it. An ad shows a service offered by someone on the other side of town. File it.
Some magazine has an article about someone in another city
and how they built up their own business similar to the one you
have in mind. File it.

Somewhere along the line, you need a separate folder for
names of people who might be able to help. These are people
who you might want to write, phone or visit some day. Underline the name. Note the reason for its selection ("possible supplier") and chuck it into the file.

On your desk, you eventually will need a little wheel or card
box for top source names, addresses and phone numbers.
These are the names you have to call or write frequently. This
file of names eventually will be one of your most valuable
possessions. Keep it sorted out and up to date.

Away from your desk, you should place medium-sized note
pads in strategic places. Every time you get an idea that might
be of value to your new venture, jot it down. I keep a note pad
by my bed and one in the car. Some self-bossers I know even
keep a pad near the bathroom john.

Wherever you find yourself thinking or stewing about your
project, make sure a note pad is handy. Ideas are extremely
valuable but many are lost because we forget about them when
some routine chore demands attention. In your car, you need a
pad because you have to note any mileage run up for business
purposes. Even if you just drive over to someone's home for a
chat one evening about your new business, jot it down. It's a
business expense. You need the date, the mileage and the
reason for the trip. You can count twelve cents a mile as a
legitimate deduction on your tax return.

I also use my car note pad for ideas. When I'm stuck in rush
hour traffic or I'm just humming along on some freeway, ideas
occasionally flip out. If it's a particularly pressing idea, I pull

over and stop to write it down. Otherwise, I try to remember it
and write it down just after I've parked. A friend of mine, Pete
Nagan, whom I mentioned earlier as running his own successful
business, uses a small tape recorder in his car. He dictates ideas
into it and his secretary takes them off onto typewritten sheets.
You can hang the little microphone around your neck so you
won't have to drive with one hand.

These little recorders can come in handy in many new businesses. I use one for interviews, but as yet haven't learned how
to use it as an idea receptacle. I, somehow, seem to "think"
better with a pencil or a typewriter.

You have to invent your own "idea machine." Use pencils,
note pads, a typewriter, a tape recorder, anything, as long as it
catches your creative flow of ideas. Build up your file with various idea folders. My early files contained folders on "radio-TV,"
"magazines," "speeches," and other areas for possible sales.
Your file might contain background information on restaurant
franchising, home decorating materials—all sorts of future sales
possibilities.

You need lots of ideas in your file, because only about one
out of twenty or so will show any early promise. Keep ideas on
file even if they don't work at first. I had a radio and TV show
scheme cooking in my idea compost heap for nearly three years
before an opportunity appeared. You have to weed the file out
now and then to refresh your memory, to recheck ideas that
didn't work the first time and to throw out stuff that you now
know will never work.

When you begin to get going on an idea that shows promise,
write out your plans. Investigate. Revise your prospective service or product description. Have people criticize it and rewrite it again. Get it ready to show to buyers. Your file and
your home office "corner" will help keep things sorted out. If
you have ideas and materials stashed away in different parts of
your home and your place of work, you're lost. When you have

brainstorm sessions, you need your idea file and all your materials handy. If you have a good meeting with someone else who has ideas you can use, get 'em down on paper (some friends use a recorder for this). Transcribe your notes onto more permanent typed pages and put each idea in its proper place.

Alex Osborn, who wrote the textbook *Applied Imagination,* says: "Millions of dollars worth of valuable ideas have been lost because of the want of a stub of a pencil and a scrap of paper." Another successful author, and scientist, Dr. Hans Selye, who wrote *The Stress of Life,* puts it even more strongly when he warns: "There's a limit to how much you can burden your memory; and trying to remember too many things is certainly one of the major sources of psychologic stress. I make a conscious effort to forget immediately all that is unimportant and to jot down data of possible value (even at the price of having to prepare complex files) . . . I manage to keep my memory free for facts which are truly essential to me."

To keep your idea notes flowing, you should even have a little pad and pencil in your coat pocket or purse. Answers to problems pop up at the strangest moments. Have you ever noticed that the harder you try to think of some name or the answer to some pressing worry, the more the answer evades you? Psychologists say that the mind, like a computer, has to make a search for the answer tucked away back in some cell. The more you push for an answer, the more the mind sends garbled messages back and forth, blocking out the answer.

When the mind is at rest or is diverted from the initial pressure, it often rattles out the answer to your problem. I find that early morning hours when I'm half awake often produce all sorts of answers. In order to get back to sleep, I used to try to forget about them. They'd be lost, and I found I didn't get much extra sleep anyway. Now I get up and jot down the flow of thoughts and go back to bed. Sleep comes almost instantly and when I wake up, there are all the ideas waiting to be clipped and used the same day or filed. Same thing happens when I'm taking a walk. An idea hits. I stop and jot it down and walk on. Pencils are easier to use because you can write up against walls and don't have to worry about the ink being level. You'll get some quizzical stares from passersby—but they quickly walk on. The main thing is: You've trapped and caged a valuable idea.

As your idea file builds and as your checking account becomes more active, you'll suddenly wake up one day to the fact that your little business is beginning to make money. Not much, mind you, but the trickle is definitely there and it has all the signs of increasing into a flow. This is a good time to make out a report on yourself. Set down all your expenditures and set down your new income figures. Based on fairly solid future sales possibilities, set down how much money might be coming in for the next six months or year and how much you think will be going out. If you can show a small but growing net profit figure, you're in business. If you're married, this is a good time to show your spouse your "annual report and future growth chart for Me, Incorporated." Make it like a real financial presentation. Write down your future growth plans and list all current and possible future contracts.

This kind of "first report" is another important step in focusing your attention on your venture. Maybe your family was dubious, even scared of your original "nutty idea." But, now you'll see that they'll probably show some interest. There's nothing like a sale to cheer you up and reassure your family that, while leaving your steady job might not be in the cards right now, going out on your own at some future date is a distinct possibility. Muttering about how you're going to do this or pursue that wild idea just unnerves people close to you. When you have it all down in black and white, so they can see where you've been and where you're going, your stock will rise in their estimation.

My wife was nice about it when I first stormed home and said I was going to show those s.o.b.'s. I was going to do a newspaper column. She knew I was unhappy with my organizational job but now she thought I'd gone balmy. "Where will your columns appear?" she calmly asked while I ranted in the kitchen as she was preparing dinner. After gulping down a drink, I answered: "I'm not sure yet, but I know it will work and then I can bust out of that place." She nodded, but I noticed she was somewhat tense the next couple of days. She was justifiably worried about what would happen if I just flipped and went charging off trying to sell newspaper columns without any idea of who would buy them.

I cooled off and wrote some sample columns and showed them to a friend who ran a news service that covered twenty-two papers. He bought one of the columns and said if I made them "newsy enough," he'd buy some more. Not a contract, but a commitment. I wrote to several newspapers around the country where I had an introduction and sold some more columns. It was at this moment that a friend who was in business for himself suggested I set up my own bank account. I thought he was kidding at first but he was serious. I set up the account, "Weaver Reports," and began to buy the materials I would need.

My wife was impressed with the sales and her whole mood changed. She saw that the thing could work, on a limited scale at least, and she saw that I was suddenly very happy. I had hope. She helped set up a little "home office" that has grown and grown. Now it covers a whole room over the garage and includes a new, three-drawer filing cabinet, two desks (his and hers), two typewriters, some comfortable office chairs, a telephone, plenty of paper and materials, a bookshelf, good lighting and a "hot-line" set of flip cards for important names and phone numbers.

You don't have to make your home office an ugly transplant of an organizational office. You can "decorate" that otherwise grim-looking file cabinet. One friend, an older woman who's doing free-lance writing from her home, pasted colorful magazine covers over her file and lacquered it. Looks nice and fits in with what she's doing.

Our home office now has two nice wooden desks, pictures on the wall and can be turned into a guest room when the occasion calls. It has a couch that converts into a bed and has easy access to a bathroom. No, your home office doesn't have to be ugly. Any married man who wants to set up a little office at home should pay attention to this: Let your wife in on the planning. Let her help select a desk if you don't have one. Let her fix it up. Tell her expenses are going to be tax deductible, but warn about overdoing it. If a wife doesn't have her own "home office," she ought to set one up. All the family finances, bills, records and consumer-related background information should be centered here. We used to have two "offices" at home. Now they're merged. We growl now and then about who is going to use which typewriter—but we work it out and are happy with the setup.

For those with children, you either have to have a place where you can close a door or do your work at night. You'd be surprised how well children react to "home office hours" when it's explained to them. We have two very active boys (ten and thirteen) and, at first, they'd come bursting into the office to relate some recent happening such as: "Guess what? Stevie just hit a ball through the kitchen window." If you limit yourself to specific times of the day and week, the children soon adjust to this and seem to like the comforting busy sounds of mommy or daddy working at home.

The home office need not be and probably shouldn't be, your

eventual main base of operations. It's a focal point for getting started. When your business gets going strong enough to run on its own, you can transfer the operation to someplace outside the home that's nearer suppliers and customers. But, if you're smart, you'll still retain "your corner" at home for doing work away from your business and for catching and jotting down ideas. You'll also need a home office as a focal point for keeping family finances, bills and other personal records in line.

I've mentioned the need for a bookshelf or bookshelves in your home office. You're going to find that several books, some inspirational, some technical, will be of great help in starting your business. I hope this book is one of them. Put it on your home office shelf and refer to it from time to time. I have a number of books that have been a great help in changing my way of thinking from the organizational approach of "climbing up," to the self-bosser approach of "moving out." I'm listing them here as possibilities for your shelf. No doubt you will pick and choose among the titles and will surely add several more of your own. But these particular books have been a great help to me and to several others I know who have also broken out on their own. I've mentioned some of them elsewhere but here they are again on separate pages you can use as a shopping list if you like.

SUGGESTED READING:

Executive Stress. Written by Dr. Harry Levinson, Harvard industrial psychologist. Harper & Row; $6.95. Don't let the word "executive" fool you. Every self-bosser is a mini-executive and this book digs into the fears managers have and how to conquer them. Levinson shows, for example, how you can channel your anger with your job into a powerful force that works for you instead of against you.

Man's Search for Meaning: An Introduction to Logotherapy. Washington Square Press; $1.25. Dr. Viktor E. Frankl, the author, is one of Europe's leading psychiatrists. He believes that the job you have in life is of utmost importance. Frankl quotes Nietzsche: "He who has a *why* to live can bear with almost any *how*." We must do those things that we really want to do, Frankl says, explaining: "Man does not simply exist, but always decides what his existence will be, what he will become in the next moment."

The Art of Selfishness: How to deal with the tyrants and tyrannies in your life. This is written by David Seabury and is published by Julian Messner; $5.95. It has a lot of anecdotes under chapter headings such as: "Never Compromise Yourself," "Taught to Fail," "How to Refuse a Request" and "When Worried About Money." It tells how to cut the emotional ties that drag many people down.

National Trade and Professional Associations of the United States. This book lists some 4,600 business and industry associations. It's a must for any new venture and can be purchased for $15 from: Columbia Books, Inc.; Suite 300; 917 15th St., N.W.; Washington, D.C.

Feel Free is written by Dr. David S. Viscott, who is a Boston psychiatrist and manager of his own sideline business called Sensitivity Games. He says: "Admit it, for once face the fact that you often feel like running." He means running from a lousy job, a lousy home life, whatever. It's a good book to shake you out of the rut you're in. Very witty, too. It's published by Peter H. Wyden, Inc.; $5.95.

Best of Both Worlds. This book was primarily written for women who want to break out of their home "establishment" to use their talents in part-time jobs. But, men can learn a lot from it too. It's written by Frances Goldman, a housewife who broke out and helped set up Distaff Staffers, an employment agency for women who love their families but also love to do professional and skilled work outside the home so they can have the "best of both worlds." It tells how to set up similar employment agencies in a sort of working "kit" form. The price is $10 from Distaffers, Inc.; Suite 1130, Western Savings Fund Bldg.; Philadelphia, Pa. 19107.

The Opportunity Explosion. Written by Robert Snelling, chairman of Snelling & Snelling, franchisor for the nation's largest chain of employment agencies, this book is aimed at: "The right way to find and get the right job." It works for finding an organizational job and it works for finding a way into your own business. It's a good book to have around whether you're able to go into your own business now or have to put it off for a while. Published by Macmillan at $6.95.

Retire to Action was written for people who want to keep active during retirement. It's also a good book for those who are a long way off from retirement but want to investigate new fields. It lists and describes every kind of volunteer job available today. Everything is in there. Names, addresses, job descriptions. Many a younger person can moonlight on a volunteer job that can eventually open the way to a business of their own. Julietta K. Arthur is the author and the publisher is Abingdon Press; $5.95.

Some of these books are available in paperback and some of them may be available in your library. A bookstore should be able to order most of them if they're not already in stock.

There are other books and booklets I rely on such as the phone book Yellow Pages. Don't laugh. It's one of the best source books available for a prospective self-bosser. Every kind of business is identified by class, by subject, by alphabetical order and a capsuled description usually accompanies the address and phone number. If you live in a small town, get your local Yellow Pages as well as those for the nearest major city. The Yellow Pages can give you ideas of areas you might want to enter with your own business and it can give you names and addresses of places where you can moonlight to try out your selected field.

I also get many an idea out of the Yellow Page listings. When I write my column, I often call various merchants and distributors listed to get more information on the product or service I'm writing about. If, for example, you think you might be interested in working with pets or want to sell pet products or even sell dogs, cats, canaries and the like, you might want to go down the list of veterinarians and pet shops. Line yourself up with a moonlighting job to see what's going on in the animal business. You may love it. And then you may not. You'll certainly learn a lot that will help when you finally set off on your own.

Part II
WHAT TO DO?

7
CREATIVE MOONLIGHTING

There are two kinds of people who are unhappy at work. There are those who would like to do something else, something specific, but are afraid to make the move because of financial and psychological ties to an organization. Then there are those who are unhappy but don't know what they want to do. These latter types often drift from job to job, hoping that their place in the sun might be just around the corner.

If you're the kind of person who wants to be on your own but doesn't have a clue as to what kind of business you could start, why not try "creative moonlighting"? This kind of moonlighting doesn't emphasize the money you get out of an extra job, it emphasizes the investigation of new ideas, the formation of a goal.

First, you've got to make a list of all the things you like. Maybe it's sports, gardening or working with people. Or maybe it's working with your hands. Whatever it is, put it down on a piece of paper. Then think of the kinds of jobs that would match up with this "happy" list. For example, if you like animals, you'd put down "veterinarian medicine" or "pet shops" as the kinds of jobs that offer work with animals. If you like working with people, you'd put down sales, running a restaurant, operating a tourist business, or some other kind of people-mixer types of jobs. Look through the index in your phone book Yellow Pages for ideas. For example, if you think you might like to produce some product or service and sell it through the mail, look under "Addressing and Mailing Services." If you like the outdoors, look under "Camping Equipment" or "Recreation Vehicles."

Armed with some general ideas you'd like to investigate, start actively looking for part-time work that relates to the kind of business you'd like to explore. Where do you look? The most painless way to get started with your "creative moonlighting" search is to make an appointment with one of the temporary employment services. You'll find them in the phone book Yellow Pages listed under "Employment Contractors—Temporary Help." Depending on where you live, you'll find local services and some that are part of a national franchising organization such as Kelly Girl, Western Girl, Employers' Overload, Manpower, Inc., Partime and Olsten's to name just a few.

Don't be fooled by the words "girl" or "man" in the titles. Western Girl has a division that hires men. Manpower hires many, many women. These temporary help services are specialists in lining up interesting work for moonlighters. They give you a thorough screening and make an inventory of your skills plus the kind of work you'd like to investigate. They determine what times of the day, week or month you'd be free from your regular job and then line you up with prospective customers who need your part-time assistance.

You say you're tired at the end of the day and don't know how you could fit in any more work? What's probably making you tired is the dullness of your job, not the amount of work you're doing. You probably have seen plenty of your colleagues complain about how tired they are while all they've done is sit at a desk. Howard Scott, president of the National Association of Temporary Services (and president of Partime, a national temporary help service), says: "Many of our temporary employees perk up when they start investigating different part-time jobs. Those who were depressed by their full-time work, suddenly realize other people want them . . . They see new faces, try out new ideas."

You can find the time, and chances are you will be less tired at the end of the week than you were when you were just handling one job. If you work the traditional nine-to-five hours, you can get temporary job assignments that provide work from 6 to 9 P.M. Or you may just want to work Saturdays. For those who get out earlier in the afternoon or have a four-day week, there's even more extra time. Some moonlighters work part or all of their vacations to investigate new businesses.

When you go into a temporary employment service office, you find out right away that it's not an employment service in the strict sense of the word. They don't get you jobs where you're paid by the new employer. You work for Kelly Girl, Partime, Manpower or whichever service you choose. The service just rents you out to its various clients. This is important, because it means the door will be open to investigate many more job opportunities. Companies often need work done but don't want to go through the expense of hiring someone full time. Full-time employees have to be put into pension plans, insurance plans and whatnot and, besides, full-salaried people have to be carried as part of permanent overhead.

Part-time employment placement is a booming, billion-dollar-a-year business. According to NATS president Scott, "There is every conceivable type of job open for talented people who are willing to work part time." He says the types of jobs are broken down into four major categories: clerical, industrial, technical and sales (includes marketing). The technical and sales categories, Scott feels, "are probably the best hunting grounds for moonlighters who eventually want to go out into their own business." But, he says, "don't overlook the less glamorous clerical and industrial fields in the probe to find a business you want to start."

Remember, the main thing you're after is commercial or business intelligence information. Fancy yourself as a sort of friendly spy who must investigate, say, the restaurant business. You take as many part-time job assignments as you can in the restaurant field. Depending on your skills, you may work with restaurant suppliers in various restaurants as a waiter, assistant manager, cashier—whatever. The temporary employment service is your "front organization," getting you into all sorts of places so you can make a final report on what's doing in the restaurant business.

Back at your "corner" office in your home, you start filing weekly reports on what you're learning from the temporary job assignments. You may pick up books, booklets, lists of suppliers, names of people who might be of help when, and if, you ever get into the restaurant business.

Same thing goes for other kinds of businesses. Say you feel you might have some product or service that could be sold through the mail. Line yourself up with some mail-order houses or organizations that do a lot of promotional work through the mail. See how the promotions are handled. How are sales fulfilled? What kind of cost figures can you get on such things as printing, mailing, addressing?

Sometimes, creative moonlighters find the business they think they might like to get into turns out to be a bore or something entirely different from the idealistic picture they had. Even if you find that you hate the restaurant business, mail-order business or any other business, all is not lost. You at least know more clearly what you don't want to do and you haven't had to commit yourself to a monumental blunder in your career.

If you have to wear a white jacket as a waiter in a hamburger haven or a leather jacket as a delivery driver for some sales service, do it as long as it brings information about the business you're investigating.

When you have your interview with the temporary employment service officer, make sure he or she understands that you have a full-salaried job and you don't want it threatened by reports of your moonlighting. You want your moonlighting work held in complete confidence. Both the service and the clients must agree to this. Some bosses don't mind their employees moonlighting as long as it doesn't conflict with regular office or shop hours. But all too many bosses do mind. They may not admit it, but deep down they resent the fact that some employee "hasn't got enough to do around here to keep busy."

Some organizations feel they own you. You're somehow "disloyal" if you aren't working and thinking about their better interests morning, noon and night, seven days a week. So it's best to keep your commercial intelligence moonlighting venture quiet. If your boss hears about it, just say it's a temporary thing you're doing to ease over a family problem. This is true, of course, even if it is a little vague. Play it down. Don't talk about your moonlighting to others outside your family or your closest friends (not those where you work).

You don't have to do your moonlighting through a temporary employment service. If you have a good idea of what you want to do, you can line up your own jobs. The "temp" services are the easiest way to get started but are, by no means, the only way. You might want to work in with a very small outfit that doesn't use or can't afford temporary employment services. Small businesses are an excellent place to moonlight because you often are given more responsibility and you work in an environment similar to the one you'll face when you go out on your own.

A friend of mine thinks he wants to do a newsletter about a very narrow technical subject. He feels there are enough people around the country who will pay for information on this subject and he thinks he can charge, maybe, $100 a year for each sub-scription. He is a technical writer for a national organization and believes he has learned all he can at his job. He has a "blah" feeling about his niche in the organization and wants to go out on his own.

He's playing it cool. He had a job offer from another big com-pany but he says, "That might be just jumping from one frying pan into another frying pan—I wouldn't even be getting into the fire." He rejected the job offer and, instead, hunted up some newsletter publishers around town. There are many of them. Every association has one and there are independents who do their own sales and promotion.

My friend signed up with a struggling little newsletter and agreed to do writing and reporting work for just a few dollars an hour—all the publisher could pay. In turn, he learned how promotion worked and how subscription orders were fulfilled. He got some good ideas and noted where mistakes were made. He was completely honest with the newsletter publisher. He told him of his own plans to start his own letter on an entirely different subject. The publisher offered to help him. My friend hasn't made his breakaway move yet but he's ready to start his own letter soon and his moonlighting employer will share office and printing expenses.

This is an example of creative moonlighting at its best. You use it to learn, to probe, to get in the groundwork for your own business. My friend and others I've talked with find that they become so interested in their moonlighting ventures—because they know they might lead eventually to their own business—that they can work much faster and much better at their regular job. One friend tells me he is able to get his regular job work done in half the time it used to take him. He uses the free time to apply to a growing family business. He developed an engine cleaning device and is now beginning to market it on a re-gional scale. When it can be marketed nationally, he will bid good-by to his regular jobs and work full time on what started out as creative moonlighting.

You usually don't make a lot of money moonlighting. At least, not at first. But over the years you can make a tidy sum. You have to be careful. Don't get carried away by the extra money moonlighting can bring in. One other friend (I can't mention names because these people are still working for somebody), got a good moonlighting offer to write monthly reports for an association. The pay was good and he was delighted. After a year or so I asked him how things were going with the moonlighting. He said: "I'm not happy with it. I just find myself working longer and harder and we don't seem to have any extra money to show for it."

On questioning, I found that he was just throwing his monthly moonlighting check into the family funds, where it seemed to "disappear" in a cloud of bills and extra expenses. This fellow and his family, without realizing it, began to buy more things and moved right up to his new earnings. Nobody seemed any happier. On the contrary, there were grumbles about the fact he had to work many nights during the month when he could have been home with his family.

Two things are wrong with this kind of moonlighting approach. The first is, the moonlighter had no goal, no plan for his work. It just came as a windfall and he took it. He wasn't learning anything new from the reports he was doing so he wasn't able to build anything that could eventually turn into a business. Because there was no goal, he was just as unhappy with his work as ever—even unhappier, because, as he said, "I'm just working longer and harder with nothing to show for it."

The second thing that went wrong with this aimless moonlighting was the emphasis put on the money angle. The moonlighter thought the extra money would make his family happy with new gadgets they could buy (they got a new car shortly after he started the project). The money was put into the family coffers instead of in a special checking account. You should never use your creative moonlighting money for family funds. Put all you make in the special "Me, Incorporated" checking account we talked about and let it build toward the business you eventually want to start. Keep living on your regular income. Don't touch the moonlighting income. It can provide the vital funds for your escape plan.

When you use moonlighting creatively, it can be a powerful force in your life. It can help you define a goal for your own business. It can steer you away from ventures you think would be great but are not for your type of personality. It can build your confidence in yourself and can often provide a sort of "halfway house" between working for an organization and being on your own. Some creative moonlighters find that their main job is too time-consuming, too restrictive. So they move to a "full-time" part-time job which requires their presence for only a half a day or just part of the week. They get less money, of course, but make some of it up from sales in their own budding business or from continuing, creative moonlighting probes on top of their regular part-time job.

If you're working for an outfit that saps a lot of your energy, another method of edging into moonlighting is the "volunteer way." Even the toughest organizations are shamed into letting their employees do volunteer community work. After all, it's for the good of the community and the organization benefits from the image of being a local benefactor.

Try lining yourself up with an interesting volunteer job in your community, one that could eventually lead you into some self-bosser business. Many community jobs can give training you might need for your own business. They can also help build a list of contacts who can be of future help. You can get a line on what kind of volunteer jobs are available by making an appointment to see someone in your local volunteer service bureau. These are listed under such names as United Way, Community Chest, Health and Welfare Council, United Funds, United Appeal, Council of Social Agencies and Community Service.

Go in and have a "job placement" talk just the way you would with a regular commercial, temporary service placement officer. You'll be interviewed and screened. Your skills will be noted and the area you want to work will be described. Let's say you think you might eventually want to go into your own business of selling recreational equipment or services. Then try getting a volunteer job with the city's recreational programs for children. Or you might want to investigate radio and TV publicity work. Many volunteer agencies need people to write and produce spot material for public service broadcasts. You may work on a fund-raising drive through a mailing campaign. This can show you how a mail-order business might work.

You won't get paid for all this. But you'll find the work gratifying, you'll be doing your bit and you'll be learning things that could help you eventually make the move out on your own. One of my wife's friends went to work for a volunteer organization that repairs and spruces up used household equipment, clothing, appliances, furniture and whatnot. Handicapped and needy workers are used to do the repairs and the fixing up and profits from sales go into training programs.

This bright gal created a "mod shop" in the volunteer organization's store. She was able to get workers to make all sorts of interesting furniture and decorator items out of junk. She also learned how to get local press, radio and TV coverage for her work. Now she's thinking of starting her own commercial decorator shop. She will continue to help the volunteer organization but she'll also have a nice little business of her own.

One disgruntled organization man volunteered to work for his city's community fund drive. He was a good salesman, so they put him to work organizing meetings with prospective donors and city charitable institutions. He was enthusiastic. He did a fine job, complete with seminars, slide shows and other meeting techniques. He did such a good job, several companies around town asked him to set up meetings for them on ecology problems and other related community subjects. Of course, they paid him handsomely for this special work. He's now getting ready to go out into his own business as an organizer of meetings, seminars and conventions for major corporations. He says he will continue to help his city with its fund-raising meetings. He loves his "moonlighting" volunteer work. It showed him he could help people and he was worth something.

As I said, moonlighting can be a powerful, positive force for those who eventually want to be on their own. If planned right, anything done outside the regular place where you work has got to be a positive force.

I can remember my first moonlighting efforts. It was back in Cleveland, Ohio, when I was working as a cub reporter for the Cleveland *Plain Dealer*. I was single then and had the most atrocious work schedule. I had Sundays and Mondays off. My friends said that having Sunday and Monday nights off for a bachelor was "like being dead, socially."

So what to do Monday nights? I found that the local community college was offering a Monday night course called "How to Write and Sell Free-Lance Articles." Just what the doctor ordered. I fancied myself as a writer, albeit a green one, so I signed up. The professor's name, I forget. What I remember is the fact that he got all of us enthused about writing our own free-lance articles and selling them around the country. He said, what I've already said in this book, "Marketing your product is 75 per cent of the battle."

We learned how to think up a good, salable subject and how to write a query letter to editors. We learned that at least twenty letters had to go out to various publications or we didn't have a chance to make a sale. We learned how to read magazines and see what kind of articles they liked and we learned which publications were the easiest to get into, which were the hardest.

I never sold any articles to *Life* magazine for thousands of dollars but I did sell some articles to *Lifetime Living* magazine (now defunct) for several hundred dollars. I was thrilled. I had no goal to be on my own then, so the money went down the drain. But a seed was planted. I liked the fleeting little business I built up providing several editors around the country with articles. I even had a primitive file and cross-check system of all the magazines that got queries and what their answers were.

Later on, when I was in Brazil as a correspondent for *Business Week* magazine, I started another little free-lance venture, supplying Copley Newspaper News Service with regular reports. Again, the money went down the drain, but it was gratifying to have this sideline business. When we moved to Mexico City, my wife took over the Copley News reports because I was too busy trying to keep up with my own company's news bureau.

These little ventures on the side actually served as the smoldering coal that eventually lit the way for my first attempt with "Weaver Reports." My wife and I had made some friends in the newspaper business and we had learned how to sell material through the mail to editors.

Unfortunately, we had no concrete goals or plans for our early sideline ventures or we might have been coaxed out on our own at an earlier stage. Even so, those few, brief jaunts in the "moonlight," eventually helped to head me out of the organizational world and into my own business.

8

IDEAS THAT WORK

When you're looking for ideas that will work, something that can be sold through your own business, you should follow your personal experience, your special interests. Almost everybody has something that they find intriguing or something that bothers them—even enrages them. Whenever you find yourself being drawn into, and wound up in, some project, you may be on your way to setting up your own business. Many of us fail to follow through on something that absorbs us and just let it sit there as a hobby, peculiar pastime or gripe.

Keen, personal interest in some subject is often the best fuel to get you started and keep you going with your own business. As I look back on the years just prior to my final break with the organizational world, I find that two key incidents turned me away from writing about business and companies and led me into the broader, much more interesting world of people as purchasers. I turned away from writing about sellers—the major manufacturers—and started writing about the nation's buyers—consumers like you and me.

I was in my office writing about some Securities and Exchange Commission ruling, when my wife called with anger and fear in her voice.

"Listen," she shouted, "gasoline is coming out of the gas tank like a fountain and we might get blown up!" I told her to calm down and tell me what happened. We had just bought a new station wagon and insisted that they install seat belts in the third seat, that faced the rear. Our two little boys often sat back there and we didn't want them crashing through the rear window if somebody hit us from behind.

So the dealer had someone put in seat belts. Apparently, according to my wife's animated description, some idiot drilled down through the wagon's frame and into the gas tank when he needed holes to screw in the seat belt anchors. It's a wonder he wasn't incinerated at the time. There was gas in the tank.

When my wife went to fill up the tank with gas, of course, the pressure forced it out and up through the little drilled holes like a geyser. My children, the seat and carpeting were soaked with gas. When my wife called the dealer, he told her: "Bring it on in later in the week, we're piled up now." When I heard that, I blew my stack. Pure, white-heat anger took over. I called the dealer and asked how much liability insurance he carried because he was within an inch of a massive law suit. The manager of the place was shocked into action and they came out with a tow truck to get our station wagon. Any spark could have set it off.

This little episode started me looking into the whole realm of manufacturers, dealers and the repair mess. This was back in the mid-1960's, about the time Ralph Nader was making mincemeat out of General Motors. My probes into the automobile and appliance businesses unearthed all sorts of repair tangles among manufacturers, dealers and customers. Consumers were becoming angry at hundreds of thousands of incidents similar to the drilled gas tank outrage my wife and I suffered. My findings got into a *Forbes* magazine cover story, and from there on in I was hooked on the consumer cause. I loved it, because I was writing about people I knew and all their daily money problems. My own problems were the same as theirs.

Not too long after the story on the repair mess, I investigated the "repairs" human beings were suffering at the hands of doctors, hospitals and medical insurance companies. My youngest boy, Mike, had to have his tonsils out. Normally, this is a simple operation, the equivalent of repairing a fender on a car. However, Mike had a fairly rare enzyme deficiency and an extremely sensitive stomach. He couldn't eat certain foods, and if his innards became irritated and he began to throw up, he couldn't take anything—food or water—for several hours. He's grown out of it now, but at the time it was a serious problem.

He was quite little, four years old to be exact, but the doctor felt the tonsils had to come out because they were enlarged, perforated, and no longer served their functions as a natural filter for bacteria. So out they came. We told the hospital people that Mike must have a special diet. The hospital frowned on parents staying all night with patients for a "simple thing like a tonsillectomy," so we were shunted out of his room. Sure enough, some half-wit gave him a big glass of water or ginger ale after he had been throwing up. He kept throwing up and began to dehydrate. He was going under and we couldn't get his doctor because he took a day off, incommunicado.

Again, the same way I had to threaten the automobile shop, I had to threaten the hospital management. Nobody seemed to be doing anything for the child. He was just going downhill. His doctor finally came and the feeding procedure was changed. They "permitted" us to be with him day and night, and he slowly began to revive. Those dumb, bureaucratic bumblers that charge the public $100 a day, and more, for hospital care, stretched a simple one-day surgery event into a five-day nightmare.

Again, the white heat of rage. Again, the muckraking cover

story. I found the mess in medicine was widespread and getting worse. Letters poured in. I'd hit a nerve. The University of Missouri School of Journalism saw fit to give me an award for the story, and I was even more convinced that I should devote myself exclusively to the investigation and reporting of all the money problems you find in the average family's checkbook. These two "happenings" pushed me, finally, into setting up my own newspaper column based on the daily money and safety traps consumers have to face. Being a business magazine, *Forbes* quite naturally didn't want me to concentrate on consumers' problems. I was asked to stick more to writing about big government, big business and big investments. I knew what I wanted to do. So the break was inevitable. The Los Angeles Times Syndicate said it would market my consumer column idea and I was off and running—and stumbling. I had plenty of problems but I was doing what my instinct told me I had to do.

I'd like to show you four cases that illustrate the point that following your own instinct, your own personality, is the best way to find ideas that will work for you.

Enter Bill Brown, sometimes called "Kwabena." Bill was working for a hospital back in the 1960's, when Martin Luther King, Malcolm X and others aroused a national wave of interest in black people—where they came from, where they were going, their culture and their ties to Africa. Being black, Bill began to investigate his own family background. He wondered where he came from, where his people came from.

His investigation led him back to the name Zaro, a legendary figure who lived on the British West Indian island of Antigua. Zaro, it turned out, was one of Bill's kin. He was a great-great grandfather on his mother's side. Zaro had been a holy man in Africa.

Along the way, Bill and his mother began picking up African culture, African music, African dress, African everything. Bill's mother, who had a city government job, began making African things. She was good with her hands and had a flair for design and bright colors. She copied African apparel and began selling it where she worked. Bill and his young wife began selling African apparel, jewelry and whatnot, where they worked.

"We could see there was a market," Bill says, explaining that "all kinds of people from the janitor on up to the top bosses where we worked . . . all of them were buying our African products." About the same time, Bill, his mother and his wife were all grumbling about their regular jobs. "I was frustrated," says Bill as his face clouds, thinking about some painful experience. "I was frustrated because I wasn't getting anywhere. They weren't giving me enough responsibility. I was tired of the organization and all its structure—all the bureaucracy. I realized that the only way is to get control of the source of your income."

The family decided to investigate the possibility of setting up a full-time business, a store, to sell African and other related foreign-design products. Bill traveled to Africa and visited scores of shops run by village craftsmen. He lined up suppliers for such things as "Dansikis" (erroneously pronounced Dashiki, he says), robes, jewelry, sculpture. He worked with a lawyer friend and got the information he needed for import licenses, store licenses and that sort of thing.

Then, one by one, the Brown family members quit their jobs and began working in the store, Zaro's House of Africa, tucked away on a street just a few blocks from the Capitol buildings in Washington, D.C. Zaro's now has an expanding list of customers—black and white, wealthy and modest means. Bill Brown, called "Kwabena" on Zaro's product flier, never sold anything before "this African thing" came along. Now he is an excellent salesman. He's good because he knows each product, where it came from, why it was made and the kind of people that use it in Africa. "Customers want to know all about what they're buying," he says. "You've got to take the time to give them a little bit of culture with each article they buy." People are tired of being pushed around in stores, Bill explains, "The soft sell is the only way." Customers want personal attention, not computerized mass marketing. With every Dansiki, every colorful robe, every decorator piece of African sculpture, Brown gives each customer "a little bit of myself, a little bit of African culture, a little something they can take with them to talk about when they show their purchase to their friends."

Frankie Greene Studios, got started with the same kind of personal interest push that spawned Zaro's House of Africa. But let's let Frankie Greene Mathews, a Denver housewife, tell it her way:

My daughter was in kindergarten and one night I had to come up with a fast idea for a little show her teacher wanted to put on in the classroom. I can't sew anything complicated. If I ever had to make a dress, I'd be lost. But I studied art in college and had an eye for good design. We dug out some bits of fairly heavy cloth and I started sewing some crude hand puppets. I sewed two pieces together that would go over the hand and then I started making heads by stuffing material into little bags. We put faces on them and off to school they went.

The kids loved them. I guess they were my first audience. They seemed to want to talk to the puppets more than they wanted to talk to the teacher or parents. Other teachers wanted some puppets. Parents wanted some puppets. I began making more and making them better. A friend introduced me to an expert seamstress and she showed me what I was doing wrong and how I could make puppets of much better, lasting quality. Another friend said I ought to look up one of these "Gift Shop Agents," you know, the kind that have showrooms and sell products to store buyers.

The agent seemed to like the puppets and put them in his showroom. Suddenly, orders started coming in from all over the place. I was so excited. I took over the basement and our big garage and began making puppets. Housewives in the neighborhood work on the puppets and they love it. It gives them a chance to work at home and make some money. It's much better than having to go work someplace.

Before all this, Frankie says, "I tried working at an aerospace plant but I couldn't stand the time-clock routine. I was bored. I belonged to some clubs but they were boring too. I wanted something to do and these puppets have changed my whole life.

Frankie Greene's husband, Lute, is a lawyer. He not only helped her set up the business but he is the main "idea man" for new kinds of puppet faces. Some of Frankie's best-selling puppets came from Lute's designs of such little faces as "cross-eyed elephant, waspish mouse and daffy dragon." But puppets aren't the only thing. Frankie has branched out into making stuffed animals, felt cloth bottle covers and potholders with animal designs. "When I run out of ideas, when I get dry," Frankie says, "I take a couple of days off and go shopping. I see what people are buying and see where I can do better. After a couple of good, all-day shopping tours, ideas just seem to come flowing in."

The Smithsonian Institution is buying Frankie Greene puppets and animals for its handcraft shop. Project Head Start is buying puppets because teachers find problem children will talk to the puppets when they won't talk to adults. The puppets serve as a sort of communication bridge. Frankie says, "They want me to set up a factory to make these puppets and animals but I won't do it . . . I want to work in my home . . . I don't want to lose control." At last count, sales were running up to $30,000 a year and rising.

Frank Payne's wife, Elaine, has hay fever and other allergies. Frank and his family live in Annandale, Virginia, where it can get nasty and cold in the winter. From fall through spring, the Paynes and others in the area have to turn the heat on. When the heat comes on, as any good heating and air-conditioning engineer will tell you, the air inside a house or apartment dries out. It dries out so much, it has less humidity (water in the air) than the Sahara Desert. This dryness works on the throat and nose membranes and makes them susceptible to irritation and eventually infection. For allergic people, air that's dried by a furnace is a disaster.

One winter, Frank's wife suffered an allergic attack that sent her to the hospital for two weeks. As a man who worked in and around heating equipment for a major building, Frank, in desperation, started looking for a commercial humidifier to get some more moisture in the air. Back in the early 1960's, Frank couldn't find a humidifier that worked well enough to get the kind of moisture to make the air healthier in his house. He tinkered around in his basement and came up with a pipe that had little holes drilled in it to allow water to be sprayed through into the furnace duct. No good. It sprayed water all over the place and would soon ruin the duct system. He went back to his bench and devised a nozzle that would spray water into a mesh-filter screen. It worked. The humidity greatly improved, and the excess water was caught by the screen and went out through a drain. The next winter, Frank's wife, Elaine, breathed easier. Frank was able to get the indoor humidity up higher than any commercial device was capable of doing. He later refined his humidifier with a "back wash" system to keep the filter clean.

Friends who suffered from the lack of humidity in winter, asked Frank to fix up humidifiers for their homes. He began installing custom-made humidifiers for seventy to ninety dollars a job, depending on the size needed. He experimented with plastic "catch pans" and they tended to break. He finally started using stainless steel pans and vinyl tubing. The size of the humidifier became standardized and he began to have machine shops around town make up batches of assembly parts.

Some local heating and air-conditioning contractors began buying regular supplies of Frank's humidifier—which he had patented—and the operation is moving into other cities on the East Coast. Frank's brother Seth helps with sales, advertising and the difficult task of setting up distributors. Frank's other brother, Grayford, set up a regular, factorylike assembly line and the humidifier is in full production.

The device, called Spra-Kleen now retails for around $150, installed, and latest figures show that more than four thousand units are being sold annually with the amount doubling every year or two. The business is taking off. Frank Payne filled a need and a business grew around it.

Then there's the "Nantucket Kite Man." Can you imagine having fun making and flying kites and getting paid for it? Al Hartig and his wife, Betty, lived in New York. He had a nice enough job working for a company that sold decorator ceramic products, but the Hartigs felt trapped in New York. They wanted to get out of the city into some cleaner air. But they couldn't. They didn't have the money, and jobs were hard to come by.

Al used to make model planes and boats as a boy and continued to make small sailboats in New York. He'd sail them in the pond in Central Park. One summer, there was a water shortage and the city didn't fill the pond. Says Al: "What was I to do? I couldn't just sit around twiddling my thumbs. While we were away on summer vacation I started to make a delta-wing kite out of cloth so it would last. The paper and plastic ones break too easy."

Back from vacation, Al, his wife and a couple of friends wandered over to Central Park with their new, and very color- ful, cloth kites. The kites flew marvelously in a fresh breeze. People kept coming up, asking: "Where the hell'd you get those kites?" Al said he had all sorts of potential customers. But he turned them down. Finally, a fellow from India who had just opened a little shop in New York called Go Fly a Kite, asked Hartig to make kites for him. He would put them in his stock of kites from all over the world. Al didn't want to do it but his wife coaxed him into building a few just to make a little money before Christmas.

The kites sold so fast, the shop owner begged Hartig to make as many as he could as fast as he could. Al started a backroom production line in his home. But first he applied for a patent to protect his unique design. His wife finally had to quit her job as a secretary to work full time on cutting patterns and assem- bling kites. Al says his boss was disturbed by his increasing ab- sence from the job. Finally, a little company on Nantucket Is- land off Cape Cod asked Al if he and his wife wanted to move there to help start a business selling handcrafts to tourists, his kite included. The Hartigs moved. Fresh air at last.

The little company folded after nine months and Al was for- tunate to be able to borrow money from his former boss to keep going. They pulled through the winter and the kite busi- ness began to fly. Hartig got Nantucket housewives to help cut and assemble kites during the winter, when there wasn't much to do. Tourists coming to Nantucket usually stop by Al's little shop on the South Wharf. Rare is the time when they don't leave with a kite costing anywhere from five dollars for a child's model on up to twenty-five for a "serious kite flier" model. A mail-order business was opened and, at last count, production was running at nearly four thousand kites a year.

Al says, "I've had all kinds of offers from major manufacturers to lease my kite designs. But I don't want to get much bigger. We make all the money we need to have fun on this island. We have all kinds of interesting people drop by to talk and buy a kite. We're happy and we don't want to jiggle it."

There they are: A man who turned a keen interest in his black heritage into a delightful family business, a housewife who made a child's kindergarten assignment into a hectic but happy money-maker, a husband who invented a humidifier to save his wife's health and a husband and wife who are merrily making money flying and selling kites.

These true stories tell a lot about ways to find ideas that will work to pay your family bills and make you independent and happy. Let's take a look at the lessons these little success stories can teach us:

★) *Strong Personal Interest* can guide you into your own business with much more chance of success than some kind of interest that's imposed on you. In every case we've just seen, there was some immediate need to fill, some keen interest, something very personal that gently pushed these people into a chance to do their own thing outside the rigid structure of the organizational world. In one case, a water shortage deprived an avid sailboat hobbyist of his time-off entertainment. So he came up with a new kind of kite. In another case, keen interest in Africa and black culture led a family into their own business. The personal interest, the personal drive has to be there. Otherwise, the mind can be lulled back into the numbness of time clocks, the coffee breaks and the rest of the bureaucratic way of life.

Everybody has something they like to do, something they're good at. If you put this personal interest to work, it could turn into something that's eventually capable of supporting you. One friend of mine loves collecting coins and scarce paper money. He's beginning to sell some of his coins and locate coins for others through a "kitchen" mail-order business. I'm sure that one day he'll open his own shop and quit his organizational job. Another friend, Dolly, tried selling wigs. It worked for a while but then the market became saturated. She loved to work with wigs and the people underneath them. She learned how wigs should be cut, shaped, cleaned, set, everything. Now Dolly is turning into a "wig and home fashion consultant." Plenty of housewives can't get out for beauty counseling, so our friend comes to them. It all started with her own wig and the need to make it look better.

★) *Family Affair.* In each case, we've seen that, somehow, the family and friends are brought in to inspire or actually help with the business. I know from personal experience that bringing your family and friends in on what you're doing can make for heights of happiness that most wage earners never experience. I don't mean you have to kneel to nepotism. You needn't have everybody in your family working for you, but you should let them participate if they want to. Encourage it, don't force it.

Frankie Greene Mathews encouraged her husband to think up designs for her puppets' faces. She says he loves it because "It's kind of like recreation or therapy after a hard day arguing with other lawyers." Frank Payne has his brothers working with him. One is good at the technical side, the other is good at sales. Bill Brown found that his mother and his wife had valuable skills that combined to develop a little business. They weren't forced to help. They just pitched in, and it worked.

In some cases, members of the family don't want to work in a business you form. Frankie Mathews' daughter (the one whose kindergarten class started the whole puppet business) helps make animals and puppets from time to time but has other interests that take her out of the home. She's not pushed. She gets paid for the piecework whenever she feels the need for money.

Neighbors like to help too. Let them. People see that you're happy and it's contagious. They want to help. They enjoy it. You enjoy it. People can be brought closer together by a little business that fills a need.

In my own business, my wife has become an important partner. Her knowledge of how an office should be run, her constant flow of ideas help me immensely. We find ourselves chattering happily away after a long day's work. We're sharing something. It takes both of us to do it right. And, our children like it. When they ask to help, we let them. Our older boy, Paul, took great pride one summer working in the office. Children should be able to see what their parents do at work. They ought to be let in on it. It's a pity that so few schools have courses that require the children to visit their parents' places of work to study what's going on, ask questions and then write reports for discussion back in the classroom. Children aren't getting in touch with the real world soon enough. We're keeping them in a hothouse education system from grade school, through high school, on into college. They don't get near enough—if any—work-study programs. They don't get a chance to develop work skills early enough and, I think, some of them lack confidence because of this.

★) *Think Small.* In most of the cases we just studied, the self-bossers instinctively shied away from bigness. Money wasn't their prime goal. Oh, they needed money to pay the family bills, but they didn't set out to "make it big" or "strike it rich," as some of the "work at home" ads put it. The kite man has turned down offers from major manufacturers that could have made really big money. He fears them, and rightly so. He would lose control. Somebody else would slowly but surely suck away his reason for being, his happiness in working with his hands and his pleasure in having, as he says, "interesting people come in to see me."

Frankie Mathews won't let them lure her puppet production out of her home into some factory. The little business she started has put magic into her life and she doesn't want to lose it. She says she runs around half the day in a nightgown and bathrobe because she often has to go right from breakfast into solving some bottleneck with the production of puppets or stuffed animals. She loves things the way they are. So why change?

We've got to have more people in this country who can "think small" instead of "think big" the way the tycoons tell it as they chomp on a cigar. We've got to think small, we've got to un-automate in some areas and we have to put more of a personal touch back into selling. Bill Brown said it: "People are sick and tired of the hard sell, they want the freedom to know more about what they're buying so they can do better."

As you look around for ideas, ask yourself what are the products or services you'd like to have but aren't really available. The more you can bring a personal touch, some personal service to customers, the more chance your business will have. Customers want to be able to trust you. They don't want to be overwhelmed. If you have to go to a customer's home to fix something in an emergency, get over there. Let your customers know they can count on you, personally, to help them with the product or service they're buying. When's the last time you encountered a sales person who really knew the products, whom you trusted to level with you on what was available in the market? Chances are you haven't run across too many sales people like this. When you do, you keep going back and you tell your friends.

With my consumer column, I encourage readers to write to me with their questions and problems. Some 18,000 have written to me in the three years the column has been going. My

staff and I answer every letter. I read every letter. These people are not just customers, they're the lifeblood of my little
news business. They tell me their troubles. They tell me what
to write.

You can work this personal touch into almost any kind of
business. A friend, Pat Goss, and his wife run a gasoline station. Nothing very exciting about that—right? Wrong. Pat and
his wife are not just gasoline station managers, they're "consumer educators." Pat gives classes at his station on how the
oil companies and the auto companies work to gyp the motor-
ist. He's sort of a Ralph Nader with grease on his hands. People
flock to his "wise up" classes. Now Pat is teaching "consumer
automobile economics" at a local community college. He fills a
need. He doesn't just pump gas. He shows his customers how to
buy, how to get more out of their machines for less money.
They trust him. He doesn't need much paid advertising. Word-
of-mouth advertising is the most powerful kind of advertising
there is and Pat Goss has a lot of it. His oil company franchisor
tried to ease him out. His classes were upsetting the mer-
chandisers. Pat took his case to the press and TV and beat 'em
back. There was so much unfavorable publicity, the oil company retreated and now leaves him pretty much alone.

Again, Pat Goss isn't trying to make a lot of money. He
seems to like using his gas station to teach people how not to get
gypped. Work no longer becomes work when you're involved
like this. You have the time to do what you want to do. Time
means everything. Money means much less. In his book *Life
Begins at Fifty,* Walter Pitkin says we're all born with the
chance of acquiring working capital of a half million. "Not dollars," he says, "hours." If we can live to be seventy and use our
time more for what we want to do and less for what others try
to impose on us, we can get a capital of a "half million hours."
Pitkin says we should get off the money standard and onto the

"time" standard. Make every minute of your working day count for something.

I've given you some ideas on how to search for ideas that will help start a business. Now I'd like to give some advice on what you *shouldn't* do.

You shouldn't fall for these advertised "make money at home" schemes. There might be some that can eke out a few pennies but 99.9 per cent of them are gyps and just detract from where good ideas can be found—in your own mind, in your own family, in your own neighborhood.

Mail-order hucksters prey on people who want desperately to start some little business at home. They usually start out with the words "no experience needed." And they usually have "make big money" or some other such nonsense at the head of their pitch. Most of the schemes ask you to send in money for the "secret" or the "key" to making all this big money. There isn't any secret and there's no key that you can't find right around you, right among your daily experiences.

These "make big money at home" sharpies remind me of the cartoon I once saw, I think it was *Pogo,* I'm not sure. It might have been *Peanuts.* At any rate, one little cartoon character said to another: "I saw an ad in the paper, it said it would tell me how to make big money if I'd send in two dollars." The other character asked what happened. "Well, I got this letter and it said to put an ad in the paper telling people I'd let 'em know how to make big money if they'd send me two dollars."

That just about sums up how the "make big money" schemes work. Don't ever send anybody any money with the promise that they'll show you how to make money. Follow your own instincts. Look around. There are ideas everywhere. Take the time. Investigate. Build up that idea file in your "corner" office at home.

9

PATENT POKER

You've got to have ideas—ideas for a new product, a new service or a new way to do something others have done before. But ideas in your head or even ideas you talk about aren't anything until they're put down on paper or into some form of a working model. Ideas are like seeds. You need them to create. But they're no good just sitting there. You need to plant, fertilize and water seeds to make them grow into something worthwhile. You need to put ideas into working form before they can grow into something profitable.

Most of the time, your idea is not completely unique or original. You're just applying a new twist to an idea that's been around a long time. Every now and then, though, you might come up with a new way of doing something that is unique. This is when many of us feel we are undiscovered inventors. Almost everyone has dreamed about inventing some gadget and reaping millions in royalties. We conjure up rags-to-riches fantasies where our basement tinkering develops a fantastic device that will clear up smog or grow new hair on bald heads.

My wife, Vida, is such a person. She has all sorts of "inventions" rolling around in her head. Some sound like good ideas. Some sound wild. I just pull my chin and murmur "mmmmm" when I hear them. One day I told her she had to quit talking about her great inventions and do something about them. She puffed up her courage and went to see a patent attorney who was recommended by our family lawyer.

Vida had three ideas for the attorney to consider. She was told that the ideas should be carefully described and that a simple drawing would be needed for the patent search to see if anyone else had come up with the same idea. The attorney decided to concentrate on two of the ideas, because the third one was too complicated and Vida didn't have enough information for the patent search.

A patent lawyer, we learned, can be initially hired by the hour to help formulate your plans and tell you whether your idea is farcical or feasible. An attorney, during this metered hour, can tell you what drawings, documents and the like are needed. The fee runs anywhere from twenty to fifty dollars an hour, depending on the attorney's reputation and the demand for his (or her) time. So Vida paid forty dollars for an hour and got all sorts of information. The next step was the patent search to see if anything similar to her two inventions had been done before. Her inventions described a new kind of pillow and a gadget for eyeglasses.

After making a probe through the Patent Office Search Center in Arlington, Virginia (a Washington suburb), the attorney found that, yes, there were patents already on file that pretty well covered the pillow design and the eyeglass gadget. There was some talk about improving the eyeglass gadget in such a way as to make an entirely new product. The attorney warned, however, that, even if a patent were allowable, the competition from similar eyeglass products would be fierce.

For the moment, the inventions are in limbo. My wife, so far, has paid around $200 for her education on the ins and outs of patenting ideas. Her attorney says getting a patent is like playing stud poker. You have to pay for each additional card you

see before you can find out whether you'll ever be a winner. To
get your idea all the way through from dream to reality, all the
way through to a final patent, will cost around $1,000. Many
drop out of the game after looking at the first couple of $100
cards. A contribution of $1,000 is too rich and, after con-
templating the fact that a patent by itself can't make money for
you, most inventions are quietly dropped. Out of 100,000 patent applications filed each year, an average of 70,000 are ac-
cepted as reasonably new ideas. Out of the 70,000 patents,
only 2,000 or so ever see their way into the marketplace. And,
out of the 2,000, only a handful ever make any real money.

So it's a tough game. But it's a necessary game if you have
something unique. Like poker, though, you can get out before
committing too much money to a hopeless hand. My wife now
knows what the patent poker stakes are and is putting a lot
more research, shopping tests and other legwork into her inventions before she springs them on the attorney.

Actually, she did start out the right way. She didn't spend a
lot of money and she didn't commit herself to some advertised
"inventor's aid" company. You've got to watch out for these
organizations that advertise to help develop, patent and market
your invention. You see their pitches in magazines and newspapers. Just clip the coupon and then wait while they clip you.

To find out just how a person should go about bringing an
idea through the planning and patent stage out into the market,
I went out to see Jack Rabinow, Chief of the Office of Invention and Innovation at the National Bureau of Standards.

Jack Rabinow has one of the sharpest inventive minds in
the country. Back in the 1950's, he quit his job with the Bureau
of Standards and started up his own company, Rabinow Engineering. He was a government engineer and inventor and when
it looked like his talents were going to be shifted into the military bureaucracy, he quit.

Rabinow had many ideas, many inventions in the stewing

stage. His new company developed an automatic regulator for clocks which is now used in most automobile clocks. He also developed and marketed a device that "reads" print for computers to store in memory cells. There were many other devices he invented, patented and marketed. Rabinow's company also did product development consulting for the likes of RCA, Univac and Philco.

Things got too big for Rabinow Engineering. Jack wanted to ease off. He was an inventor, not an industrial magnate. He had many offers from companies who wanted to buy his business and he finally sold the whole works to Control Data Corporation for a figure in the millions. Now Rabinow is back at the Bureau of Standards but, this time, he has an open book on what he can do. He invents, he putters, he investigates products and they leave him alone. He can go in and out of the establishment whenever he wants.

Having been in and out of both worlds, Rabinow has some sound advice for "basement or kitchen inventors." Listen to what he says:

> When you have an idea, get it down on paper and consult with some technical people, people you can trust who are recommended by friends. If it's a product that involves some sort of engineering or design expertise, an engineer ought to look at it to see whether it even has a chance to work. A lot of people have great ideas that are technically impossible.
>
> It's always a good idea to get a lawyer or someone else to witness your invention and make a notarized and dated statement to that effect. This gives you some protection in case an unscrupulous person wants to run off with your idea. Then you make a patent search. If you live near Washington or plan a trip to Washington, I suggest making the search yourself. It not only saves you money but, more

important, it will teach you a lot about the whole patent system. It kind of humbles you. You think you have a brilliant idea and then you find out somebody had the same thing down cold in 1910.

Once you find that your idea is new and can be patented, you file for a patent. This takes three years or more but you have another, stronger form of protection in the application itself. That's why you see "pat. pending" marked down on so many product labels. After your application is filed, you can start work putting your idea into production and sell it.

There are two ways of marketing your patent. First, you can get someone to market it for you. They're called patent brokers. Some are honest and do a good job. But there are others who take your money and give little in return. Your attorney may know names of legitimate patent brokers, if you want to go that route.

Personally, I think the second way is best. People should try to develop their own product. Naturally, if it's some kind of mass-produced component for automobiles, you can't very well make it yourself. Try to license it and sell it to somebody. If an invention can be developed through a basement or garage, at least for the first sales samples, it's best to build your own business.

Get a local machine shop, instrument shop or other manufacturer to make the necessary components. Retailers and distributors can give you names. So can local engineering companies.

Once you get some good-looking samples made, take them around to local stores or distributors to see if they'll buy your product. If they won't give a firm order, ask them to put your product up for sale on a consignment basis. They get a commission on each item sold. Once your product starts selling and you can make a profit on it—you're in business.

Jack Rabinow and others who have successfully marketed their inventions, say you must realize your selling costs will far outshadow your production costs. You can't have production costs that are more than one fourth your product's final retail price or more than one half the wholesale price, if you go through a distributor. Marketing, then, is 75 per cent of the battle. Remember it. If you make something that will eventually sell to the public for twenty dollars, it can't cost you more than five dollars to make—and this includes your profit. The more you get your production costs below that one-quarter break point, the more profit you can make. More profit, that is, unless you cut costs so much your product is cheapened to the point where nobody will buy it.

You've also got to realize that your product has to make some money within a year. If the product can't make some money so you can see your way clear within a year, drop it. Your product has to pass the test of the marketplace. The fact that friends and neighbors say they like what you've invented isn't any help. They tend to flatter you. Let some hard-nosed store buyers see if they can sell it. If they can, then figure your costs and see whether you can make any money. Be pessimistic on your cost and profit figures. Remember, this is a gamble you're taking. Gamble only that money you can afford to lose. Use the money you've built up from investments or moonlighting. Move cautiously. Once you get going with some local sales you've got a nice record to show prospective sales representatives who can market your product in other cities around the country.

Frank Payne, the man in the previous chapter who invented a new kind of humidifier, is a classic example of the cautious development of a product and a market. Frank, with the help of his brothers, began developing his invention from machined parts done by local shops. As he got going, he got regular suppliers and finally moved the whole operation into a small assembly plant. He sold his first products by word-of-mouth advertising. Then he and his brother visited local heating and engineering contractors to get them to market the humidifier. Now, sales representatives are being lined up in other cities around the country. Frank says you can get names of reliable sales representatives from the local stores that sell your product. They know who the good ones are.

A big company can start making a product similar to the one you've patented and there isn't much you can do about it. As soon as Frank Payne's nozzle spray type humidifier began to gain ground in the market, other companies came out with spray models. But, Frank claims, they're not as good, and so far he's well ahead of the competition.

"The main reason for a patent is to discourage the smaller, local companies from jumping in and skimming the cream off your market," Frank says. If a big organization wants to go after you, they usually try to buy you out first. If that doesn't work, then they come out with something close in design to what you're making. Unless you have a friend or relative who is a lawyer and will work for nothing, it's usually too expensive to take a big company to court.

Aside from protecting against the small-fry local competition, Frank says a patent is "good for your image." He says prospective buyers like to see that patent on your product. They know you're not running some basement bench shop. You're not just a fly-by-night. It costs time and money to get a patent and they know it.

As for the protection, you've got it for seventeen years from the date the patent is granted. If you have just a simple design patent, your protection runs from three and a half years to fourteen years, depending on what fee you pay (they range from $10 to $30).

If you have your product name protected by a registered trademark, and you should, it lasts for five years. Then, you have to pay a $10 renewal fee. Original filing fee for a trademark is $35. You have to pay from $25 to $50 for a search to make sure someone else doesn't already have your mark or name. Your patent attorney can handle the trademark search and application as your business begins to develop.

A trademark does not have to be linked with something you've patented. It can be applied to any catchy name you have for something you're selling. It can even be your own name. You can get a certain amount of protection through "common law" channels by publicly displaying your trademark on your product, but you get much more, clear-cut proof of ownership by an official registration.

Copyrights are another matter. They're handled through the Library of Congress, not the Patent Office, which is in the Department of Commerce. You need a copyright for three basic kinds of products you might want to sell—music, games and written work. You can get a copyright for art work, movies, photographs, certain maps, catalogs, even ballet and opera (if they can be put down on paper). But songs, games and salable writing are the main areas for copyright action.

Not to be discouraged by her patent setback, my wife picked out a catchy tune on her guitar and got the neighborhood kids to sing it caroling last Christmas as a project to raise money for our local Children's Hospital. It's a sort of religious rock song and the kids loved it. So did the neighbors who heard it. Now the song is being put down on paper in the form of musical notes and words so a local sales agent can see it.

Does my wife need some sort of copyright protection before she takes her song out to sell? Indeed she does. It doesn't cost much (six dollars for the copyright registering) and it discourages plagiarizers.

There are two kinds of copyrights for music. One kind protects an "unpublished" work. This means my wife can have her song played before an audience, can have it played on the radio or TV, and be protected. Then there's a copyright for published sheet music. If the music is to be sold in sheet form, it needs a special copyright. As of February 15, 1972, you can have a recording or tape protected with a copyright. Before that anyone could copy a recording and sell it.

When you get a copyright, you're really just getting a formal registered date of disclosure. There's no search to see if someone else has a song similar to yours. All this kind of argument has to be hashed out in court. The date you got your copyright is the evidence you need to protect yourself in court. If the copyright examiner sees you coming in with a neat new ditty called "The Star-Spangled Banner," he'll tell you to get lost. Any such obvious copy will be turned down.

If you invent a game, you can copyright the container as a form of permanent advertisement. You can also copyright most game rules, unless they're too simple. You can copyright the game board design and the wording and design of any cards or other props the game uses. You can also copyright a game as a whole unit, like a book. You can even patent the action parts of some games.

The Monopoly game we all played as kids is a good example. The inventor of Monopoly protected himself with various copyrights on the board design and the wording on the little cards. The container design was also registered. The name Monopoly was given a registered trademark and the overall dice action, hotels, houses, markers and other functioning elements of the game were patented. A triple-threat protection.

As for written work, this book, my newspaper columns, magazine stories and other writing I do, are all protected by copyright. One thing I quickly learned is the fact that you can't get a copyright for a literary work in unpublished form. This means any manuscript you have or any article you send in to a publisher, cannot be protected by a copyright. You can retain a copy of your work, have it dated and witnessed by a notary.

This will help if anyone tries to steal your priceless prose before it's published. In many instances you are protected by the common law of unfair competition from deceptive business practices. This means that somebody can't obviously steal your stuff and get away with it even if you don't have a copyright. You can copyright art, movies and such before commercial sales take place.

You can't copyright an idea or a title. Some complete thought must be committed to paper, whether it's one paragraph long or twenty volumes. You can get more information on the copyright laws by writing: Copyright Office; Library of Congress; Washington, D.C. 20540. Ask for the booklet *General Information on Copyright*.

For information on patents and trademarks, any field office of the Department of Commerce (found under U. S. Government in your phone book), should be able to supply you with three basic booklets: *General Information Concerning Patents . . . An Information Aid for Inventors . . . General Information Concerning Trademarks*. The first booklet lists names of the public libraries around the country where you can initiate your own patent search. The booklets cost just a few cents and are worth getting for your home office bookshelf.

You might also want to buy or borrow *The Inventor's Patent Handbook,* written by Stacy V. Jones and published by Dial Press. Jones, who also wrote an earlier book, *You Ought to Patent That,* has a column on patents appearing every Saturday in the New York *Times.* His column investigates interesting new patents. It can give you some ideas.

Most libraries carry these books and major libraries probably carry the Saturday edition of the New York *Times.* While you're browsing through the library, look up the *Thomas' Register."* It's a massive, multi-volume work that contains the names of suppliers of almost everything. If you need some components or some raw materials to make a model of your invention, you can find them in the register. Also, once you have your patent application in, you might want to see if any manufacturers show interest. The *Thomas' Register* reveals, with all sorts of cross-references, who makes and sells every conceivable kind of product. If you're a budding inventor, look through the register.

A little note about how you can tell whether you have an inventor's mind. Jack Rabinow says: "It's simple. An inventor is the kind of a person who stubs his toe on a piece of flooring and stops to contemplate instead of curse. He asks himself if there's some way flooring material can be made not to buckle up like that. The non-inventor just stumbles, curses and passes quickly by."

Howard Head, the inventor and successful marketer of Head Skis, is a perfect example of Rabinow's "Inventor." While skiing down a hill at great speed, Head was disturbed by the flutter in his skis. Instead of cursing and diminishing his speed, Head went home and figured a way to put a damper in the middle of the ski to stabilize it. He is an aeronautical engineer, so he had some basic concepts. The damper worked and the skis stopped fluttering at high speeds. Head started selling his dampered racing skis to exclusive shops and they went over big.

The rest is history. Sales boomed and, finally, the American Machine and Foundry Company bought out Head's little company and retained him as consultant. He now has plenty of money to visit the world's winter resorts and his skis don't flutter when he zooms down the slopes. Meanwhile, my wife is still back at the drawing boards. Some day, maybe . . . ?

10
FRANCHISING: INSTANT BUSINESSES

For those who want to get into business on their own, franchising has the allure of making it quick and clean. They set you up with an instant business and you're off, happily making profits into the sunset. At least, so it seems. The trouble is, a good percentage of the hopeful self-bossers who are lured into owning a fast-food franchise, coin-operated laundry or whatever, either go broke or are limping along as slaves of some national franchisor. Many have later found the "be your own boss" franchise pitches to be a hollow mockery. All too often, the franchisor is the real boss and you have to do what you're told or the contract will not be renewed and your entire investment evaporates.

I'll admit I'm somewhat prejudiced against most forms of franchising. There are some excellent franchising organizations and you can make a lot of money and, for the most part, be your own boss if you're smart enough to learn the business before you jump. I'm suspicious of most franchise pitches because I've seen too many people lose their entire life's savings after franchisors fast-talked them into basically bad business deals. You should never be *sold* a franchise. You should go out and carefully investigate the whole field of franchising and settle on the type of business that you and your family like. Hopefully, it will be a type of business that you know, one where your own personal skills and experience can be used. The more any advertisement or franchise salesperson pushes, the less chance you have of making it after signing on the dotted line. The really good franchisors, such as McDonald's, Colonel Sanders' Kentucky Fried Chicken and Holiday Inns, don't push at all. As a matter of fact, they're very choosy about the kind of people they even agree to negotiate with. They investigate you and your experience even more than you investigate them.

Unfortunately, these good companies form just a small percentage of the total 1,500 or so franchisors roaming the land. The rest are mediocre, incompetent or outright frauds. My personal bias against most (not all) franchisors started a couple of years ago, when a California reader of my consumer column wrote in a pathetic letter describing how he and his son had been taken by a smooth-talking franchise salesman. The Californian wrote:

"I was talked into a franchise agreement with Mini-Gifts, Inc. I paid $6,000, all I had saved, with the understanding that a factory representative would be here within a few weeks to place on location some merchandise racks I purchased as part of the franchise agreement. I waited and waited. Four months after taking my money, they finally sent a representative. He stayed a few days and signed 23 locations (11 less than the contract called for) but he didn't place any of the gift racks. The gifts they sent me for the racks were just pieces of junk and way over-priced. Many of the gifts were substitute items that were not shown at the signing of the contract. I'm now stuck with 50 of these racks filled with worthless gifts. I am out $6,000 and I so badly needed the extra income I thought I was going to get from the franchise."

Sad, isn't it? But there are thousands of tales like that. I found that Mini-Gifts was a Miami, Florida, outfit that sold some $300,000 worth of unsellable gift racks and then quietly slithered out of existence.

Want to hear another one that helped turn me off hard-sell franchising schemes? Listen to this letter from a Charlotte, North Carolina, widow:

"In May I was talked into investing $15,000 (40 years of savings) for a franchise to open a Bavarian Alpine Inn. The company man drove around with me, discussing locations and showing me plans. I spent a day in Atlanta, their home office, and was assured they would send someone to Charlotte the following week to get things started.

I have not received a single word. I called their office and either got no answer or no one could take my call."

This is incredible. A whole life's savings and they wouldn't even answer the phone. I got in touch with Mary Gardiner Jones, a commissioner at the Federal Trade Commission. Commissioner Jones got an FTC attorney in Atlanta to "make a little visit" with the Bavarian Alpine Inn enterprise. The visit from a "Fed" really shook up Alpine. The company said it was having "some difficulty," but agreed to pay back the Charlotte widow $1,500 a month with 8 per cent interest. They made good on several payments and then went bankrupt.

Admittedly, these cases are among the most rotten apples in the franchising barrel. Many others sort of fall in the middle between success and failure. People rush into an advertised "fascinating new career . . . be your own boss," only to find that they have to work twelve hours a day, seven days a week. Still others make some money but they "hate the business." Serving a few chicken dinners to smiling faces is one thing. Serving hundreds of thousands of chicken pieces to a sometimes grouchy public is something else.

One husband and wife "team" got into a shoe store franchise operation. The business failed and the marriage almost went on the rocks. Why? Because, in order to make the place profitable, both the husband and wife had to work long hours selling shoes and the wife said she "hated smelling those feet all day."

"It all seems so simple the way the franchisor explains it," says a retired military officer who wanted to go to law school and needed the extra income to make ends meet. He saw a glowing "get in on the boom" franchising article which mentioned several "hot prospects," including Chicken Delight fast-food stores. The retired officer thought running his own franchised business was just the thing he needed to pay his way through graduate school and, who knows, it might even make him independently wealthy. He warns prospective franchisees, however, not to be fooled by the claimed simplicity of the business. He describes his interview with the Chicken Delight representative:

"The smell of success was everywhere. Everyone was smiling. The sales representative showed me how I was going to make money right off the bat. He started adding up the cost of a typical Chicken Delight dinner. The chicken would cost, say thirty-five cents, french fries a nickel, a nickel for rolls, a few cents for sauce and the plate package with Chicken Delight's name on it would cost seventeen cents. So this put the total cost for the dinner at around sixty cents. The dinner was to sell for $1.39. To the untrained eye this looked damned good. Man, you say, how can you beat that?"

Later on, after he'd opened his Chicken Delight fast-food store, the retired officer found that his "cost" was a lot more than sixty cents for each dinner. The food was just the raw material and he had to "manufacture" it into a dinner and serve it. Along the way he had to pay for his help, operate and maintain several cars to deliver dinners (the franchisor advertised "free delivery"), pay for workmen's compensation, all kinds of taxes, payroll for his help and a jillion other things.

And the seventeen-cent plates—don't forget those. The franchisee discovered that he could have purchased the same kind of paper plates for a few cents each through local suppliers. The plates were a "tie-in" purchase all Chicken Delight franchisees had to make. This served as an enormous hidden fee franchisees had to pay and it ate hungrily into profits. Chicken Delight's tie-in purchases were later challenged in court by some California franchisees in a class action suit and the company had to give it up. When the company tried to charge a 5 per cent franchise fee off the top of each franchisee's gross, there was a revolt. Most franchisees wouldn't pay it and the great Chicken Delight boom went bust.

The retired officer continued the fast-food place on his own after canceling his Chicken Delight contract. He found he could make more money on his own with different kinds of foods to offer. He came up with a new style of serving barbecued ribs and made some money. The retired officer finally dropped out of the fast-food business altogether because, as he put it: "I liked the idea of owning my own business, but I didn't like having to work all that time in a fast-food store . . . it was too much of a repetitive business to keep my interest." Will he ever go into another franchise deal? "Maybe," says the former officer, "but I'll take much more time to investigate and I probably won't go into the fast-food business." He thinks the fast-food bubble has broken.

Now, let's take a look at another case, one that shows how a franchised business, if carefully investigated, can make for a profitable and happy venture. Jerry Derry (that's his real name) worked for an engineering company in the Boston area. His wife Winifred worked for Western Girl, a temporary employment service that operated through a franchise chain. Jerry and Winifred wanted to be on their own. They decided to investigate the possibility of running their own temporary employment service.

The Derrys figured they had special skills and background.

Winifred had been seven years with Western Girl's office in Providence, Rhode Island, and Jerry had considerable financial and business administration background as the operating manager of an engineering department. They carefully mapped out their plan of attack. To get more experience, Jerry even worked in a Kelly Service office (another temporary employment service) in Florida. From time to time he would farm himself out as a temporary employee to "get the other side of the picture."

Jerry and Winifred toured up and down the East Coast looking for the right location for a temporary employment service. After nearly a year's investigation, the Derrys picked Washington as the most promising place for the fast-growing temporary employment business. Then they had to pick a franchisor. After talking with several, they picked Partime, a relatively new national chain, because the company at the time seemed to offer more freedom of individual action.

Why did they pick a franchised service instead of setting up their own temporary employment agency? Jerry says, "They offered a complete bookkeeping service, co-operative advertising and all the legal and technical backup we needed." Also, the national chain kept a continued stream of memos coming in on new sources of business. In the employment business, one franchisee can often channel business to another as customers move around the country.

This is the ideal kind of franchising situation. The franchisee knows the business ahead of time. The franchisor charges a fair fee and in return gives the franchisee a national name, plenty of advertising power, backup technical and legal advice, and a bookkeeping service that eases administrative pains.

Franchising for a certain select few can be a relatively quick way to get into a business. But, as Jerry and Winifred Derry showed us, you've got to take from six months to a year to investigate before you decide to risk a sizable chunk of your life's savings, and even more of your own time, on a franchised business. As the Derrys case proves, it's even better if you work for a while, even as much as several years, in the kind of business you eventually want to manage as a franchisee. This way, you'll find out whether you really like it and you'll pick up the necessary operational skills to make your own business successful. As one franchisee says: "You've got to be fascinated with the kind of business you want to operate on franchise. You've got to be willing to spend seven days a week working and worrying at it. It's total immersion. Absentee ownership never really works for very long."

Even after you've picked the kind of business where "total immersion" will make you sublimely happy, you should ask yourself: Why franchise—why not set up my own, independent business? Remember, you've got to pay the franchisor a percentage right off the top of all sales. It can run from a low of around 3 per cent (for some of the best) on up to 7 per cent and beyond.

You've got to add up all the services the franchisor offers and see what they total in dollars and cents. You've got to know how the money will flow, what all of your costs will be. Then you've got to compare a franchise deal with a theoretical model of an independent business. For example, let's say a franchised fast-food or laundry service is expected to gross $200,000 a year. If the franchisor demands a 5 per cent fee off the top (and many do), this means you'll be paying out $10,000 a year to the franchisor for the bookkeeping, legal and other services. For $10,000 a year, you can buy an awful lot of local consulting help for these same services and when you're independent you only buy help when you need it.

Jerry S. Cohen, an attorney who has represented the National Congress of Petroleum Retailers and the National Automobile Dealers Association, two of the biggest franchisee organizations in the country, says most people don't go through the necessary steps of comparing the cost of an independent business with that of a franchised operation.

Cohen, who once investigated the whole field of franchising as chief counsel for the Senate Antitrust and Monopoly Subcommittee, says, "You have to watch out for tie-in purchases." He says most tie-ins are illegal nowadays but some still persist in subtle form. One major movie theater operation is a good example. The franchisor is fighting a lawsuit because it is alleged that the franchisees had to purchase projection equipment from one of the company's subsidiaries. The franchisor's projectors, it was claimed, cost considerably more than projectors an independent movie theater operator would pay in the regular market. Aside from tie-ins, Cohen says you should not be fooled by just a few percentage points the franchisor says have to be charged for the chain's services. One or two per cent off your gross can break you or make you as far as your final profit is concerned. Again, add it up. See what the total money flow will be. It's even a good idea to hire an independent accountant to go over the whole money-flow model of your prospective franchised operation. You do all this, of course, before you even think of signing anything.

At every turn, you should see whether you can get a certain service offered by a franchisor at a better price somewhere else. If a franchisor says the company will teach you how to run a fast-food shop or a motel, find out how much it will cost you to take a university course to learn the same thing. Or, maybe, you can learn by moonlighting for someone else who already operates a motel or food shop. Wherever possible, use someone else's money to do your investigating and learning. Maybe, if you own your own business outright instead of franchising it, there's an association that can offer some of the backup legal and technical services you need. Get in touch with the association that covers your type of business and see what they have to offer.

After this kind of detailed investigation, if you still decide—as did Jerry and Winifred Derry—to sign up with a franchisor, then make sure you get a long-term contract and, if necessary, a long-term leasing arrangement. "Otherwise," says Jerry Cohen, "they can twist your arm with a short-term lease. . . . You either do what they say or, after a year, you're out and your investment is gone." You need a long-term arrangement with option to renew. This can serve as insurance to protect your independence. "In some sad cases," Cohen says, "a man and wife will beat their brains out building up a franchised store's business. . . . Then, when they're really going good, the franchisor steps in and won't renew the short-term contract. He takes over the profitable business they built up."

You need an attorney to go over any agreement before you sign. Actually, it's a good idea to talk to an attorney before you even start out to investigate a franchised business. You need a lawyer that's expert in franchising and they're sometimes hard to find. The best way to handle it is to have your own family lawyer, someone you trust, find out who's the best franchising expert in town. If there isn't someone who has handled a good number of cases for either franchisees or franchisors, then ask your lawyer to get the best name in the nearest major city. A tough franchising specialist can save you thousands of dollars and untold misery by not letting you get into a bad contract.

If you decide not to franchise but still like the idea of getting a fast start with an existing business, you might consider buying out some local owner-manager of an independent business. It's a good idea to look for a business in your field of interest that's doing only moderately well. Those that are doing a highly profitable business, will either not want to sell or will want to charge so much it's prohibitive. Find a place where the owner wants to retire or where the younger members of a family business want to get into something else. You have to get a business that has a steady income and a track record that can be analyzed by a professional accountant. You have to know you'll have a certain basic income, albeit a small one, that you can build up with your own ideas for new services or new products. Before you can do this, of course, it's always wise to have spent a considerable amount of time moonlighting in the kind of business you want to buy so you'll know exactly what you can do and what you can't do. You will find all sorts of consulting talent around most major metropolitan areas, and, in certain cases, it's even free.

As a first step to investigate franchising or buying into an independent business, you should do some reading. I particularly like *Franchising—The Investor's Complete Handbook,* written by Robert M. Dias and Stanley I. Gernick, published by Hastings House. It tells how to investigate a franchising business and how to spot the more obvious frauds and traps. The Dias-Gernick book even goes into such things as "Estimating Your Profits" and "What to Ask Your Accountant." It's not a tedious, technical book as so many of them are. It's written in easy-to-understand, lively English. I personally met Bob Dias, one of the authors, when he testified during the Senate hearings on franchising. At the time he was considered the "Ralph Nader of the franchising business."

There are other books you might want to read, such as *The Franchise Boom,* written by Harry Kursh and published by Prentice-Hall. This book, has a "friendly, come on in the water's fine" approach that tends to gloss over some of the negative points in franchising. Then there's *Franchising, Trap for the Trusting,* written by Harold Brown, published by Little, Brown and Co., which is just the opposite. It's almost completely hostile towards franchising and is quite naturally despised by many a franchisor.

Your library may get *The Franchise Directory,* which is the bible of the franchising business, listing more than a thousand franchisors and what they offer. The same company that publishes the *Directory* also puts out *The Franchise Journal,* a monthly magazine that notes and analyzes the latest franchising offers. The annual and the reports are written by Thomas H. Murphy, one of the best informed and most impartial experts on franchising. For more information, write Thomas H. Murphy; Continental Reports, Inc.; P. O. Box 6360; Denver, Colo. 80206.

"Investigate Before Investing" is a handy little book that shows you how to evaluate a franchise opportunity. It costs $1.00 and is published by the International Franchise Association; 1025 Connecticut Ave.; Washington, D.C. 20036. While you're at it, ask for IFA's free "Membership Directory." It lists 160 of the country's leading franchisors by franchise category and address.

Part III
AGES AND STAGES

11

FREE FROM PARENTS—THEN WHAT?

For the adolescent, independence has to be wrenched, inch by inch, from parents and from an obstacle course of teachers and campus administrators. It's a tough and sometimes frightening process but every young person who wants to make their own way in life has to go through it.

One of the most unsettling moments in this form of human chrysalis is when the young man or woman actually does break free from parental direction. The big question then is: Where do I go from here? Just getting a job to support a family is no longer the main goal. Young people want more than a job and money, they want to do something "meaningful." Sometimes the definition of "meaningful" sounds weird to adult ears. No matter. The young are aiming in the right direction even if there are times when they are not quite sure what step to take next.

According to Margaret S. McKenna, assistant director of health services at Harvard University, in an interview with the Los Angeles *Times:*

"Young people are turning inward to try to find something they can do free from political manipulations, from financial squabbling. They want to do something that can bring them some sort of inward satisfaction. . . . A lot of them are turning to things that can be done with their hands—pottery, woodwork, weaving, things like that. This parallels the rush of students—and it's fatastic—back to law and medical schools. In both cases you have something independent. If a patient gets better, you doctored him well. If, in making a piece of pottery you realize your artistic intentions, you have a similarly tangible reward. . . . I'm talking about the middle class. They're not worrying about survival, but whether it is worth surviving."

When a young person today goes out to get a job, he or she wants to do something important, something significant. Having your own, individual trade or skill, is one way. Trying to break into an important and relevant establishment job is another, much more troublesome way. According to labor writer Sam Zagoria, "If the young people don't find things as they want, they won't hesitate to move." Whenever the young get stuck in a dull job—blue or white collar—they either move on in a restless search for meaning in their work or they turn their anger inward against the employer. You see these feelings expressed in absenteeism, shoddy work and even sabotage. As United Auto Workers Union Vice-President Douglas Fraser puts it: "The young people are rebelling against the system."

Fine. But, having rebelled, then what? To be truly independent, you've got to be able to control your own income. You can't keep sponging off your family. As one well-off college girl, who is working as a waitress to pay her own way, tells it: "For every thousand dollars Daddy gives me, I get ten thousand dollars' worth of advice." There's a real dilemma here. How can you be financially independent and still do something meaningful?

One of the troubles can be found in our education system. We put our kids into a long line of grades and studies. It's a sort of hothouse, unreal, existence. From kindergarten on up through graduate school, most of our young aren't exposed to enough real-life work situations. Oh, they get part-time jobs but very few get early work experience in fields they may want to enter for their life's work. Says Harvard psychologist Harry Levinson: "Most adolescents cannot have had sufficiently varied work experience out of which to make career decisions. . . . As a result, they have a certain reserve about committing themselves to a decision." This accounts for the bouncing around from one job or one place to another. They want to do something, but they don't want to get caught in the same "rat race" in which they believe their parents are inextricably caught.

Back to the original question—how can you eventually be independent, be your own boss, and still make enough money to live the life you want to live? Sit back and listen. I have a plan. It's based on my original premise, stated in earlier pages, that one should learn to use, and not be used by, the establishment. Rent them your body for a while as you learn some portable skills and then shove off. Unfortunately, many young people today look at the establishment as something to fight (anti-establishment violence) or something to hide from by taking whatever job you can get, using drugs, music, communes or whatever as an escape. There's a third alternative to throwing rocks or buckling under. It's "Use, don't be used." For college students, I call it "paid graduate school." You work at jobs in careers you want to sample, careers that can lead to an independent business, trade or profession. Make a life plan. It doesn't have to be rigid. You can change direction, modify or cancel any time you want.

The first step is to find out the kind of things you do best. Usually, these are things you like to do. You delineate basic areas such as working with people or loner-type occupations such as handcrafts or other creative work that doesn't depend on a constant flow of people. Then you sample jobs in these areas. Use summer vacations or weekends to shop around various jobs. Don't be afraid to accept some menial job in practicing what I call "foot-in-doorsmanship." If you think you might like being a medic or a paramedic, get your foot in the door of some hospital. Sign on as an orderly. They're always looking for someone to empty bedpans because few people want to make that their life's work.

You don't have to make bedpan emptying your life's work. All you want to do is get into that hospital so you can hobnob with doctors and technicians. See what they're doing, how they live, how they like their work. Make the rounds with some doctor in your off time. Ask questions. Volunteer for jobs that will get you around inside the hospital. In short, use that so-called "lousy job" as a vehicle to investigate and pick up skills you may need later on, when you're on your own.

One boy came to me dripping with frustration. He wasn't sure, but he thought he might want to be an architect. He didn't want to commit himself to years of engineering and architectural training only to find out later he didn't like the business. I asked him why he didn't work in the summer for some architect. He said he tried, but none of them wanted to take on temporary, summer employees.

I made a bet. I said he should go back and talk with several architects and offer himself to work for a month for nothing. The work could be anything, such as retyping and revising the files, running to get blueprints or answering the phone. If, after one month, the architect didn't think the work was worth it, the boy could leave and no money would change hands. If, on the other hand, the architect found the work useful, he could pay the boy whatever he thought it was worth and they could try another month. The main thing, I emphasized, was the fact that the boy must tell the architect that he was making this offer because he was fascinated with the idea of building and designing and wanted to learn all he could by just being around a good architect.

The boy lost his bet but he got the job. The architect was flattered by a young person showing such interest in his work. The architect, being a somewhat conservative fellow, was also impressed by the boy's willingness to work and learn. Several times the architect told the boy, "You're different from those hippies . . . they don't want to work . . . not many want to work these days." Naturally, the architect wouldn't let the boy work for nothing, explaining, "I wouldn't work for nothing and I don't want anyone working for me for nothing either." Problem solved. Boy got job. Boy learned about architecture and architects.

You've got to get inside, get your foot in the door to pick up the skills and earn some money. You've also got to take another look at the kind of education that's being thrown at you. Some of it is good, but some is irrelevant, tired theory being palmed off by teachers and professors who haven't been in touch with the real world for so long, they don't know what's going on. You should have a proper mix of a liberal education and one that gives you work-study experience. You can't just have a pure liberal arts education, nor can you have just a plain trade school education. You should combine both.

If young people went to work earlier in jobs that were related to their studies, they would have much more confidence when they began to work full time. They would have the confidence that comes from being judged by outsiders who are unrelated to parents and teachers and they would know more precisely what they want to do.

I think the growing number of community colleges are where the action is. They are newer and much more flexible than the older, tradition-bound, four-year universities and colleges. At Lansing Community College (Lansing, Michigan), for example, you get "prescribed education." This means each student gets an individual prescription of courses to fit his or her personal needs. And you study at your own pace. There are very few classrooms as such. There are group discussion meetings, but most of the time students come and go on their own schedule, using self-teach "learning laboratories" that are open from early morning to midnight. You meet with professors on a one-to-one basis to discuss problems and make progress reports.

Students have a wide variety of work-study programs to choose from. If you're interested in eventually doing veterinarian medicine, you work with a veterinarian. You get regular college credits for your work and you get paid for it as well.

At Orange Coast Community College in Southern California, students can get all sorts of jobs in the community that are directly related to their studies. The college even has its own store in the community. Students bring work problems back into college meeting rooms and laboratories to work out with professors. And the reverse is true. Students bring study problems to work to discuss with their employer. By the time the community college graduate transfers to a regular, four-year university, he or she knows a lot more about a chosen career than most "native" sophomores who started out as freshmen in the same university. Studies by the Department of Health, Education and Welfare show that community college transfers do just as well, if not better, than those who started as freshmen at a four-year institution.

Paralleling work-study experience, students should also concentrate on building portable skills, things that can be used anywhere, things that can make you less dependent on working for some organization all your life. Examples of portable skills are the ability to write quickly and clearly; the ability to speak clearly and forcefully before an audience; the ability to draw, design or photograph; accounting and bookkeeping;

the ability to use equipment such as typewriters, calculators, computers and recorders.

These are some of the basic portables. There are others that are more specialized, such as medicine (paramedic, veterinarian, doctor, dentist), engineering (mechanical, electrical) and law (not necessarily as a lawyer, but how to use the law). Nutrition is another special field that has long been neglected and is now coming into its own. Nutritionists are in demand for all sorts of consulting work. Being an independent nutritionist who works through consulting contracts and helps educate the public through articles, appearances on TV and radio, is my idea of a nice life for someone who is interested in both food and people.

As soon as possible, a student or a young person new in the work force, should consider setting up an independent business, even if it's just for a summer or a string of weekends. You need to pick up administrative and marketing skills that are best learned through running some little business. You need to know how to deal with customers and suppliers. You need to know how to keep costs in line and how to test a market to see if your service or product can make it.

A good example of this kind of foot-wetting procedure can be found in General Eclectics, a micro-business founded by Georgetown University chemistry major Ralph Gitomer. Ralph read about a NASA program where the agency leased products and techniques it developed for the space program. One technique in particular interested Ralph. It concerned a process that NASA developed to coat the inside of the astronauts' face masks with a liquid that would prevent fogging.

There are all kinds of anti-fogging sprays on the market now, but none of them last very long, especially under severe temperature drops. Ralph wanted to make an anti-fogging spray that would endure for weeks, maybe a month or more, on such surfaces as the inside of glasses, car windshields, scuba masks and even the surface of bathroom mirrors.

The trouble is, the NASA product has to be applied in a laboratory under specially controlled conditions. Ralph Gitomer took the NASA process under license and altered it so he could apply it on any surface without the need of a laboratory. He calls his product Space Anti-Fogger.

The young chemistry major then learned an important lesson. Having a good product is only half the battle. Getting it distributed and sold is the other half. He got several hundred plastic squeeze bottles for his anti-fogger liquid and tried to sell the packaged product. He got the city bus company to try the anti-fogger and a major taxi fleet said it would give the product a test. Both organizations liked the anti-fogger and said it helped their drivers see through windshields during stormy weather.

Ralph Gitomer was then faced with the problem of trying to study for finals and trying to scrape up enough money to get more of his product sold. He is thinking of asking his university's school of business administration to help sort out the financial tangle. Meanwhile, Ralph has come up with two more new products. One is a coating for marine propellers which makes them move faster through water and much more efficiently. The other is a chemical kit that pharmacists can use to test for dangerous quantities of lead in household dishes and lead in paint. The chemical kit was snapped up by the American Pharmaceutical Association and will be tested by pharmacists in several cities to see if it's worth marketing on a national scale.

Ralph Gitomer is getting a running start at managing his own business. He's weak on the financial side but he understands this and is taking courses that will improve his money knowledge. The main thing is the taste of freedom this student got running his own show. He'll never forget it. He may work for a company somewhere to gain more practical knowledge and skills but he's convinced now that having your own business, as he puts it, "is the only way to really enjoy what you're doing, the only way to keep growing."

In the Boston area, several college students put together a "Junior Catering" business to make money during the summer vacation. They had a good idea. Every parent knows that putting on a birthday party or some other party for children can be an awful pain. You have to do it. You want to see your little one have fun, but you have to cope with all the preparation, the screaming, the mess, the cleaning up. Junior Catering filled the need for someone to "take over your child's party." Agents from the little company would come by to discuss the party, would buy all the necessary comestibles, such as ice cream, hamburgers, chicken, whatever. They'd even make the cake unless pride forced you to do it. They'd get the paper hats, the little prizes, games, everything. They had drama students who could put on a pretty good show with clowns or magician acts. And, what's more important, they cleaned up everything afterward. Parents could relax and enjoy the kids.

The idea caught. Orders came in by the hundreds. More caterers were recruited. At last report, there was talk of branching out to other cities or even franchising the business. Every city has drama students who would like to work for any kind of paying audience—even kids. There are always home economics majors or others who are willing to do food planning and catering for parties. Why didn't these Junior Caterers appear sooner on the scene? We could have used them for a long line of hectic birthday parties. When you find a need, fill it with your own service or product. You may not make it a lasting business but the experience will be filed back in some brain cell to be used later on when you finally go out—and stay out—on your own.

Unless you happen to hit a little business that really grows into a self-supporting, lasting sort of thing, or unless you're independently wealthy, you will probably have to go out to work for a few years, or a lot of years, to make enough money and gain enough experience to be able to make it eventually on your own. As you look over the job field, you want to pick places that can teach you the most. The pay should be secondary. Ideally, you should look for a place that can teach you the skills you need and can give you enough time off to practice moonlighting with your own little business projects.

A number of companies are moving into a four-day work week. This can give you time to work on your own business projects. Other companies are giving employees time off for special training. If you need the training, grab it. Always do your best work for your employer. But, when you stop learning, you should move on to something that can teach you more or, if you're ready, move out on your own. I've discovered that after three to five years working for some organization, you stop learning. That's the time to leave. The work often becomes dull and repetitious. Remember, you're using these jobs as a sort of "poor man's graduate school." When the learning stops, you stop.

Some companies are even beginning to let their employees have paid sabbaticals so they can work on their own projects. Xerox Corporation, for example, grants a few of its young employees the right to take a year off to do "something socially useful." Employees are working on projects that include drug control, civil rights and literacy efforts. This kind of experience can be invaluable for those who eventually want to be their own boss. As in the military, you do your duty for your company, but when it's done, you leave and run your own show.

Polaroid is using job rotation to keep its employees from becoming bored with their work. Some technician can work for a while in accounting, some accountant can work for a while repairing cameras or other equipment. Out of this rotation, you should be able to come up with a combination that could click with your own business. Get as much free or paid training as you can get to help toward your goal of having your own business. Give them the use of your services for a few years while you build up your special investment account, and then say good-by. You may owe them a few years, but not your life.

These are just a couple of examples of the kinds of opportunities you should be looking for. There are thousands of others. Sometimes it's better to work for a much smaller company than one of the giants. You may get less pay but you also may get a chance to have more responsibility and can get a better feel of how a small business is run. Willing workers are often given much more responsibility in a small company than they are in one of the giants. You get this extra responsibility because they can't afford to pay for more help. You can also get plenty of diversity handling customers, producing the product or service, working on the books, handling labor problems—the works.

As you cast your line for the kind of job that can give you the best training, it's a good idea not to cast in stagnant ponds. Some kinds of businesses and skills are not growing very fast and others are declining. Schoolteaching, for example, is on the downswing. So are certain kinds of engineering. The Department of Labor puts out a handy guide called *Occupational Outlook Handbook*. It's a bit heavy but it shows what careers are on the upswing for the next ten years and what kind of jobs show less promise. The last edition showed computer programmers, recreation workers, psychologists (not psychiatrists) and social workers would be in high demand. Other areas where there are likely to be shortages of talent and therefore fertile grounds for creative job hunters are in the fields of geology and geophysics (plenty of consulting possibilities here for an enterprising rock collector). The whole area of urban planning, counseling, children's day-care planning and administration will also be fertile grounds to probe.

These are just ideas. And, as I've said before, ideas are no good until they're put into action. To put your ideas into action, you need to think out, and commit to paper if necessary, an escape plan that is much more detailed and much more personally tailored to your own needs, your own likes and dislikes. The main thing is to realize that you don't have to work for the establishment all your life. You only have to spend a few years learning the skills you need. Use the establishment. Don't let it use you.

I'd like to add a personal note on how a young person who wants to get into journalism should go about it. I have a lot of experience in this field—both in and out of the establishment—and maybe you can profit from it.

First off, you've got to learn to write clearly. By this I mean so anybody can understand what you're saying. Obscure, far-out writing may be okay for some little literary review but not for the general public. If you want to write far-out stuff, write it for the little magazines—on the side. If you want to make a living as a writer and be your own boss, you've got to learn how to write clearly so rich, poor, old and young can understand you. Clear writing is sorely needed these days.

You can write much more clearly if you know what you're writing about. You can always tell when a writer is "faking it." There are vague words, soft words and hedge words all over the place. To know what you're writing about, it's necessary to be a good researcher or reporter. You've got to know how to use libraries and reference material and you have to know how to interview people, especially people who have information but don't want to give it out.

The best way to learn and polish these skills is to work for some newspaper, wire service or newsletter that offers a lot of work but little pay. Don't aim for a prestige outfit like the New York *Times, Newsweek* or the Washington bureau of the AP. Head for the suburbs and the small towns. The newspapers and wire service bureaus in the boondocks need writers and reporters but they can't pay much. Besides, all the image seekers are flocking to the cities and the big, prestige jobs. You will get lots of writing and reporting with a small outfit and that's what you want. You want the experience of having to write over and over again under pressure. You want to be able to sharpen your nose for news and new ideas to write about. You want to be relaxed interviewing everyone from the janitor in the school on up to the governor of the state. You can only get this by doing it over and over again.

Some little papers even have reporters double in brass for all sorts of things. One week you'll be an assistant printer, another week you'll be out selling ads and yet another week you'll be writing the guest editorial on why the schools stink in your state. This is good. Soak it up.

I mentioned newsletters along with newspapers and wire services. They're the sleeper in modern journalism. Most young people scoff at newsletters because they know nothing about them. There are thousands of little newsletters in production around the country. Every association has one and there are 4,600 associations. There are all kinds of special newsletters on such subjects as pollution, consumer fraud and various facets of the ecology problem we face (water, natural resources, atomic energy, air). The newsletters may not pay much at first but you can get plenty of reporting and writing experience and can choose your own special field of interest. Look at the end of the chapter on "Your Own Corner." In the list of books I recommend putting on your own home-office shelf, you'll find one that lists all the associations in the country. Pick out some and try catching on with one of their newsletters. A good number have their main office in Washington, a town that has more information, more ideas for writers than any other place on earth.

Get your foot in the door. Get started. Volunteer to report and write anything. What you need is plenty of work to get your brain used to telling your fingers what to write and how to write it fast if necessary. You need to get published. You need to gain confidence in your ability to go out to get information, check it and write it on a tight deadline. Once you have that confidence, you can begin to think about branching out on your own.

About branching out. Many have asked me about writing an independent column. Writing a column is a lot of fun and can provide a base of operations for someone who wants to be on their own. But, unless you're Art Buchwald or some other such famous name, you're not going to make enough money to live by writing a column and nothing else. Sure, there are quite a few writers who make good money writing columns, but most of them took a long time getting there and most of them do many other things, such as lecturing, TV and radio work, writing books and putting out special newsletters of their own.

So you have to be able to line up some basic contract for a column, radio series, newsletter or whatever, and then build on it. If you want to be on your own, you ought to know how to do newspaper writing, magazine writing, radio or TV specials, public speaking for pay, teaching, newsletters, photography—everything you can get your hands on.

When I was on the Cleveland *Plain Dealer,* they stuck me on the police beat for nearly three years. It was supposed to be an ignominious job. I made the most of it. I learned to write fast. I learned to squeeze information out of the chief of detectives (and was told that if you can get information out of him, governors, senators, heads of corporations, even Presidents, seem easy by comparison). I got some confidence.

Then I moved on and learned magazine writing with *Business Week* and *Forbes*. I learned to speak another language and I learned how to take pictures that were readily acceptable for magazine publication. I also learned how to use a tape recorder as a stenographic device to make interviews go faster. I learned how to take the information quickly off the tape recorder and edit as I transferred the thoughts from tape to paper. All these skills were vitally important when I pushed away from the established job and went out on my own.

If you initially have trouble getting work, think up stories for editors and for broadcasting program directors. I've never seen an editor turn down a really good story. Get your foot in the door. Get one account. Then get another. A young fellow in our building looked at the list of weekly newspapers in the country—some ten thousand of them—and figured he might be able to sell a service from Washington. He had to keep it cheap because these little papers are unaccustomed to paying more than three dollars or so for anything.

He came from Ohio and he knew the state well. So he started there. He lined up seventeen little weekly papers around Cleveland, owned by a chain, then went downstate and lined up a whole list of others. He wrote a regular column on Ohio news from Washington. He also wrote special reports for any given paper for extra money. He's their man in Washington. They couldn't afford having their own Washington bureau and they like the idea of having something special for their own readers. They don't like having to rely on canned stuff put out by the local congressman or some other special-interest promoter.

This young Ohio self-bosser even passed the hat among his list of papers and got enough money to cover the national political conventions. There's nothing to stop him from doing

his own, Ohio radio show and there's nothing to stop him
from doing a whole lot of other things on his own now that he
has the bug. He had a tough time for a while, operating out of
a corner of someone else's office to keep costs down. But he's
making it and no editor tells him what to do. He's the boss and
he's still in his twenties.

12

THE MANGLED MIDDLE

At age forty-two I found myself a card-carrying member of America's "mangled middle." I was middle-aged, I was middle-income and my middle was hanging over my belt. I was frustrated, wondering where I was going, realizing that there were only so many weekends left in life. My job was no longer challenging because I'd learned all my company had to teach and found that I was giving more to them than they were giving to me. Bosses seemed to sit heavier and heavier on my back. I wanted out.

Perhaps you're in this "mangled middle" position in life. Maybe you're a member of the over-the-hill gang, just putting in time, or maybe you've been fired or feel that your job won't be around much longer. If so, join the club. There are millions in it with you. I'm still middle-aged and middle-income but I'm no longer mangled and even my middle isn't as big as it used to be (that's from all the work and worry that went into starting my own business—thins you right out).

When you're in the middle like this, you think everything's going against you. You're stuck in one dull groove. You're burdened with commitments, bills and responsibilities and are absolutely horrified if some nut like me suggests breaking out on your own. You may secretly want to do this but you're horrified because it's all unknown out there and your confidence rating is hitting a new low. When your employer puts you on a shelf or treats you with ill-disguised contempt, your confidence goes even lower. You think (erroneously) that, because the organization doesn't seem to love you with the same fervor it did when you were young, you're no good any more.

If you have these middle life blues, you need a shove to get out. Something has to knock you off dead center. You need to face up to the fact that you're not doing what you want to do and you don't have very many years left to make a fresh start.

Dr. Harry Levinson described this frustrated and fed-up phase very neatly after he had a session with a forty-two-year-old management man who was caught in the middle. The man felt he was going nowhere and was having an identity problem.

"A few questions quickly revealed," says Levinson, "that this man would prefer to be in his own business. But, every time we touched on this subject of running his own business, he was full of excuses and wanted to turn away from it. He did indeed know what he wanted to do. He was just afraid to face it. He wanted to be independent but he could not break away from the security of his company. He had maintained the fantasy that he might some day be able to make the break, but as the years drifted by, his conflict increased in intensity."

This conflict or anger with oneself is a common plight with us middlers. If you let the anger turn in on yourself and burn inside—you can get into a depression. You find yourself doing more drinking, battling with your spouse and, in general, moving slowly around in tighter and tighter circles.

But, if you turn this anger outward and focus it on a plan of action, it can be a powerful force, a powerful engine, to drive you out of the dumps and into the sun. Anger, if it's used for constructive purposes, can keep you going, keep you motivated to do the painstaking research that's needed to find and develop your own business.

My anger with myself and my dull job was hurting me until I begin to turn it like a white-hot laser beam on the task of setting up my own newspaper column and my own, independent business. If your anger can be harnessed to drive you so you will spend nights researching possible projects or take on moonlighting jobs to learn new skills, you'll find that it can keep you going through the hard spots. Your health—mental and physical—will improve, because this anger will no longer be burning up your insides.

The thing is, you have to realize that you're the only one who can really turn this anger and frustration around into a positive force. Nobody is going to come along with the magic wand and spring you free. You're the one. You have to quit worrying about some sort of image you have in the organization and have to start coolly and calmly looking outside the organizational world for the things you've always wanted to do. You've got to find something that has meaning. It has to be something that is really "you." Once you've found out what this is, then you can begin to design an escape plan that will lead you out of the mangled middle mess you're in.

Maybe you aren't boiling with anger. Maybe you're just occasionally fed up or even "sort of satisfied." You're not brimming with happiness, mind you, you're just "sort of satisfied." In this case, you don't have enough of the really hot anger to harness as a motivational force. You've got a low octane rating as far as the anger engine is concerned. What you need, then, is not anger but something to challenge your curiosity. You need to investigate a moonlighting job or some very small project you can quickly work into a success. Maybe you're good at accounting. Get an off-time contract with some small business managers to unravel problems they may be having with their books. Maybe you make some pretty good carvings, trout flies or whatever. Sell some through a local gift shop or sports store. Make your goal small and fairly easy to achieve. Aim in some direction you've always wanted to aim. Set your sights low and accomplish one little success at a time outside of your organization.

You'll love it. Then, feeding on the first little successes, try for more. If you're tied to some desk job and want to get out more to meet with people, try working in a store where you're on the firing line with customers. Do this evenings or Saturdays. Keep stringing your little successes like pearls, one at a time. Your confidence will rise and you'll have a positive charge to keep you going further until you finally find your way out into your own business. The negative charge of well-focused anger works. So does the positive charge of a string of successes you accomplish outside of the organization and outside the watchful eye of your bosses. You'll find that your attention is more and more drawn outside the organization and is less and less attracted to the futile game of "going up the ladder" where you work.

Sometimes it's hard for us middlers to find the direction where we want to aim. We know we want out—but where can we go? M.I.T. professor Richard Beckhard, who is a business consultant, has some tricks that might help find out who you are and where you want to go. "First," he says, "answer in ten different ways the question: Who am I?" He explains your answer can be that you're a father, mother, good cook, good fisherman—whatever. Have your spouse or someone else close to you also make a list of who they think you are. Compare the lists and knock out as many answers as you can and still retain the "core you." Keep working back to the number one answer you placed in the priority list.

"Then," Professor Beckhard says, "build a fantasy of a perfect two days—ten years from now." What will those two days be like? Where will you wake up? What will you have done to get to these two "perfect" days ten years from now? After this exercise, look at a peak experience or experiences in your life. Pick a moment or a weekend where everything went right. Then think of what you really want to do, something that would put you close to feeling the high you felt during that peak experience. Go back to your priority list and reshuffle the items that you selected to form the "core you." Add some, subtract some. The number ten isn't really important.

Finally, do a self-inventory. Make a list of the things you do well—even seemingly trivial things. You work well with people. You're a good cook. You're good at telling stories, making people laugh. Whatever. Get it down. Then have your spouse and some close friends make up their lists of what they think you do well. Then write down things you do poorly and things you'd like to do better plus things you'd like to stop doing.

After this kind of self-inspection, you should begin to get an idea of what you really want to do. Then try to match various fields of work that are complementary with the things you want to do. You can make a list of types of specific jobs you'd like to investigate with the possibility of eventually setting yourself up in your own business. Your own, ultimate business doesn't have to be the same kind that you select for investigative moonlighting, it can be something related to it. For example, if you like dealing with animals, you might work in a pet shop for a while or for some veterinarian. Then, after a year or so, you might find that there's a real need in your community for a grooming center for dogs and cats. Or you might find that there's a need for a pet supply store. See what I mean? You find out what things you'd really like to do, investigate through moonlighting jobs and, finally, design your own business from what you've learned.

You may have to take an organizational security blanket along with you when you finally make the break. It's not a bad thing to do and it can be of great help if you or members of your family worry about your image. You might try to get a contract with a big name organization for your new business. It may only be a small contract to do one specific project or service, but who needs to know?

I signed a contract with the Los Angeles *Times* to market my column. I could say my column was syndicated by the Los Angeles *Times*. I left *Forbes* magazine but picked up as good a name, or better, with the Los Angeles *Times*. It's true that it was just a sales contract and that I wasn't actually working for the *Times,* but nobody cared. They just knew that I was doing something with that big name paper.

A friend of mine is working with a big organization, very big, and he wants out. His wife is quite upset. She will no longer be the wife of a man who works for an organization that draws ohs and ahs from the multitude. They are invited everywhere and sought out because of his "connection" with this prestigious organization. What will happen when he leaves? Will he be dropped by certain friends and business contacts? I know it sounds like snobbery but it's very real. We all suffer from it. Spouses and children become insecure when they can't say what their father does. Not everybody needs this kind of crutch but it's handy if you can grab one. It not only helps with the image problem but it can also serve as a door opener for prospective customers you're trying to line up for your new business. It's not as hard to line up one of these contracts as you might think. Big organizations often need part-time help or someone who can do special projects. They need the job done and they don't want to hire somebody full time to do it.

Up to now, I've been dealing with the frustrated and the fed up. What happens if you're fired? That's a real disaster for a poor middler. What little confidence you have goes down to zero when the "Dear John" letter comes along. In heart-thumping panic, you tear around trying to "line up something else" with a competing organization. It's usually no good. You spend long, anxious days looking, looking, hoping for some opening back at the old grind.

It's kind of like the proverbial canary that's let out of the cage. Instead of trying to fly free, he always tries to get back in the cage. The same thing happens to some of the mangled middlers when their organization gives them the ax. They try to get back into the same, hopeless situation.

According to Frank Holt, president of Forty-Plus in Washington, D.C., "When you've been let go, you should get some part-time job quick. Get anything even if it's pumping gas. . . . Get some money coming in and have some kind of a base to work from while you look for something more permanent." Forty-Plus is a non-profit employment placement service for mangled middlers who get the rug pulled. There are chapters in several major cities, where members have a place to go to look for a new job and a way to rebuild their lives.

I'd take the whole thing one step further than just "get some part-time job," as Frank Holt suggests. It's a good suggestion, but I think you can do much more. I think you can look at the firing or phasing out (whatever you want to call it) as an opportunity. The firing is something final. You don't have to wonder where and what you're going to do in your organization. You're out and, you should say, thank God. In some cases a firing is a blessing in disguise. If it shakes you up and gets you started in another direction, you may really be able to make something out of the rest of your life.

You should look at yourself as if you were starting a new career. No matter that somebody back at your organization hurried up your decision. You should look at getting a new job the same way I suggested young people should look at job hunting. Try to get into something that really interests you, something that can teach you a new skill that might help when, and if, you can break out on your own. You can try the temporary employment services to see what's doing around town. Or you can work on some down-the-line job in a field you're interested in cracking.

For example, a dear friend was fired from his job in New York just three days before Christmas. He had a wife and two children to support. He'd been working with a firm that did market research and polling. When the recession came, the company lost a number of contracts and my friend was fired. He was stunned. It could never happen, he thought. He went through the motions of trying to get other jobs with various other marketing organizations. Nothing seemed good enough. As time dragged on, he even tried to get a job at a gas station.

He made his prospective employers feel he was "overqualified" and was just looking for something temporary while going through the help wanted ads. What he should have done was sign up with a chain of stores, gasoline stations, whatever, to do on-the-line direct selling to the public. Sure, he'd get a "cut in salary" from what he was making before. But underline those words "was making." He wasn't making anything *after* he was fired. He should have leveled with a store owner or manager and explained that he wanted to work for a minimum of a year or two and that his experience in market research would come in handy. He could do special studies for his new employer as he learned what goes on at the consumer level. He could do marketing projects for various clients while he learned marketing from the point of sales. The combination of his new direct selling experience and his past market research experience could work as a base for setting up his own consulting firm.

No way. It seemed beneath him to have to "work for wages

selling gasoline or groceries." He finally went back with some other organization and seems "reasonably satisfied under the circumstances." But what an opportunity he missed. Somehow he got hung up on his "image" and what "people would think."

I came close to being fired once and I got an ominous suggestion another time that I should show more loyalty to my boss's decisions—even when he was wrong. The first time, I was in Brazil working as a correspondent for various business magazines published by McGraw-Hill. Some bright beaver in the home office figured all the news correspondents could double in brass as market researchers for the company's clients. After all, we were already out on the scene. Why couldn't we just gather a little extra information from local businesses and government sources? What this bright type had in mind was "commercial intelligence" information—spying, if you will. We were supposed to act as if we were getting information for *Business Week* or some other McGraw-Hill magazine. I said that if I told somebody I was getting information for a magazine, then that magazine was going to get a story.

One time I got information for a client who wanted production, sales and other information on possible competitors in Brazil. I got the information and published it in a survey story in a McGraw-Hill magazine that dealt with electrical equipment merchandising. The client, who had paid good money for the survey, read most of it in a fifty-cent magazine and rightly blew his lid.

I got a phone call, long distance and the rage was awesome. I was told I was going to be fired for doing such a stupid thing as getting a "private survey" published. When I went home that night I told my wife and we had a long talk. At first we were scared because it looked like we'd have to pay our own way back to the States if they fired us. But, as we talked it out, we decided to stay in Brazil, put our few bits of furniture in storage and head off around South America, writing and reporting for various newspapers or magazines that would give us assignments. Interest was picking up in the area because of the so-called "communist threat" and papers could afford giving out assignments to free-lancers on the scene even though they couldn't afford sending their own correspondent.

We were excited about our new plan. We felt relieved. We were looking forward to it. Then the cable came. Big mistake. Canceling whole survey program. Please accept apologies. I wasn't fired after all and, frankly, I was sort of disappointed. We never got to do our fling around South America.

Much later, I was again threatened with firing and this time I decided to plot my way out of the place—even if it took years doing. I realized that they always have the threat of firing hanging over you and the only way you can be free to do what you want is to get control of your own income and your own time. The only way to really do this is to be your own boss.

Firing is, indeed, a trauma and plenty of agonizing and suffering follows in its wake. But, as I said, if you take a look at yourself and your real worth, firing can bring a change for the better. After all, we mangled middlers do have *some* things going for us. We have experience. We have learned several skills and some we might even be very good at. We have a lot of bills to pay, true, but we also might have some equity. We have a house or some other property that can be sold or hocked. We have a track record of accomplishments. Remember, organizations aren't set up to evaluate real human worth, they're set up to make a profit through administering some set policy. Their idea of someone's worth is often far from reality. Just because a human being is no longer useful to a specific organization doesn't mean he or she is worthless.

Let's take a look at a case where a firing changed a man's whole life around—for the better.

Tom Shepard was an engineer and product designer in the

aerospace and defense contracting business near Boston. He worked for several major companies on such projects as the Hawk missile system and atomic bomb triggering devices. He was making good money, but there was always that threat of a contract not being renewed or a change in a company's engineering emphasis.

Tom says: "Any engineer who has an ounce of creativity feels trapped in our system. You can't see what you're doing, what your work really accomplishes. You work on one small piece of an enormous project and you're lost." You also have to work on some things that you're morally opposed to, such as a missile system or a bomb device.

So Tom was disenchanted with the aerospace business. He said when shifts were made, "They traded human beings like a commodity—buy and sell, or, worse, buy and then dump." You were either "bumped to a lower job or bounced" when cutbacks came. The fear was always there and many a boss played on it to get more work and more "loyalty" out of his staff.

Tom's disenchantment with his work was solved one day when he was told he was "overqualified" for the job and had to be let go. "Overqualified," says Tom, "means they want to hire someone who's cheaper." Tom decided not to try to go back into the engineering business. He began to collect his unemployment compensation checks and finished a course in pottery making he was taking at a local museum. He tried to sell his pottery but found he wasn't much of a salesman and didn't have the necessary confidence or boldness to push his wares.

A local cabinetmaker knew that Tom was good with his hands and took him on to repair furniture, install cabinets and otherwise act as troubleshooter and handyman. After a year or so, the owner decided to quit and asked Tom if he wanted to take over the lease and put his own ad in the paper. Tom did and soon business began to roll in.

He has become an expert carpenter and designer of kitchen cabinets. He has plenty of work. He enjoys seeing his work "completed and in useful form." He's branching out to help some condominium builders design and supervise cabinet and carpentry work. Tom says he's making about the same kind of money he was making in the aerospace business, maybe a little less, but he's happy. His wife set up her own typing service, which has also blossomed into a full-time, going concern.

"You need to spread out the power they have over you," says Tom, explaining that he now has twenty or so bosses (his steady customers) instead of just one. "This way," he says, "you vastly dilute any one boss's power and get almost complete control of your income and your time."

Henry Mitchell Havemeyer wasn't fired from his job, but he feared his position was becoming less secure every day. Mitch worked on "Mad Ave" (Madison Avenue, New York) in the hectic and highly competitive advertising business. He was a designer and art director for various advertising programs. Says Henry: "I suddenly learned that when you turn forty they think you're too old . . . they want somebody younger to keep up with the times. Nobody announces this. It just creeps up on you."

He found that it was increasingly difficult to sell his design work. "I just couldn't make a psychedelic poster for a rock record album . . . things like that," Mitch says. Madison Avenue is caught in the youth culture and if you aren't young, you're suspect.

Henry Mitchell Havemeyer and his wife, Mary Allen, had been summer-commuter residents on the island of Nantucket four seasons and loved the place. One summer, they noticed that there was no bookstore in the little town of Nantucket. There had been several bookstores but all had failed. The Havemeyers wanted to get some special books for vacation reading and none were available. A wild, almost impossible idea hit them. Why not start up a bookstore right on Main Street near the ancient wharf? Obviously the failure of the previous bookstores had to be investigated first. Maybe the island just didn't have enough people who wanted to read.

The Havemeyers learned that the previous bookstores had either been poorly managed or in a poor location. Also, every one of the previous stores had been grossly undercapitalized and only had a small selection of books.

When they returned to the New York grind after the last vacation, the Havemeyers had worked out a detailed and well-thought-out escape plan. Mary Allen went to work for a bookstore in Westchester, their suburban home. She was only paid $1.50 an hour as a sort of permanent, part-time employee. She didn't care. What she wanted to do was "learn the business inside out." She sold books, arranged purchase orders, took inventory, managed the books—everything. She knew what books sold, what books did not and which publishers delivered on time. Henry hung around the store on weekends to pick up what lore he could and to get a feel for bookstore advertising techniques.

After two years working in the bookstore, the Havemeyers were ready to make their move. On a vacation visit to Nantucket, they checked every available building on or near Main Street to see what they could get. After making a head count on how many people passed each crucial corner during the day they selected a building on the corner of Main and Orange streets—a busy and historic spot. They got an architect who had designed many bookstores to help with their newly selected building. The place was gutted and a bookstore was built inside to use every inch of space to best advantage. The purchase of the building was signed in April 1968. The Havemeyers said good-by to the Madison Avenue job and moved to

Nantucket in May. The sale of their home in Westchester produced much-needed capital and they got a loan for the rest.

At 3 P.M., June 28, they rang up the sale of their first book. From there on in business has boomed. They set a target for the first year at $50,000 in sales and they surpassed it by $5,000. After four years, total sales rose to $122,000 a year. Every June 28 at 3 P.M. the cash register is closed down and a little party ensues. The Havemeyers religiously celebrate each anniversary of their departure from the "New York rat race."

Mitch Havemeyer found he could write ads as well as design them and his little announcements in the Nantucket newspaper have become classics. The Havemeyers are expanding with a mailing business and have seen the once restricted tourist season (June, July, August) stretched earlier into May and picked up again between Thanksgiving and Christmas. As a matter of fact, Mitch says, "the day before Christmas, sales are absolutely wild . . . there are many visitors to the island for the beautiful season here and everybody panics the day before Christmas . . . they all want books for presents." The Havemeyers' bookstore, called Mitchell's Book Corner has become a specialist in marine lore and technology. It has books on whales, old sailing ships, marine life, sea gulls, everything to do with the sea and ships.

One day a couple came into the store and showed more than a casual interest in the books. The couple, Tom and Dorothy Jeglosky (in their thirties) were from the Midwest, where he was vice-president in charge of promotion for the Dayton-Hudson Corp. (a billion-dollar-a-year chain of retail stores). They got to talking and the Havemeyers' "escape plan" came out in the open. The Jegloskys confided that they also "wanted out." He had a promising career ahead as an executive—but he felt trapped, unable to do a lot of the things he wanted to do with his family.

A second escape plan was hatched—this time for the Jeg-

loskys. They worked in Mitchell's Book Corner with the Havemeyers in order to learn the business. They had talks into the
night discussing the mistakes the Havemeyers had made and
what things were successful. Tom Jeglosky surveyed the New
England coast for a site to open the Jegloskys' own bookstore
and picked Kennebunkport, Maine. It's a quaint town and the
little building the Jegloskys selected had an aura of charm and
history. The Jegloskys' escape plan went into high gear. They
quit the prestige position with the big company, moved to
Maine and were suddenly in business for themselves. They're
doing even better in their first year than the Havemeyers did,
having profited from the advice they got during their Nantucket
"moonlighting." It was a gamble, but Tom moved his wife and
four little girls to Maine and a new life as master of his own
business, his own time and his own income.

Mary Allen Havemeyer is proud of her "pupils," explaining:
"We loved helping them. Those of us who have broken out get a
vicarious pleasure out of seeing others escape. We loved seeing their little plan grow."

People who have taken the big step out on their own seem to
enjoy helping others do the same thing. I know I do. Obviously, the Havemeyers do too. When you feel fed up and get
the itch to do something on your own, start seeking out others
who have made the break. Buy something from them and strike
up a conversation. Or offer to work for them, as the Jegloskys
did, or invite them to lunch or dinner. See if their happiness is
catching. Ask for their advice and help (but don't move in on
them and become a bore). You'll find that most of us who have
broken away have an informal brotherhood. We enjoy helping
others escape. Use some of your spare time or vacations to
learn from us. See if you can catch the spirit.

For many, this spirit is not as catching as I'd like to think.
For every Tom Shepard or Henry and Mary Havemeyer, there

are thousands of others who don't like what they are doing, realize they should move out, but keep putting it off. It's like
diving off the high board for the first time or like diving into an
icy lake early in the morning. You can think of all sorts of reasons why you ought to turn back and forget it. You admire
others that make the leap, but shudder at the shock you, personally, have to face.

Such a case of shuddering at the brink is Ted Holton (not
his real name). Ted has been with the same big company for
fifteen years, working in various fields as a salesman and administrator. He's completely fed up and his company is slowly,
but surely, pushing him further and further down the shelf.
He's an excellent salesman, in his thirties, yet his company con-
siders him "stale" or "burnt out."

Ted realized he was on a closed circuit to nowhere after
he'd been ten years with the company. But, because of a juicy
profit-sharing plan that allowed an employee to be fully vested
(in control of his or her share of the money) after fifteen years
of service, Ted decided to "stick it out so I can get my hands on
that money." He stuck it out. He got his hands on the money,
a tidy five-figure sum, but he's still with the company, brooding
away, unable to make a move.

Friends have noticed that Ted seems to be drinking more,
eating more and otherwise going to seed. The one thing he
clings to with a passion is golf. He loves golf, golfers, pros,
tournaments—everything about the sport. Talking about the
long putt on the eighteenth hole is a happy moment for Ted.
The reality of his deteriorating situation back at the office
seems to fade away for a while. But there's always Monday
morning and another tense note or call from his boss.

Ted is a failure. He can't get off dead center. He knows he
has to do something but he just lets the days pass by until he
can get to the golf course. He has far more going for him than
most of us have. He has an outstanding record as a profes-

sional salesman (until they made him an administrator and he went sour). He has a bundle of cash he could use for investment capital. Apparently, having a bundle to invest isn't enough. It may even be a drawback for those people who fear they may lose some or all of it. I'm not sneering at this. It happened to me for a while. I wanted out at least eight years before I actually could muster up enough courage to cut the ties. I had some money but I was afraid I'd blow it on some stupid "breakaway" scheme—and then where would I be?

But let's get back to Ted Holton and analyze his case to see what could be done if he'd only make the effort. It's always easier to tell other people what to do than to do it yourself. Ted is a good salesman with a proven record. He has a charming personality. People like him (except that tense boss, of course). He has a sizable chunk of cash and he has a considerable amount of equity in his home. He loves golf and everything that goes with it. He knows golf equipment and he's a top player.

Pop! Light bulb flashes on. Why doesn't Ted Holton work into becoming a manufacturers' representative for companies that sell equipment and clothing to golf clubs and pro shops? If he was selling something he really liked, he could be an even better salesman. He'd be getting paid for doing what he now dreams of doing for free every weekend.

Manufacturers' representatives have their own companies. They take on a number of lines of products to sell and they hire their own subsidiary salesmen if necessary. They plot their own course, they set their own hours and they don't have one, powerful boss. They spread their allegiance out over a number of companies so that no one has any heavy, unhealthy power over their actions.

How could Ted begin to experiment with this manufacturers' representative scheme? He could begin to combine some of his golfing weekends with a little side business. He could write to several manufacturers of golf products (or golf course equipment manufacturers) to see if he could represent them in his area. Manufacturers will scrupulously keep these side deals confidential. Ted's company need know nothing about it. He'd be working on his own time and it's really none of their business.

After six months' or a year's selling and experimentation, Ted could start up a whole line of products to sell. You need some capital to get going in this business, and he could use some (not all) of that nest egg he's guarding. He could pretty well calculate how much money would be coming in over the next year or two and, when the time was ripe, he could say "bye-bye" to his employer. Both sides should be relieved. Another eager cog in the organizational wheel would slide into his slot.

If this kind of a situation fits your case or that of a friend, there's a good source of information you can use to start investigating. First, check the libraries in your area for a magazine called *Agency Sales*. It's published by MANA (Manufacturers Agents National Association) and contains articles on what steps others have taken to set up their own businesses. It also shows mistakes representatives make and warns about traps some manufacturers set.

If you can't find the magazine, you can get a subscription by sending ten dollars to: MANA; 3130 Wilshire Boulevard, Suite 503; Los Angeles, Calif. 90010. If you don't want a subscription, you can ask for a couple sample copies of the magazine and you can ask some questions. You can describe your qualifications and your desires and get some advice. For answers to specific questions, address your letter to J. J. Gibbons, MANA's executive director. He has his own manufacturers' rep business and can give you an idea of what's needed to start your own.

By writing letters or poking through libraries to get more information, you will be taking the necessary first step into the sometimes tortuous escape route. To keep going, you have to begin putting down on paper a balance sheet of pluses that will help and the minuses that will hinder along the way. Be realistic about your minuses but don't dwell on them. Chances are your confidence has been beaten down enough as it is.

Remember, going out on your own may seem preposterous at first, but you've got a lot of things going for you that you may not realize. As a mangled middle-ager, you've probably built up an interesting record. Here's a tentative list:

★) Experience. You've developed specific skills after working ten to twenty years. You know how to sell, how to handle books or other such skills. You've helped somebody else make money all these years, now it's time to use this experience to help make money for yourself.

★) Capital. You may have a savings account, some securities or equity in a home. You do have capital—much more than you had when you started out. See how you can commit at least some of it to an investment in yourself. You have the credentials to get some fairly good-paying moonlighting jobs and can use them to put extra money into your capital fund.

★) Contacts. You probably have a number of friends and business contacts by now and some of them may be quite helpful in getting your business started. Some of them might even be your first customers. A friend of a friend may be just the person to give you the advice you need to make the big decision.

Instead of whining about all the reasons why you can't make it on your own, start writing down all the reasons why you just might be able to make it. It won't cost you anything and you can make your list some night in secret. Don't think that being on your own is the same as "being alone" just because it rhymes with it. Those who have broken away will tell you that they have more close friends and business associations than they ever had back at the old office or shop. When you're on your own these friends and associations aren't forced on you, you meet them on much more equal terms.

The first days out investigating any escape plan might make you feel lonely for a while because you're the key person. Nobody else can do it for you. It's your life and you're the only one who can make it mean something. Dr. Viktor Frankl says it clearly, right to your face:

"The striving to find meaning in one's life is the primary motivational force in man. . . . This meaning is unique and specific in that it must, and can be, fulfilled by you alone. . . . Only then does it achieve significance."

You alone have to make the decision. But, once you've made it, you can count on those of us who have made our own breaks to help you with yours. By working with others, we confirm our own faith.

13
HOUSEWIFE HORRORS

Working wives. They're all over the place. Get a job—any job
—is the thing to do. Women are breaking out of their "establishment," which is described by one harassed housewife as:
"Cleaning crud out of diapers, instant chauffeur, trying to get
endless piles of laundry and dishes done, supermarket carts
and crying children, and . . ." She ran out of breath. It seemed
wiser not to prompt her any further.

There is one big problem with all this. Housewives think if
they could just get a job, all their problems would be solved.
For a while, maybe, it works. But, as time goes by, more and
more housewives begin to realize they've been had. They've
just exchanged one establishment trap for another. They find
that their job hours are usually rigid and they also find that
they are discriminated against—either subtly or openly.

Many organizational jobs have unwritten limits on how far
"up" a woman can go in the hierarchy. Others have double
pay standards. Some have both. This kind of discrimination
against women as workers is illegal and it's all spelled out in
Department of Labor booklets. But it's still there and is extremely difficult for any individual woman worker to combat.
One of the reasons it's so hard to combat is the fact that all too

many housewives are so glad just to get a job they don't want to jiggle their luck by protesting unfair salary situations.

On top of all this, working mothers (around twelve million of them) find that a full-time job takes a lot out of them. When they come home, they still have a family to contend with and in many instances small children demand immediate attention. How to cope with having a family and working on an outside job is the big hang-up women are grappling with. How can you have it both ways?

First off, getting a full-time job isn't the answer unless a woman is divorced, or widowed, and just has to have the money. If a husband can bring in enough money to provide a home (roof, clothing, food and all that), a woman should use this solid base as a place to work from, not as a place to escape from. I know, I know, you ask: "How can I work in this place? Kids yelling. Husband demanding. Housework to do." You can work from your home, at least a few hours a day, if you begin to set some new rules and, more importantly as far as many husbands are concerned, have a plan to bring in some extra money.

What housewives need just as much as wages is time. Time is money. That's an old adage. Time is also peace of mind, gratification and all sorts of other things. By hooking up with some organization on a nine-to-five schedule, you may get money but you sure lose out on the time side of the equation. You lose badly. You not only trade one establishment job for another, you often find that you have two establishment jobs on your back (home and office) and your back gets near the breaking point.

What a wife and mother needs as a first step in breaking out of the home establishment is an interesting part-time job. Aha, you say, just try to find them. It's true. Part-time jobs for women who want to enjoy both outside work and a homelife are hard to find. The jobs are there, all right, they're just hard to find. Sometimes employers don't even know they're there. You have to show them by using my old "foot-in-the-door" employment technique. You have to get inside a place with whatever job you can get and then see what you can learn so you can build up portable skills that are useful to a whole list of employers on a part-time basis.

Let's back up for a moment and try to spell out a plan that will give you more control of your income and more control of your time. Isn't that what it's all about? Isn't this what I've been saying all through the book? Your goal should be to build up an interesting work schedule that will give you more control over your time and money. At every turn you will be experimenting with various combinations of those two crucial wheels —time and money.

Okay, where do we begin? Fran Goldman, who started her own non-profit employment agency for harassed housewives, comes right out and says, "Most wives who haven't worked for a while need to build up their confidence. . . . Many of them are beaten down. They don't think they have much value for an employer and some are even afraid to ask for fifty cents an hour."

Why is this? "Because," says Fran, who is a housewife and mother herself, "they're afraid of rejection or afraid of failure." I guess in this case they're no different from men who have been beaten down by their organizational job. Like the men, housewives are afraid to move out of their establishment because they might be rejected or they might fail. Of course, as I've said before, anger is a powerful force and can drive a distraught housewife out of her home "organization" just as fast as it can drive a man out of his office or plant job. Uncontrolled anger, as we've seen, can be dangerous. Control it and guide it and it can be a powerful, motivating force.

But, for those who aren't on the verge of divorce and aren't hopping mad at their "world" at home, the key to getting more independence is to build what I call a series of "success steps." Use the temporary jobs you can get outside your home as steps toward a goal of setting up your own business or professional service career.

As a tactician, you have to look for jobs in fields where you have a strong personal interest or aptitude. You've got to analyze yourself. Do you like to work with people? Do you like to work alone? Are you good at selling? Don't pass this last question off too lightly. Many women turn up their noses at selling careers because they lack experience or because they frankly think it's some kind of lowly occupation, something for "peddlers to do." What they don't realize is the fact that, as wives and mothers, they're often very skillful salesmen (I mean salespersons). Firing up a child's interest in arithmetic or reading takes considerable sales ability. So does organizing church or other social events. So don't knock it. If you're good with people, put selling down on your list of possibilities.

If you've ever been good at writing or drawing or even cooking, put it down on your list. Then add up the various things you're good at and see if they indicate any category of job that might be worth investigating. If you've been the one that has kept the family budget and books straight, and like that sort of thing, then why not polish up your bookkeeping skills to help small businesses with their books?

Alice Carter now has an accounting business of her own. She sets her own schedule so she can be with her husband and three boys when she wants and still do her bookkeeping work. She started out by keeping the family accounts because she likes fiddling with figures. When her husband, Arthur, decided to leave his law firm and put up his own lawyer's shingle, she took over his office books. Business acquaintances began asking for her help to the point where she began studying accounting in earnest so she could pass the certified public accountants' exam. She passed with flying colors and began to line up a whole list of clients. Most of them run some kind of small business and can't afford a full-time accountant or bookkeeper. Alice has her own office, her own hours and her own money. On top of all this, she's able to spend more "meaningful" time with her husband and boys. She has what most housewives want—the best of both worlds.

Best of Both Worlds, by the way, is the name of a book Fran Goldman co-authored with a friend, Renee Taft. These two Washington, D.C., housewives, set up a part-time employment service called Distaff Staffers. Renee has branched out into doing foundation-backed studies on jobs for women and Fran is opening up a Distaff Staffers branch in Philadelphia.

The trick is to be able to ferret out part-time work. Fran's organization limits itself pretty much to finding "professional" part-time work with a minimum wage of five dollars an hour. You don't have to limit yourself to that. Using my "foot-in-the-door" theory, you can infiltrate any organization on a part-time basis by taking almost any kind of a job. The secretary or typist route, of course, is one of the easiest. There seems to be an insatiable need for secretaries. Once you're in your part-time secretary's job, you don't just have to sit there typing away. Analyze your boss's needs for extra help. If you want to polish your writing skills, offer to work on a company brochure or annual report or advertising campaign—in your spare time. Take work home and bring it back well done. You get paid extra for this, of course. It may not be much pay but, remember, you're building a visible record of professional work.

Getting that first part-time job will do a lot for your confidence. Unless you are fantastically clever or lucky or both, you'll find it hard to start up a home business from scratch. But, as I've said, just getting an organizational job is not enough. You've got to get one that can help you develop "portable skills." You've got to build up skills and an aura of professionalism that can be used anywhere, so the word "boss"

evolves into the all-important word "customer" or "client."
Once you have a list of customers or clients, you'll be able to
have far more control of your time and income.

Set yourself a goal. What kind of a professional or skilled
service would you like to offer? Even if you're not particularly
good at the skill you admire most, aim for it. Wherever you
need to polish auxiliary skills, such as salesmanship, accounting, writing, whatever, get yourself a part-time job that will do
the polishing. As I've told college graduates who are just starting out to work, you should look at your part-time jobs as a series of graduate schools that pay you. Put most of the money
away in your capital fund and use the part-time jobs to pick up
portable skills, skills that can eventually form the base of your
own business.

I keep saying "portable skills" over and over again. Have
you noticed? The reason, I guess, is that I know professional or
"portable skill" workers always seem to have much more control of their income and their time than organizational "ladder"
workers. The more self-contained the skill, the less you have
to depend on any one organization for your livelihood. The
more self-contained the working skill, the less power or control
any one organization has over you.

In the case of the housewife, or married woman if you prefer, this portability can be extremely important. Marina Harris
(not her real name) has a husband who works for a major corporation. Every two or three years, the corporation moves her
husband "up the ladder" to a theoretically more important job
in another city.

How can a woman build up her own business in any given
community if her husband's company is forever moving him
around the country like a chessman? Well, it can be done but,
as you can imagine, it depends heavily on your ability to develop a professional skill that can be used anywhere.

Marina went to art school and got a job with an advertising

agency when she graduated. She got married and later transferred to another agency. Just as she began to develop her job
and get more pay, bam, her husband's company decided "it
was time to move again." It was hard to get a job with an
agency in the new town, so Marina decided to do free-lance
work. She had a portfolio of past commercial jobs she'd done
and went right to the clients, major government and industrial
prospects.

She now has a list of her own clients and does graphic design
work for them on individual projects. She has her own "basement office" and also spends some time at clients' offices working out final details. With certain limitations, Marina can now
move to almost any major city and begin to pick up her
graphic design business from scratch.

"It's not easy," she admits, "and it takes time to build up another list of customers." At this stage of the game, Marina and
her husband, Jerry, had to have a long talk about "this moving
around from city to city syndrome." It's not only tough on a
wife and children, it's also tough on the husband who's being
moved. Marina says she's seen "many friends in the corporation
who seem to be burnt out when they're forty . . . corporations
seem to slowly eat them up and then spit them out when
they're finished."

Couples have to look at jobs as a team. If you believe that
women are discriminated against in work—and I firmly believe they are—then the man in the house should try to get the
full-time job that can teach him the most and bring in the major portion of the family's money. The woman in the house
should use this money and home base perhaps to develop an
individual business before her husband is able to take this step.
Or maybe they can have a goal which would use both of their
developed skills in a family business or in businesses that
would complement each other. Alice Carter's bookkeeping business developed out of her husband's law business. It isn't too

important which partner takes the first steps toward building their own business. What is important is the fact that a married couple should work as a team so each individual can get as much control of time and income as soon as possible. If a couple looks at using the establishment in a joint effort, this crucial control of time and money can come much sooner. If they work at cross purposes, it can retard this freedom for many years and quite possibly can make the whole thing end in divorce.

The reason I mentioned the fact that a husband might well be able to make the most organizational salaried money first so a wife could develop an individual business is because it fits the facts of life. Organizations, for the moment, seem to pay men more and advance them further than women. But married women, especially those who have had to manage a house full of kids (and two grade schoolers can be considered a house full), seem to be in an excellent position to develop an individual business. I think many housewives, if they'd just stop to think about it, are in a much better position than their husbands to begin to plot and plan to manage their own business.

Why? Because by nature the housewife has had to learn how to operate on her own. She is usually the purchasing agent for the family. She is often the "chief maintenance engineer" for household equipment. She knows how to find and handle repair people. She has had to learn to live within a budget and this means she has had to become a smart buyer. In short, she is running a small business already—the home. Many households today are more complicated and have a bigger cash flow than many small businesses.

The housewife hasn't been working in an organization as such and has had to be on her own. That's why you always see these stereotyped jokes about the hapless husband trying to manage the kids and the leaky faucets while his wife is away. A competent housewife has learned a lot. Because her husband is usually "too caught up in his job," the housewife has had to fend for herself, feeding, supplying, educating, transporting and entertaining everybody.

In order to recognize this "on-your-own" experience she already has, a housewife must make a list of everything she does —I mean everything. Fran Goldman says that housewives are pathetic at making up a job résumé because they don't put any value on many of the things they've accomplished. "We've found that women who come to us tend to undersell themselves, playing down or even omitting important things they've done." Women, for example, tend to leave out any volunteer work they've done. This is wrong, because being able to do volunteer work and still run a complicated household ain't easy. Any employer likes to know if a woman can handle a job project and the home scene at the same time. It's quite an accomplishment. The same goes for part-time study a housewife may have negotiated while she was helping rear children. It shows, as Fran says, "that a woman knows how to make the necessary arrangements to meet commitments outside of her home."

Any studying you do, unless you want something for purely cultural or amusement reasons, should be part of your plan to get a job that might eventually propel you into your own business. Volunteer work should be looked at in the same light. Responsible volunteer work can teach you a lot. In many instances it can teach you how to be a manager. It can get you into a social service field where you can develop skills that people will pay for later on.

Let's take some f'rinstances:

Likes to cook—Working in day-care centers or with feeding the poor, elderly or handicapped can teach you a lot about food management, nutrition, bulk buying. It could lead to setting up feeding programs for other day-care centers, schools or industrial feeding. It could lead to a catering business that works with major commercial or government cafeterias. It could lead almost anywhere.

Likes to write or draw—Working on a fund-raising campaign can teach you how to write radio and TV material, how to write, design, print and publish booklets and sales (contribution) letters. It can introduce you to people around town who are in the writing business and who might be future customers.

Likes small children—Working in the administration and formation of day-care centers. Government money is going into this now and volunteers are needed to help with the social work backing up the centers. Later on, your intimate knowledge of how day-care centers work could lead into a business of setting up and managing day-care centers for industrial and commercial employers who need to attract female employees.

You can probably think of many more opportunities that could spring out of doing responsible volunteer work. You never know until you investigate. Because they don't pay, volunteer organizations often give great responsibility to volunteers. One housewife we know, helped Goodwill Industries set up a "mod shop" to sell furniture and appliances that had been renovated by handicapped workers. As a "buyer" this housewife learned to work through the press, radio and TV to get citizens to donate used household furniture, appliances and whatnot.

As "sales director," the same wife was able to move all kinds of renovated objects that had once been considered junk. With the trend toward mod and camp furniture or decorations, the "mod shop" was an instant success. At some time in the future, our friend should be able to make the move to her own shop but, this time, she'll get paid by her own customers. Her volunteer job taught her the ins and outs of managing and marketing a decorator shop.

So there are three basic ways to take the first step out of your home to get a part-time job that might lead into your own business. First, there are the part-time employment agencies that specialize in getting people to work at odd hours. Because schoolchildren come home around 3:30 P.M., you might have to work from nine to three. The second place to look for a job that will get you started in the right direction is in responsible volunteer work. The third way to try getting started is to make the direct approach to employers, selling them on the idea that they need your part-time work. If you can convince them that you can do more work in your short work day than many full-time employees can do in an eight-hour day, they might take you on. Use the "foot-in-the-door" technique of offering to do one project as a trial. If they like it, then they can make a more permanent arrangement.

When you make a résumé of your talents and background, Fran Goldman suggests you break it down into two categories —professional work experience (or whatever work experience) and any volunteer work you've done for your school, church or community organization. One woman omitted the fact that she had edited her husband's book because she didn't get paid for it. Put down things like that. Put down any special skill you have. You may be good at tennis. Put it down because some part-time employer may want someone to deal with sports equipment sales. Who knows? Wherever possible, be able to show samples of work you've done.

In the book, *Best of Both Worlds,* the authors suggest:

"Résumés should be easy to read; sparse, not in essay form. The point of a résumé is to tell enough to whet an employer's interest in having an interview. Two pages is more than sufficient. You should write your own résumé. It reflects who you are. Professionally written résumés are out . . . they look as phoney as a $3 bill." As you keep adding nuggets to your résumé, remember what you're aiming at—a self-contained profession or skill that doesn't depend on working for one organization. Eventually, your résumé of work experience should be able to be translated into part or all of a sales brochure that can be used to get individual clients or customers for your own business. Use your series of part-time paid (and volunteer) work as steppingstones toward selling your own products or services.

One way to get sales experience is to sign up for a franchise with one of the nationally known direct selling companies such as Avon, Amway or the kitchenware manufacturers. You sell these products around your neighborhood, sometimes through sales parties given at someone else's house. There's nothing to stop you from also selling some other product you may be making on your own. You can carry two complementary lines—the nationally advertised brand and your own homemade clothing, pottery or whatever.

Be careful when you get into one of these mini-franchising deals. Remember, you may be signing a fairly long-term contract and you have to know in detail all your responsibilities and all of the franchiser's responsibilities. Frankly, I'd never sign one of these contracts, nor would my wife, without having a lawyer go over it. You have to know who's responsible for any warranties, how refunds are handled and all that. The Uniform Commercial Code says you are legally just as responsible for what you sell as the manufacturer or distributor. For a list of names of the top home sales or party-plan franchisors, you can write: Direct Selling Association; 1730 M Street, N.W.; Washington, D.C. 20036.

Be wary of companies that advertise "make big money at home" deals. I went through this in a previous chapter on "Ideas That Work" but it has to be emphasized again in this chapter. Frustrated housewives are a prime target for these hucksters. Don't fall for their gimmicks. If they knew how to make big money at home, they'd be home making it instead of conning other people. If you want to do mail-order selling from home, you'd better first take a part-time job with a local mail-order company to see how things work. You have to have some product to sell that's unique or you should have an increasing line of products you've selected for a catalog. It takes a certain amount of capital and experience to start up a mail-order business. Don't let the advertisers fool you with "needs no experience" come-ons. If you have a product that you think could be sold through the mail, get in touch with a local mail-order consultant, pay for the advice, and see if he or she is willing to take you on as a regular client. For names of reputable mail-order consultants and mailing-list brokers in your area, write: Direct Mail Advertising Association; 921 National Press Building; Washington, D.C. 20004.

As you range down the list of ideas that may develop into your own business, don't overlook certain mechanical or repair jobs that are usually thought of as "men's work." I mean such things as TV, radio and stereo repair, auto repair, household appliance repair, things like that. You may have done makeshift repairs at home and you've certainly learned how to deal with the repair problem. Maybe I should say "cope" with the repair problem. You're probably the one at home who's stuck with the job. Any aptitude tester worth his or her salt will tell you that women often score much higher than men on things that require manual dexterity. You can learn electronic equipment repair, auto repair, air-conditioning repair—any of these —through local adult education classes or classes held at a nearby community college. Who knows? You could start up a repair business. Husbands may even take more interest in home repairs if the repair "man" turns out to be a bouncing woman in well-fitted overalls. There I go again, looking at women as "sex symbols." Got to watch that.

Isabelle S. Streidl, chief of the Economic Status and Opportunities Division, Women's Bureau, Department of Labor, says: "A small, but increasing number of talented women are finding the repair business to be quite interesting. Women are supposed to make excellent workers on the assembly line in electronics plants, why shouldn't they be good in the more lucrative repair business?" It's true that unions dominated by men might try to keep you out, but if you operate out of your own home they can't stop you. Women, who for years have had to struggle with mediocre repair work done by others, might be able to do a better job at handling customer complaints than men. Just a thought.

Now, how about handling husband and family? It can be a major hang-up or it can work fairly smoothly. You'll need all the support you can get and must keep resentment at a minimum. A husband may suddenly be grabbed by fear of rivalry. He has depended on his wife to "handle things at home" while he was out winning bread in his career. When a wife asserts her independence by going out to work, the husband may feel threatened. Bring your family in on your plans after you've thought them out and, hopefully, have lined up some sales or other signs of your project's possible success.

When you ever do begin to work out of your own home, set some specific hours. Martha Williams, who works with me as an editorial assistant, does much of her work at home. By helping me, she is also learning how to run her own, free-lance writing business from her home. Here are some tips she's jotted down for doing "home work" (other than housework):

★) *Set specific hours*. Tell children, husband and others what your hours will be at home. If you say you'll start at 9:15 A.M., then start at that time. If the breakfast dishes aren't done. Leave 'em. After all, if you were tearing off to the office, you'd leave the dishes anyway. Give yourself a set quitting time, too. You're more efficient when you have some deadline and you won't feel guilty when you knock off.

★) *Household duties*. Take a hard look at the work you're doing around the house. How important is a made-up bed? Wouldn't it be a good "character building program" for your husband and children to do a lot more of the work around the house?

★) *Handling the children.* Explain to your children what you're doing. Have an "office" or place where you can shut the door. But don't "shut them out." Have specific times when you come out of your cave to talk and relax with them. If they have questions or problems, they should save them for your "off" times—unless it's an emergency.

Explain the nature of your work and, wherever possible, bring your children in on it. Let them help address envelopes, cut out clippings, file things, whatever they can handle. Give them piecework pay for their "jobs." If they feel they're a part of it, they'll help you and will be co-operative. They won't feel that the work is competing with them for your attention.

Martha Williams' advice should be good, because it's working for her. She's married to an Air Force attorney and has three very lively youngsters in the grade school stage.

If you have smaller children, you may not be able to handle the situation at home unless you get some outside help. Even Mrs. Williams and others we know who have older children have to get paid baby-sitter or child-care help. The great thing about getting this kind of extra help is the fact that you can now get sizable tax deductions for it if you're working at home or at somebody's office or plant.

Here, according to the Internal Revenue Service, is how it works:

If you have dependent children under age fifteen or even have a disabled dependent such as a parent or a spouse, you can qualify for up to $400 a month ($4,800 a year) income tax deductions for such household expenses as child-care service, cleaning service or even full- or part-time maid.

You have to be "substantially employed." This means you have to be working at least six hours a day (this includes lunch hour). So, if you're working at home, you should be working

from, say, 9 A.M. to 3 P.M. with an hour off for lunch, reading
the mail or playing with your children. This covers regular jobs
too, providing you get those six hours in—nine to three, eight
to two, ten to four—whatever. Or you can work thirty hours a
week by working three days for ten hours each day. However
you slice it, the total hours should come out to thirty a week.

You also must be within certain income limits. You and your
husband's combined income cannot exceed $18,000 a year in
order to get the full tax deduction benefit. If you and your husband make more than $18,000 your deductions are reduced by
fifty cents for every dollar of added income. This means a joint
income of more than $27,600 won't bring any new deductions.
These figures will surely be raised over the next couple of years,
so be sure to check with your local IRS office (found under
U. S. Government in the phone book).

The total amount of deductions you can get per month depends on how many children you have or how many total dependents. If you only have one child and must put the child in
a day-care center, you're limited to $200 a month for these
expenses, which can include day care, nursery school or even a
summer camp. Regular school (first grade on up) expenses
cannot be included. But summer camp for children who are of
grade school age (up to fifteen years old) can be included. So
can transportation to and from day care, nursery or camp.

If you have more than one child in day care or camp, you
can get other deductions on up to the $400-a-month limit. If you
only have one child, you can build up your deductions by including housecleaning and maid service costs. You can even
count such commercial cleaning services as those offered by
Servicemaster and others. Maid service and in-home laundry
can also be included on your expense list. You cannot include
any payments you make to members of your family for this
work. Sorry. That's too cozy for IRS.

To see what kind of money can be saved under the new tax

law, let's look at a family of five where both parents work, their combined income is $18,000 a year and all children are under fifteen. You have to file a joint return (single return for widows, widowers and divorced parents) and you must itemize regular deductions. Let's say your regular deductions for such things as local taxes, medical expenses and charities come to $2,500. Add to this your full $4,800 yearly allowable deductions for child and home care expenses. Then add the $3,750 you normally get for five dependents (everybody in the family counts). You'll come up with a total of $11,050 in deductions, which whittles your $18,000 income down to only $6,950 for tax purposes. This leaves a final tax bill of $1,180.50. Without the special child and home care deductions this sample family would have to pay a total tax bill of $2,205. So, with the "working wife" deductions, there's a saving of $1,024.50 a year.

Getting good day care for your children is not all that easy. You can't just plunk them down in any old place. More and more businesses (hospitals, factories, offices) are opening up day-care centers for their employees. These are usually pretty good and you don't have to pay. But, if you have to work at home or for some employer who doesn't have an entrée to a day-care center, you have to pick your center as carefully as you'd pick a private school—even more carefully.

Dr. Carol Seefeldt at the University of Maryland Early Childhood Education Center, says: "It's not a good idea to ship a child off to a day-care center during the first six months of life. A child needs a mother's warmth and close attention for at least six months to a year."

A center should have a staff of one trained adult for every seven to eight toddlers. For children who are from four to five years old, the center can have one staff person for every twelve to fifteen children. Don't rely on state laws to provide satisfactory regulations for day-care health, education and safety standards. Dr. Seefeldt says, "Some states have standards for dog kennels that are better than those for day centers." You've got to look the place over carefully and talk with the staff. Any center or nursery school which doesn't permit visitors or resents inquiries into accreditation and qualification of the staff should be suspect. There should be ample indoor and outdoor space. Medical exams should be required for all children and the place should have plenty of liability insurance.

You can get an excellent guide on how to select a day-care center by writing in for a booklet called: *Some Ways of Distinguishing a Good School or Center for Young Children.* It's published by: The National Association for the Education of Young Children; 1834 Connecticut Avenue, N.W.; Washington, D.C. 20009.

In the hiring and handling of domestic, household help, you can get a *Code of Standards* booklet from the National Committee on Household Employment; 1725 K Street, N.W.; Washington, D.C. 20006. The NCHE suggests you have a two-week trial period for your prospective employee and if it works out well, you can make a deal for a year. You should spell everything out for your employee. Guides for this "meeting of minds" are contained in the *Code of Standards* booklet. Also, the NCHE has many chapters around the country and the chapter nearest you might be able to help find good, reliable domestic service. It's not easy. But when you can get tax deductions of up to $4,800 a year, you might better be able to afford domestic help.

There you have it. These are just some ideas for a job plan and some suggestions for handling the home front while you build up your experience and, eventually, your own business. Time's a wasting. Get to work. Maybe you can have the "best of both worlds" after all.

14

SENIOR SHOCK

If you've opened your so-called "golden years" retirement package of Social Security benefits and, hopefully, a pension plan, you may already know what I mean when I talk about "senior shock." Unless you're one of the lucky ones, the drop in income from your salary to your fixed retirement income resembles a leap from a ten-story building. Joseph A. Pechman, director of economic studies at the Brookings Institution, flatly states that "for most people, retirement is an economic catastrophe."

It is indeed. Let's look at some figures supplied by Social Security. Many, many retired people are actually getting less than 20 per cent of their pre-retirement income. This means, for example, that a person living on $12,000 annual wages will suddenly take an income plunge to $2,300 at retirement. A couple would get $3,400. Now, what are you supposed to do with that piddling amount of money? How are you going to eat, get around and keep a roof over your head? Those "leisure years" and "golden years" they talk about are a hollow mockery.

What about pension plans? They usually aren't much good. Many people don't stay long enough on one job to have their pension money "vested." Vesting means ownership. I worked for the Cleveland *Plain Dealer* newspaper for six years, McGraw-Hill Publishing Co. (*Business Week*) for ten years, *Forbes* magazines for five years and I don't have one damned cent in pension money to show for it. All those years I was working for these organizations, I was dutifully enrolled in what they called their generous pension plans. They may have been generous, if you'd stayed with each organization fifteen to twenty years.

James H. Schulz, professor of welfare economics, Brandeis University, calls this the "myth of the private pension plan." He says most people are lulled into a false sense of security, believing they are covered by a pension plan. In fact, only 15 per cent of retired people today are getting benefits from pension plans and when they do get benefits they average less than $1,000 a year. Big deal. Don't spend it all in one place.

This is why you have to start making extra money on the side while working for some organization. You not only need the money to put into that voracious retirement kitty, you need the skill and service experience to have something going before the watch presentation and "retirement luncheon" routine. Professor Schulz says you have to put money aside because neither the government nor your organization is going to do it for you.

Schulz says that you should have an income during retirement of around two thirds of what you were getting on your regular job. You don't have to pay as much income tax, you don't have to save as much, and you supposedly have lower living expenditures. This means if you're making $20,000 a year in your early sixties, you could live on $13,200 or so a year. In order to do this, you have to put around 11 per cent of your working wages into savings and investments during your entire working life. Now, you know you haven't been saving that amount of money. And, remember, this amount of savings (added to your Social Security) doesn't provide much, if any, cushion for calamities. If you have any serious illnesses or economic crisis in your family, they could wipe out much of your savings and you'd be right back on the floor again comes retirement time.

Obviously, if you want to avoid becoming an instant pauper at retirement, you'll have to think of something to do that will bring in a good amount of extra income. Your organization may retire you at age sixty or sixty-five—but you should never really "retire" as such. You may slow down or try to work the kind of hours and kind of jobs you like, but don't stop working. As you've seen, you're liable to starve to death if you completely stop working. Also, gerontologists (those who work with the problems of aging) claim you can deteriorate mentally and physically much sooner if you stop working, stop being involved in things.

Dr. Morton D. Bogdonoff, chairman of the department of medicine at the University of Illinois, describes this "retirement syndrome" in an article he wrote for the *Archives of Internal Medicine*. When a person has been retired by his or her organization, Dr. Bogdonoff says, some minor physical ailments often begin to occur. There's a little backache, some leg cramps; "then the patient encounters a decrease in appetite, some fullness and gas, and is tired after the least bit of effort."

As time goes by, things get worse. More ailments and "symptoms" appear. People who continue active on into old age, don't seem to be afflicted by this "retirement syndrome."

"What is being suggested here," says Dr. Bogdonoff, "is that in order for an individual to remain healthy, he must have a specific reason for being alive and well beyond mere survival . . . Insistent demands for continued involvement with the details of daily work constitute an important factor in maintaining health. The requirement to be some place each day, to be performing some task, to provide some service, to be with certain people in some planned manner may not necessarily be the chains of responsibility so much as the lifeline links to the future."

Actually, this "retirement syndrome" Dr. Bogdonoff describes can be applied to people who haven't officially retired from their organization but who have been mentally or spiritually retired. Remember the depressed fellow in his early forties who felt he was all washed up with his company? You have to be doing something that other people need. Other people must want your services or skills.

You may be happy in what you're doing but the system picks an arbitrary age for retirement. According to doctors, this age—sixty-five, sixty or even earlier—is not related to your actual mental and physical capabilities. They picked this retirement age for Social Security purposes because they quite frankly wanted to get people out of the top of the labor market so young workers could more easily enter at the bottom. Organizations believe they have to work this way. I don't believe they do. But they think mandatory retirement at a specific age is necessary, and that's what counts. That's the way it is.

If you face retirement or have recently been retired, you've got to fight the system that keeps trying to push you out. Don't be pushed out. Hopefully, you've been able to work on some moonlighting that can be continued on after your organization drops you. That's what much of this book is about. It's about getting something going *before* they retire you and not waiting until the day arrives.

You can find work after you've been retired, but it isn't easy. You have to make a determined effort, just as determined as if you'd been fired earlier in the game. Regard retirement as being fired and get cracking on lining up other work. By now you know my feelings on the kind of work you should line up. You should plan to get into things that can help polish skills that can be used in your own business. First off, you're going to run smack bang into outright discrimination. Maybe you weren't a member of some oppressed minority group before you retired. Well, you are now. Politicians, government agencies, industry, labor unions and others pay lip service to being concerned about the problems of the elderly but most of them don't do much more than talk. They usually just want your votes or your money.

If you're job hunting, you'll find many a door closed in your face. The organizational world doesn't seem to want to employ older people. There's a stereotyped opinion of an older person's capabilities. They think you're not as dependable, which is not true. They think you'll be absent and not capable of doing the job, which is also not true.

You'll also find that your own personality might have become set and somewhat inflexible. Maybe you don't want to work certain hours or claim you won't do anything other than what you've been doing back with the old organization. You've got to be flexible. You've got to be willing to try new things, take on training courses if need be. There are all sorts of organizations that can help you get training. There are the various state employment services, the U. S. Training and Employment Services (federal government), rehabilitation services and others. One problem with getting training is getting the transportation you need. If you still drive a car or have enough money to take buses (if there are buses) or taxis, then you're all set. But many in the senior shocked set don't have too much money. Some volunteer organizations around the country are beginning to organize transportation pools for elder citizens who want to get job training or ride to and from a new job. If you have transportation problems, try calling your local women's clubs, United Givers organizations and other volunteer organizations.

You may believe the old saw: You can't teach an old dog new tricks. Nonsense. Dr. Robert Butler, gerontologist and research psychiatrist who is consultant to the U. S. Senate Special

Committee on Aging, says: "Depending on whether there are physical handicaps, you can teach people to do all sorts of things on into advanced age." Dr. Butler knows a woman in her seventies who learned to type. She now does work for various authors and works on institutional reports. She doesn't have the speed of a young typist so she can't really work in an office. But her work is neat and accurate. She enjoys typing authors' works and talking with them about it. Keeps her up on things, she says.

The same thing goes for bookkeeping. There seems to be a great demand for bookkeeping skills these days and elder entrepreneurs have been able to cash in on it. One woman in her seventies has her own list of clients for her bookkeeping service. Many small businesses in a metropolitan area cannot afford a full-time bookkeeper. I know I can't. So they look for someone who can come around once a month or once a week to pay all the bills, do the billing, keep tabs on all the taxes (and there are many of them, including federal, state, local, Social Security, Workmen's Compensation) and, in general, keep the books in order.

I hired Gerry Boudreau, a woman who was retired from government service. Gerry comes in one week every month, pays all my bills, deposits my checks, pays my taxes, keeps the books and, if she has time, files things and gives me ideas for my consumer newspaper column. She makes extra money and has a feeling that she's really needed by someone. Which is absolutely true. Those books and tax deadlines were driving me crazy. Gerry learned how to manage quickly and is now considering expanding her services to take up more days of the month with other clients.

You have to find needs in your community that aren't being filled. Mrs. Emogene Baxter helped start an organization that finds these needs in the community and then finds older people who can fit them. The organization is called Over 60 Counselling and Employment Service and it has offices throughout

Maryland and Virginia. "People who have been shocked by retirement," says Mrs. Baxter, "need turning around with some counseling." If you can find a local organization that specializes in finding jobs for older people, you can get this kind of counseling. One such national organization, Mature Temps, specializes in getting part-time jobs for people over fifty-five. For further information, you can write Mature Temps' main office at: 521 Fifth Avenue; New York, N.Y. 10017. There are others, such as Opportunity, Inc., in St. Louis and the Civic Center and Clearinghouse in Boston.

An increasing number of universities are starting special courses aimed at "turning around" older people who are in economic and cultural shock. One of the best can be found at George Washington University in Washington, D.C. The G.W.U. course is called "New Horizons" and is aimed at getting older women back into meaningful work. Mrs. Baxter got her start through a "New Horizons" course and was able to help build a network of non-profit employment training and placement centers for older workers.

"I think volunteer work can help you take your first step out of retirement and back into things," says Mrs. Baxter. She cites the case of a widow in her early sixties who had quite literally gone into a form of shock. She was depressed and had every reason to be. This widow found that almost all of her savings had been eaten away by inflation and an illness. She was lonely and didn't seem to have any real reason to continue living.

"She went to work for a small volunteer organization at her doctor's suggestion," Mrs. Baxter explains, "and the transformation has been almost miraculous." The widow opened up and got out of her depression. She was put to work and realized that somebody really needed her. Now she's taking a training course in bookkeeping and feels she can make some money and help others with her own accounting service.

To get going again, Emogene Baxter claims you need counseling with someone who will listen and who knows how to spot your skills and put them to work. If you can't get counseling, or don't need it, talk to others who have made it out on their own after retirement. They not only serve as an inspiration, but they can give valuable leads on what you can do and where you can get help.

We've all heard the admonishment: "You need to have a hobby to keep busy when you're retired." It's a hackneyed phrase, but it's true. Hobbies can be a great help after retirement and not just to keep your hands from reaching for that whiskey bottle too often. "I believe in hobby polishing," says Mrs. Baxter. She means you should polish up your hobby and put it to work. Some people have marketable expertise if they'd only realize it. Some examples: One man had been a stamp collector most of his life. Retirement hit him and, of course, he had much more time to put into his collection. But he needed money and, frankly, he wanted something more to do. A counseling advisor told him to put his collection together and show it around to some of the stores that sold stamps and coins. Collecting, in case you haven't heard, has become a booming business. This fellow got not just one, but several job offers to manage stamp sales in hobby shops. He's now working in a shop and is building his own sideline "special request" service for stamp collectors.

Another fellow loved old books. He collected them and enjoyed picking up old-book bargains. Just for fun, he set up a small stall in a "flea market" where people could buy, sell or trade old books. After a while, a small crowd began to gather around the old-book stall. Finally, he made enough money to invest in more books and some advertising. His business is increasing steadily.

There are other avenues besides hobbies, avenues that many of us don't think about. The whole field of home health care, for example, is wide open for older workers. Emogene Baxter's Over 60 Counselling and Employment Service designed a course to teach retired people how to be family aides or home health aides. "We've gotten jobs for many of our family aide graduates," says Mrs. Baxter, "and we're now getting ten requests for every graduate . . . there is an enormous need for this sort of person."

Family aides get training in nutrition, psychology (handling of the sick, aged and children), proper dispensing of medicines and hygiene. The course is short and intensive. Aides can be used by doctors, nursing homes and social workers. Psychologists claim that it's much better for an older person to stay in their own home instead of being shipped off to a nursing home. Wherever possible, they like to keep a person in their own, familiar surroundings. In order to do this, trained professionals or para-professionals have to be available to feed, medicate, bathe and supervise the handicapped elder who wants to stay at home.

There are never enough people to help with long illnesses where a person has to remain at home—no matter what age. There's also a need for taking care of children while a mother works or is sick and unable to give the necessary care. There aren't enough professional nurses to do these jobs and, actually, nurses with their highly specialized skills are more needed elsewhere.

You can learn how to become a home health aide by checking through your local United Givers (Community Fund) headquarters to see what organizations have training programs. United Givers, in most cities, serves as a clearinghouse for volunteer information. The Red Cross, for example, has an excellent home nursing course which could get you started on being a home health aide. The course is not exactly designed to be used to make money but it certainly could be used as such.

One of the problems with the home health aide or family aide career for retired persons is the stigma some people attach to it. It's fading fast, but there's still a feeling that working in someone else's home seems too much like being a maid or cook. When these programs first started some of the families that were receiving family aide service tended to treat these para-professionals as domestic servants and there was some ill feeling. But, with more training, strict rules and the fact that they're often so hard to get, the home health and family aides are usually treated with great respect, as much respect as nurses and other professionals get. Aides get less per hour than nurses, something in the neighborhood of $3.50 an hour, depending on the locality and the demand. But that's not bad when you consider they can also get some meals and even transportation paid for. Even more than the pay, these para-medical aides seem to be getting satisfaction out of seeing how their patients and families respond to their care. It's gratifying to see some other human being be able to cheer up and even conquer an illness because of specific help you have given.

As you look around your community, you can see other needs that aren't being adequately filled. The whole field of minor repairs seems to be wide open. Over 60 Counselling and Employment also started a training course for men and women who seemed to be handy at fixing things. Professional carpenters and shop experts were brought in to teach students how to fix windows, doors, screens, broken furniture, and make all the other minor repairs that plague the average homeowner.

At first the trade unions objected, but when they were brought into the program and limitations were set on how big a repair job a part-time carpenter could do, there was peace and the program was able to get moving. If the home repair business appears wide open for retirees, so does the home landscaping business. With the exception of a few, winter months in cold climate areas, lawn care, tree care and all that goes with it, can be a good business for anyone who has the health and the inclination to work outdoors. Some pretty sizable businesses have been built up by those who are doing contract landscaping and lawn care.

Your county's Co-operative Extension Service (found under county or city government in the phone book) probably has several courses on landscaping and lawn care. You can get training on the types of equipment and products to use and how to handle various soil conditions. The extension service agents also have other courses in nutrition and home repairs, any one of which could be turned into a business. The nutrition course could be turned into expertise that would fit into home health aide work. The more you know, the more doctors and others are willing to pay.

Try to find out what jobs are going begging in your community. Then design your own business to fill the particular job that interests you. For example, I just learned that "key-lining and pasting" is a job that never seems to attract enough qualified help. This is the job of taking a commercial art director's layout for an advertisement, poster magazine, magazine cover or whatever, and translating it onto a board to be ready for a camera to shoot. Headlines, artwork, copy, everything, has to be just so many inches from each edge and each corner. This is where the key-liner and paster comes in.

Young graduate art students don't seem to want to do this exacting, mechanical work (they have bigger ideas). Yet advertising agencies, publications, government agencies and others have an enormous demand for the service. One commercial artist we know says she could move to almost any city she wanted to and get work right away as a key-liner and paster. There's that much need. But who ever heard of it? Local art schools or trade schools probably offer courses in this kind of work and, if you have some skill with measurements and design, you might give it a try.

Copy editing is another field where they never seem to be able to get enough help, especially for odd hours or weekends. If you know the English language, know punctuation and spelling fairly well, you might be able to make it on a copy desk. Copy editors go over writers' work, make corrections, check for facts and write headlines. The interesting part is the headline writing. If you're good at "Scrabble," you ought to be good at headline writing. It takes a good knowledge of words to be able to fit a headline in a precise amount of space. Some newspapers give their own copy editing courses in order to attract extra help and most university journalism schools offer them.

Finding the need and getting the training are only half the battle. You've got to know how to sell your services. You may be the best home health aide, the best repair fixer or the best copy editor in town but who's to know if you don't advertise and make your services visible? You have to make a job of getting a job after retirement. Set up the little home office I outlined earlier. Get some letterheads, cards or fliers made that describe your service. In the case of home health aides, leave your cards around at doctors' offices, hospitals, clinics and medical schools. You can also leave your name and qualifications with your local social service agencies.

Use the phone book Yellow Pages for leads. In the case of typing, copy editing, key-lining and other work related to the communications field, possible customers will be listed under publications, advertising, printers and other such categories. If there's an organization such as Over 60 in your area, be sure to ask their help in lining up jobs. You'll find that there are many employers who will buy your part-time services for various projects but would never hire you full time. As I said, there's still a wall of prejudice that blocks many elder workers from jobs. There seems to be far less prejudice against hiring elders as part-time or contractual project workers. Your best advertising will be word-of-mouth advertising. Do good work for one client or customer, and word will begin to get around. You will still need cards and fliers to describe your skills to prospective customers, but the word-of-mouth recommendation will be one of your most valuable allies. Once a customer realizes that an older person is often more reliable than a younger worker, the word will spread.

You may move slower but you're often more dependable and more exacting than a younger person. You may be more willing to use patience and get the job done right the first time. It's a matter of time. The young are in a hurry. You're not. Time is your biggest asset in setting up your own list of clients. You've got a lot of time. Your organization no longer demands your entire day, five days a week. You have time to plot your course. You have time to get some extra training and you have time to market your services. You'd better occupy your time doing these things or you might slide back into senior shock to become a geriatric dropout with all the psychological and physiological consequences.

As you move out to make money after retirement, you'll come up against a nasty little surprise the government has worked out for you. The Social Security laws say that you can't make more than $2,100 in any given year, or part or all of your Social Security checks will be cut off. Their misguided reasoning is that when you're retired, you're retired, and you're supposed to stay retired. Some of the best fiscal and tax experts in the country claim this Social Security law is way out of date and should be changed to give elders an incentive to work in later years. But we're stuck with a law that was designed in the 1930 depression years, when the government wanted to get as many people out of the labor pool as possible.

Until the law is changed, you're going to have to learn how to use every available opportunity. The one big opportunity you shouldn't miss is the one that says you can count your earning limitation two ways. You can take $2,100 a year as your limit or—and get this—you can go on a monthly limit basis, using $175 a month as your income limit. If you multiply it out, you'll find that $175 is just one twelfth of $2,100. That's all right, because the law further states that if you make more than $175 in any given month or months, you will be docked in your benefits for only those months where you exceed the limit.

It sounds complicated, I know, but it's clearer if we look at an example. Let's say you can get a job or jobs during the holiday rush. Maybe you're good at sales, maybe you're good at bookkeeping. No matter. You have a skill that's desperately needed on a seasonal basis. So you work November and December, and let's say you make $1,000 in each month. For those months, you won't get your Social Security checks. Let's say you're supposed to get $216 a month from Social Security (this is on the high side for an individual and near average for a couple). So for two months out of the year you won't get $216 a month or a total of $432 from Social Security. But you will get your Social Security checks for the other ten months, which is a total of $2,160.

Still with me? Now, let's say that you are able to do part-time work several days a month and this pays you right up to your $175 maximum allowed by Social Security. You do this for ten months and you get $1,750. When you add up your big two-month wages, your regular ten-month wages plus your ten months worth of Social Security checks, you get a grand total of $5,910. If you had been doing nothing, just receiving Social Security checks, you only would have received $2,592. If you had worked but had kept at the $2,100 yearly limit set by Social Security, you would have received $2,592 plus $2,100 for a total of $4,692. This is still much less than the $5,910 you would have received if you'd worked those two big months.

The point of all this is the fact that many government offices out in the hinterlands have personnel who aren't up on this loophole and continue to tell retired people they can't earn anything over $2,100 a year without losing their Social Security benefits. This is not true. You could make a million dollars in one month and still would only be docked one month in Social Security benefits. Every year you have to make out a form that tells Social Security whether you plan to have yearly earnings that go above the $2,100 limit. Just say "no," you don't plan to. Then, when the month or months come along where you do exceed $175 in earnings, you'll still get your Social Security checks. Don't send them back. If you have enough reserve savings, you can spend them. If you're tight on cash, then put these Social Security checks in a savings account and just live off your regular earned income for the months you exceeded the $175 limit. Later on, in a few months or so, Social Security will catch up with the months where you exceed the limit and won't send you a comparable number of checks. You'll be "paying back," as it were. If you know that you will be having a good-paying, seasonal job, you can work all this out in advance with your local Social Security office.

This is complicated but is well worth figuring out, because you can make more income and still not lose the bulk of your Social Security checks—if you know what you're doing. If you can eventually work into your own business with your own direct customer relationship, the Social Security scene is even further complicated. When you're the boss and are not working for one individual employer, Social Security uses time instead of money limitations on your earnings. In general, the limitation is forty-five hours a month. If you work more than that, you might have to explain your actions or lose your Social Security check for the month.

The same "big month" choice is still available to the self-employed. You can work for one, two or three big-pay months that require much more than forty-five hours of your time each month and still be docked benefits for only those months.

You can be working on some home-base business that brings in a little money each month and doesn't require too much time. Then, if there is some kind of seasonal "rush" period, you can work full tilt those months and only miss a total of those months' Social Security checks.

These loopholes are especially important if you can take advantage of big seasonal pushes in certain businesses. For example, you may have a rooming house, store or whatever that does very little business in the off-vacation season. But in June, July and August, you could do a whopping business and still be docked only three months in Social Security checks. Same thing goes for winter resorts, the real estate business, special sales seasons or the two months before tax time for accountants.

I've only touched some of the bases for working after retirement. You can get in more groundwork by reading a couple of books that are highly recommended. They're mentioned in the chapter on "Your Own Corner" as part of a suggested self-bosser's bookshelf. But, for emphasis on post-retirement projects, here they are again:

Retire to Action, written by Julietta K. Arthur and published by Abingdon Press. This book is a must for retirees or those contemplating retirement within the next few years. It describes in detail every kind of volunteer job, employment service and job training service available. It gives names and addresses of every organization that can help retired people. They're also broken down into categories such as "special help for rural areas." Even if retirement is as much as ten years away, this book can get you started in the right direction.

The Opportunity Explosion, written by Robert Snelling and published by Macmillan. Snelling is the chairman of Snelling & Snelling, franchisor for the world's largest chain of employment agencies. It's not written especially for older people but it has many tips for people of all ages who want to work. A person facing retirement can get plenty out of this book.

These are the two basic books. If you are feeling sorry for yourself and are somewhat depressed, I suggest you read *Man's Search for Meaning,* written by Dr. Viktor E. Frankl. I've already mentioned Dr. Frankl several times because he is the founder of "logotherapy," which works around the theory that the striving to find a meaning in one's life is the main thing that keeps us going. Dr. Frankl was a prisoner in a Nazi concentration camp and describes his survival through that ordeal and how he became a better person afterward. After reading this book, you'll feel a lot less sorry for yourself.

The Department of Labor puts out a well-organized booklet called *Back to Work After Retirement.* You can get a copy by writing: United States Department of Labor; Manpower Administration; Washington, D.C. 20210. It gives ideas for post-retirement work but is mainly valuable for its complete listing of the government agencies that can help retirees and the bibliography of books and booklets related to continued employment after retirement.

As a little inspirational fillip, the following list is quoted from *Changing Times* magazine:

★) Cervantes completed *Don Quixote* when he was nearing seventy.

★) Clara Barton, at fifty-nine, founded the American Red Cross.

★) Goethe finished the dramatic poem *Faust* at eighty-two.

★) George Bernard Shaw wrote his famous drama *Saint Joan* at sixty-seven.

Part IV
THE FINAL BREAK

Hardly a day goes by in our legalistic society when some document, some harsh words, some misunderstanding presents itself as a possible legal trap. Think about it. You are faced, for example, with all sorts of contracts. Some of them are simple enough but others are quite deceptive and can lure you into long-term agreements you may not want to be bound by.

Even when you fill out a coupon and send away for something in the mail, you are completing a form of contract. You have to read what those little book club, record club and other "coupon" agreements say. Then there are the big contracts, such as marriage, or the breaking of contracts, such as divorce. There are written contracts between employer and employees and subtle unwritten verbal contracts that can hang you just as sure as the written ones.

Aside from the contracts, you're faced with the almost stupefying complexity of our tax laws. For those who do not understand the tax laws or don't hire someone who does, much money can be lost because rights are not claimed and legal loopholes are not used. Every time you change your status, you can run afoul of the tax laws and can be taxed more than your fair share. When you marry, when you have children, when you buy a house or sell a house, when you retire, when someone in your family dies—these are all important stages in your life to know your legal rights. And, for those who are contemplating going into business for themselves, a whole new field of legal problems presents itself. Many a struggling new business has become needlessly tangled in legal snarls and has been dragged down to failure.

Some of us fancy ourselves as a sort of a Clarence Darrow or Perry Mason type of legal hero. We throw legal terms around and when we're involved in certain business negotiations we talk too much. We need a lawyer to tell us the right moves and when to keep our mouths shut. We don't need to call a lawyer for every problem that passes by but we need to work with a lawyer fairly early in our complicated lives. We need to talk calmly with a lawyer to get advice *before* a crisis occurs. In short, we need a "family lawyer" just as much as we need a family doctor. We need preventive legal care just as much as we need preventive medical care.

My family is blessed with a truly creative family lawyer. I found him by asking around, just the way my wife found a pediatrician and dentist for the family. I only wish we had gotten a family lawyer much sooner. But no matter, we got a good one and he has gotten us out of some family difficulties (a nasty fight with the moving company) and has helped me avoid several dangerous legal curves in my new business.

Our lawyer is Alan Y. Cole, who is as much of a psychologist and observer of human behavior as he is a legal mind. Alan Cole became intensely interested in the law while serving with the U. S. Army at the Nuremberg War Trials, where Nazi war criminals were given trials and prison terms after World War II. From there on in it was Yale Law School and a career that took Cole into the Department of Justice and into the Supreme Court as a clerk to Justice Robert H. Jackson. Alan Cole is now in private practice, where I dropped by to get some pointers on how those going into business for themselves should use a lawyer to best advantage.

"When you're looking for a family lawyer," says Alan Cole, "it's much like looking for a general practice doctor or internist. Not every doctor is a surgeon and not every attorney is in fancy trial cases. The glamorous surgeon and trial lawyer are certainly necessary, but most people hope they will never require services from either of them."

What's needed, then, is not a fancy specialist but an all-round "general practice" lawyer, one who knows many facets of the law.

You need somebody to supervise your legal problems. This doesn't mean the G.P. lawyer you get can't bring in a specialist when necessary. Lawyers bring in specialists or call them for advice just the way doctors do. And it's far better for your own family lawyer to be calling the specialists than for you to do the calling. I've found that good doctors know how to find other good doctors. The same thing goes for lawyers. Also, your G.P. lawyer can translate the specialist's technical advice and can better fit that advice to your overall needs.

The public has come to look at lawyers as "costing an arm and a leg" every time you need them. This is because most of us wait until disaster hits before we call the lawyer—and, at that stage of the game, lawyers are expensive. "If you consult a lawyer too late," says attorney Cole, "after a suit has been filed or some other crisis has occurred, the lawyer hasn't much flexibility. He must either go to court or negotiate under difficult circumstances."

If you have a family lawyer and use the lawyer as a sounding board before problems arise, you can avoid much of the expense that's attributed to doing business with the legal profession. A fifteen-minute phone chat with your family lawyer can sometimes save thousands of dollars and months of anguish later on. When you spot trouble brewing or are poised to make some major move in your life, let your lawyer know. The lawyer can help you keep out of trouble. You can practice "preventive law" just as well as you can practice "preventive medicine."

So how do you find a good lawyer? It takes patience and time. Like doctors, lawyers can't advertise. You can best find them by word-of-mouth advertising. I found my lawyer by asking a friend who had successfully broken out into his own business. He told me he had used Alan Cole for eight years or so and hadn't made a wrong turn yet. I met the lawyer at lunch with my friend and we had a friendly general discussion with no commitments. Some rapport began to build.

Then a crisis hit and it took us by surprise. When we moved from one side of town to the other, the moving company charged three times more than was stated on the original estimate. I refused to pay any more than 10 per cent above the original estimate, which I thought was a fair limit. A sheriff came to my door one evening and handed me a summons to appear in court. I was being sued for the unpaid remainder of the bill by the moving company. I was outraged. I felt like calling the moving company up and threatening. I felt I was right and had a sudden vision of handling the whole case myself just the way Perry Mason would do it. Fortunately, after talking it out with my wife, I put in a call to our new-found family lawyer. We won the case and I learned a lot about the law and lawyers. I also spent some money and some time away from my work. Had I thought about letting my lawyer look at the moving company contract *before* I signed it, the whole bizzare mess might never have happened.

When you're looking for a lawyer, you want to get someone who will keep you out of court and out of trouble. The court scene is often interesting, even exciting, as long as you're not one of the participants. As you ask around among friends and business associates for names of lawyers, try to find out how each recommended lawyer operates. For example, it's important to know whether the lawyer is "issue oriented" or "people oriented." Some of the new breed of lawyers may not be nearly as interested in the fact that you were evicted from your apartment as they are interested in making an issue out of the entire procedure by which courts should decide eviction cases. This may revolutionize the field of landlord-tenant law and, in the long run, be helpful to thousands of people. This type of lawyer is extremely useful in our society today but may not be the kind of lawyer you need to handle day-to-day family and business problems.

Many lawyers—young and old—will go to great lengths to help clients solve seemingly unglamorous problems. If you have a young family, you probably should look for a lawyer around your own age. He or she may lack experience but this will be more than made up by the extra care and attention you'll get. The young lawyer may take a little longer to research your problem and call around for advice but the fee will still not exceed the older, more established lawyer's fee. One charges less for the time but takes longer, while the other charges more but uses less time.

Young lawyers these days are often more creative and vigorous in defending their client's interests. They're less willing to accept old answers to legal questions. A young family can grow with the young lawyer as they work to sort out family problems. If you're middle-aged or beyond, you might do better with an older lawyer. It's often hard for an older person to muster up the necessary trust and respect for a younger lawyer. It's not impossible, don't get me wrong. The main thing is to build a relationship with your lawyer that can continue on through the twists and turns in your life.

Aside from picking up lawyers' names from friends around town, you can also ask your banker, service club members and can even pick up names to check out from the *Martin-*

dale-Hubbell Law Directory in your library. It lists lawyers' names and specialties in glorified Yellow Pages fashion. You should probably steer clear of choosing the same lawyer that represents your bank or other major enterprises, because this kind of lawyer usually is establishment-oriented and is more adept at handling the complexities of corporate and banking law. Corporate lawyers have their place—but it's usually not in an opposite chair chatting about down-to-earth "people" problems.

It might be a good idea for you to start off with your chosen lawyer on basic family law issues, such as your will (you should have one of these) and estate planning. When you take on a family lawyer, you have to confess yourself economically just the way you medically confess yourself to a new family doctor. You have to list all your assets and liabilities, names and ages of family members and any kind of contractual agreements you have signed. You must also discuss your hopes and aspirations for yourself and your family.

At this stage, a lawyer might suggest that a young couple set up a ten-year limited trust for the children. If properly done, one of these trusts can eventually pay for a child's college education with virtually tax-free money. But this kind of trust has to be set up when the child is around age six or eight, because the law requires a minimum of ten years duration. It's no good trying to set one up when the child is a budding teen-ager. It's too late then.

You may also tell your lawyer that you're thinking of selling your house and buying a new one. You'll be advised to buy the new house within a year after you sell the old one. This is because you may well have made a profit on the sale of your old house and this profit will be taxed unless you parlay it back into the purchase of a new house within a year's time.

These are just a couple of examples of how a family lawyer can save you money and worry by spotting a potential problem in advance. You needn't have an "annual legal check-up" the way you might have an annual medical checkup, but you should report in to your lawyer any time some sort of long-term agreement appears or any time you're making a significant change in your life. As you prepare to go into business for yourself, you'll probably be making more than the usual calls to your lawyer. Going into your own business is a whole new field for you and you will probably feel unsure of yourself. New problems come up every week. You have contracts to sign, agreements with employees and, of course, the whole question of what kind of business structure fits your particular needs.

At this stage of the game, you might be seriously considering taking on a partner. Your insecurity tends to push you toward the comforting image of a partnership. "We can do it together," you say. You won't have to face all those decisions alone. I know, I was looking around for a partner in the early stages of my break-out. I must have looked pathetic, like a dog searching for a friend or a child hunting for the security blanket.

It's a dangerous stage in your business venture and you should be most wary about taking on a partner. A partner's all right, providing you've thought the situation out and have planned the whole thing very carefully with your lawyer. You shouldn't even talk to anyone about the possibility of being your partner or of your being someone else's partner, until you have thrashed the whole thing out with your lawyer. Many of us who have looked at taking on an early partner through the cool, analytical eyes of a lawyer, have given up on the idea.

Many lawyers will tell you that entering into a business partnership is more serious than getting married. At least when you are married you can sleep with your partner. You can't do that with a business partner. In a partnership you will have all the disadvantages of a marriage and none of the advantages. You could be liable for all your partner's debts and bad business decisions. If the partner is sued, you can be dragged in on it. You can get around this, but it has to be carefully worked out by a lawyer in advance.

When a tax lawyer hears the word "partnership," all sorts of flags wave and gongs sound. Partnerships have a way of creating nasty tax problems. You may have a dear friend who you'd feel would make a dandy partner and would give you great comfort in the lonely, scary first days your business is in operation. Resist the urge to merge. Talk it all out with your lawyer and friends who have been in business awhile. Don't talk about the partnership with any prospective partner before you talk to your lawyer.

Sometimes with a partnership negotiation or with any other such crucial business negotiation, the other party might seem miffed or outright insulted by your bringing a lawyer into the act. Reassure the other party that your intentions are honorable but insist on getting your lawyer's advice. Good fences make good neighbors. By making nice clean fences in your business relationships at the outset you can avoid many problems later on. If you do eventually work out a partnership agreement, be sure you have your lawyer build into it a method by which it could be dismantled so that there would be less problems if you should later change your mind.

Once you get going in your business, you'll learn when to call your lawyer and when not to. The fees, of course, keep you from making frivolous calls. But don't let the relatively small fee for a short phone call prevent you from making the call if you've sensed a problem brewing. Any time you are faced with some sort of an agreement or a change in relationship with customers, suppliers, employees or whatever—give the lawyer a call. It may seem like a deceptively simple answer you get, but it will set your mind at ease and might save you money in the long run. Any major turn, such as a contract, licensing agreement, new form of compensation, bonus, anything like that, should be aired with your lawyer, if only through a phone call or a brief office visit.

Sometimes you can get advice from friends who are in business for themselves and this can cut down the need for phoning the lawyer. Even so, you may spend a little more in legal fees your first year by making extra calls to your lawyer. You can consider this as part of your legal education. I probably made too many calls the first year, but I learned a lot. I think I have at least partly learned the art of when to call a lawyer and when not to. But don't get too cocky. If some hidden sensing device inside your head gives a warning, call your lawyer.

Any time you get a letter from an employee, a customer, your landlord, anybody, who talks about "referring this matter to our lawyers" or if you get an ominous note from somebody else's lawyer, always make an immediate copy and bounce it over to your lawyer. Don't reply until your lawyer gives the go-ahead.

I made this mistake once. I wrote a column about a business organization in Florida in rather uncomplimentary terms. My facts were straight and they were checked out with various government agencies. I even called the head of the organization and told him of my intentions and read my first draft. We argued and I modified my writing, but the end result was still uncomplimentary. A while later, after the column appeared around the country, I got a letter from this organization's law firm. It was a modulated letter but it contained a request for a "retraction." "Suggested wording" was even included in the letter.

I fired back an answer because I felt the lawyer who wrote the retraction request was trying to push me around and I resented the fact that the head of the organization never called or wrote. Nothing came of it, but my lawyer was upset. I could have been trapped. I could have let my anger trip me up. "A goldfish shouldn't start swimming with the sharks," says my lawyer, adding that "next time you get a letter like that from a shark . . . call in another shark."

You never know when someone's "shark" is going to come back at you. That's why you have to avoid dangerous legal lagoons. If, for example, you are leaving your organization to set up your own business, a business which will be in direct competition with your old employer—watch out. Sometimes bitterness or frustration with one's employer can lead to the rationalization that the employer owes you something. You may feel that you can steal some of your employer's people or you can line up some of your employer's customers for yourself.

If you're going into competition with your employer—keep it clean. Don't steal anything. Don't steal your employer's time by working on setting up your own business during office hours. Don't entice his other employees, don't steal your boss's customers and don't steal any technical or trade secrets. Don't steal anything. Talk to your lawyer before you make any move to go into competition against your old outfit. Some horrendous court judgments have been handed down against people who have used their former boss's employees, business information and customer lists in direct competition. Even if you're sued by your ex-boss and you win, you'll still probably lose the war. Big organizations have much bigger financial and legal resources and they can lose a court case and still kill off your new business. If the legal fees don't bust you, your time and attention will be taken from your business in its crucial early development stage. You'll be spending all your time in your lawyer's office or in court. If you're going into a business that doesn't compete with your employer, almost anything goes. Employees and customers are open game.

It's also not smart to set up a business that depends on some iffy or shady situation. One company wanted to sell a certain product in a Latin American country. It was a new business and it had all the shipping arrangements worked out. Their lawyer asked about import restrictions and possible duties. The business partners replied that their Latin American associate "had the customs people all taken care of." No dice, said the lawyer. You can't build a business on a principle that isn't absolutely straight. In this case, they could change the customs officials some day and the whole business could collapse. This group finally did open an exporting business to the other country, but they did it the right way. They didn't make as much money at first but the business can now continue for years without the fear of "customs arrangements" falling in on them.

In talking over your business with a lawyer before you actually take the first major steps, you may well spare yourself some grief, even disaster. In the case of the exporters, a possible disaster was averted. In the case of two friends who opened a highly specialized employment service, they didn't talk to a lawyer first and their business plans had to be drastically changed because of one seemingly innocent legal question.

In the chapter on "Housewife Horrors," I spoke of a new employment agency, Distaff Staffers, opened up by Fran Goldman and Renee Taft. These two housewives wanted to start a special agency to help get other housewives part-time professional jobs. They got encouragement from all sides and made their plans. One of the partners even quit her job to devote full time to planning and launching the new agency.

The two women's initial cost analysis counted on the fact that they would use one of the partner's homes as the employment agency's office. After the business got going, they figured, the whole thing could be moved to a proper office. Gotta keep overhead down, they said.

But they learned to their horror, when they went to apply for a business license, that local laws would not permit cooking or sleeping arrangements on the premises. This meant a private home was "out." The partners had originally hoped they would not need a license because they were working for a non-profit cause. They just wanted to help other women and get paid enough to keep the whole thing going. Nope. They had to have a license, they had to keep their books in a special way, they had to have special receipts for customers' payments, they had to record all job orders and applications and they couldn't even restrict the whole thing to housewife applicants (male civil rights).

A lawyer was called in and the situation was sorted out. The women finally opened up shop in a proper office that complied with all the weird, local legal requirements. Had they praticed "preventive law" with their own lawyer, they probably could have saved some money and they certainly would have saved a lot of time and frustration.

One of the crucial decisions a lawyer can help with as you start up your own business is the question of what kind of legal structure you should work under. Basically, there are three types of structures—sole proprietorship, partnership and a corporation.

A sole proprietorship is the simplest and the least expensive but is not necessarily the best structure. You can operate under a proprietorship, perhaps, in the early stages of your business when you're moonlighting and are still riding on the financial coattails of your employer. But when you decide to operate on your own, you should investigate setting up a corporation. I've already mentioned the dangers of setting up a partnership and it should only be considered if you have other people with the necessary capital and expertise needed to form a going business. As I said, don't even discuss a partnership with anyone until you've talked the whole thing over with your lawyer.

For the majority of self-bossers, the corporate structure seems the best. Until recently, the corporate structure was far too cumbersome and far too expensive for the average professional or small business owner, and there could be adverse tax consequences. Now it's just about as easy to set up a corporation as it is to form a partnership and it costs very little. Depending on the complexities of your case, the cost of setting up your own corporation will run from $250 to $500 and this includes all filing and legal fees.

The advantages of having your own corporation are many. Under special provisions of the tax code you can set up a little "Subchapter-S" corporation where income can flow directly through to the owner without getting taxed twice. In the standard corporate structure (the only one possible before Subchapter-S), both the corporation's income and the owner's income were taxed. Double taxation. To qualify for Subchapter-S treatment, you must have less than ten stockholders and can have only one class of stock. Usually, members of your family are owners of the stock and they can serve as your board of directors, too, if you like.

Aside from the obvious tax advantages of having a corporation under Subchapter-S, you have the advantage of being shielded from personal liability. If you are working under a proprietorship or a general partnership, your company can be sued and the plaintiff can make a grab at your private assets as well as those of your company. For example, say you own a hamburger haven and one night when business is booming, you ask a seventeen-year-old employee to use your car to pick up more paper plates. The teen-ager, in the rush, crashes into a child on a bicycle and kills the child. The teen-age driver was acting as your business agent and the grieved parents can sue your company. If you had inadequate insurance, you could lose your savings and even your home as part of the judgment. Unless you're operating through a corporation, you have no protection.

If you have a corporation, your loss is limited to whatever's in the company. Usually, with a Subchapter-S corporation, there isn't much money in the kitty. It's mostly passed out pretty quickly to the owner.

Later on, when you are making more than enough money to pay your salary, you can use your corporation to set up a pension plan or profit sharing plan to defer current income into investments that can be tapped later. This can get you out of paying taxes now on income that can be used later in semi-retirement, when your salary has diminished and there's less of a tax bite.

If they incorporate, professionals, such as doctors, lawyers, dentists and other small business owners can be eligible for the same kind of liberal tax benefits executives have been getting in the major corporations. After considerable agitation by professional groups, laws have been passed in almost all states to let them come to the tax table along with their big business brothers. You should, by all means, investigate the advantages of a Subchapter-S corporate structure for your own business.

The disadvantages, on the other hand, are relatively few. You have to set up records, keep minutes, and you have to send in annual reports to local authorities. My lawyer helps me with this for a modest annual fee but you can do your own minutes and filing if you want to. A lawyer should get you started with the first minutes and after that, with a little coaching, you can take over. My brother and my wife are officers in my corporation and my wife and children are stockholders. We all have a great time at the "annual meeting." Seriously, my brother, Bob, is not just a figurehead officer. He has been a great help to me in organizing my company and in keeping it going. As a matter of fact, because he is a management consultant, his advice and suggestions have been invaluable in the writing of this book. You can make use of your corporate structure to get good advisors as officers and board members. You may want to take your lawyer on as a director. Other people in business sometimes enjoy serving on the board of a struggling little company. You either pay them a small annual fee or buy them a fine steak dinner some time when you feel in an expensive mood.

Speaking of steak dinners, your lawyer and other professionals you'll be working with often turn out to become close personal friends. We call each other for a friendly lunch now and then so we can listen to each other's problems and otherwise share the comradery self-bossers usually enjoy when they meet.

Building this kind of rapport with a professional advisor is not only personally gratifying but it also allows the professional to get a good idea of what you're like as a person and what goals you have. Then, when a big business problem or opportunity comes along, the professional has extra dimensions to work with to steer you in the right direction.

16
ACCOUNTANTS, BANKERS
AND OTHER PROFESSIONAL HELP

Some people who want to go into business for themselves claim they can't afford to buy consulting services from lawyers, accountants and other professionals. I say you can't afford *not* to pay for good professional consulting advice. I suppose you could afford to "go it alone" if you're independently wealthy. You'll get an education out of your own mistakes but it will be costly.

It's ironic, but the people who financially are in less need of professional help are the ones that use consultants the most. Your business executive, banker and others all use tax, legal, engineering and other consulting services. They gladly pay the fees because they know that, when you're in business, mistakes can cost much more than the fees you pay the professionals to keep you out of trouble.

I've already talked about getting "free" advice from those who have gone into business for themselves. You can, however, overdo this free advice routine. After a while, if you keep asking the same person to help solve every little problem that comes up in your plan for your own business, you'll become a bore. Your free advisor will more often than not be "in a meeting" every time you call. You have to use your own judgment on how much you can lean on another person. I've given many hours of my time to others who want to start up their own column, newsletter or other journalism business. So far, nobody has abused my willingness to help. However, I often advise a prospective self-bosser up to the point where I suggest that he or she get in touch with a good lawyer, accountant or other professional who charges a fee for service, and I give some recommendations.

Free advice is fine in its place. It can help you make up your mind whether you really want to go into business for yourself and it can give you good leads on where you can get more, specific advice and help. It can be a great morale booster too.

But there comes a time when you have to start spending some "research" money. As I've said, a lawyer is one person who must be paid a fee to hear out your plans and give you guidance on the pitfalls to avoid. Another key person you'll be needing is a certified public accountant (CPA). As your business develops, you'll probably see a lot more of your accountant than you will of your lawyer, or, at least, you should hope so.

You can find good accountants through recommendations from your bank, business friends and especially from others who have started out into some sort of business on their own. You want to get the names of prospective accountants who have successfully helped others get started with small businesses. You don't need a fancy accounting firm that's primarily concerned with auditing balance sheets for big organizations.

However, you might just find an up-and-coming young accountant in a big firm who is willing to do some moonlighting. This young accountant may well be a person who will soon break out into his or her own business. My friend Peter Nagan, who has his own newsletter publishing business, found a good accountant this way. The accountant went out on his own and was able to give my friend much more personal attention than he could have gotten from a big, established firm. The accountant has seen his customers' businesses grow along with his and has been able to guide them as they continue to grow.

The first meetings you have with your accountant should concentrate on the "numbers'" in your new business. By numbers I mean, how much will it cost to produce your product or service and how much do you expect to make in the first six months, first year? You also have to confess yourself financially with your accountant just as you did with your lawyer. The accountant has to know all your family financial obligations, your savings and securities, insurance, everything that involves the flow of money in and out of your family coffers.

To get an idea of what kind of information you should have when you begin your first talks with your accountant, I asked Eugene Fisher, taxation chairman, District of Columbia Association of Certified Public Accountants, to make a little checklist:

1) *What are your fixed costs?* These are the items you have to keep down to a minimum and they include such things as rent (if you're not using your home), utilities, employees' wages and financing charges (loan payments). These are just some of the more obvious fixed costs. There are others. You have to pay insurance premiums, all sorts of taxes and license fees. You have to go down every possible cost and tote it up. You should never commit yourself to any new business without having some hard figures on fixed costs and good, conservative estimates when hard figures aren't readily available. Then you should see if some of these costs can be eliminated or reduced. For example, do you really need a secretary, or can you operate out of your home instead of a fancy, downtown office? A good accountant has been all through this many times and can help you keep in touch with reality.

2) *What are your variable costs?* As the title suggests, these

costs can vary all over the place. They include such items as inventory if you're going into some sort of store or other selling enterprise and they always include all selling costs, advertising and public relations. In my business, my selling costs are often quite high, especially when some new project is getting started. Don't skimp in figuring estimates for variable costs. Talking with people who are in the kind of business you're entering or moonlighting in the business can greatly help get meaningful cost estimates. One thing I greatly underestimated was my long-distance phone bill. To keep on top of things, without actually having to take a plane to any given city, I found I had to use the phone a lot—like $175 a month.

If variable costs are hard to estimate, an accountant can give a conservative percentage estimate out of your estimated gross. An equation can be worked out where you list fixed costs and make an estimate, based on a feel for the business, what your variable costs will be as a percentage of annual sales. From this figure, you can compute your "break-even point." For example, let's say your annual fixed costs are $5,000 and your estimated variable costs will be around 25 per cent of sales. Your break-even point would then be $6,667 in annual sales when you figure 25 per cent of it to cover variable costs. The variable costs come to $1,667. After figuring out your break-even point, you and the accountant will then have to see what realistic estimates you come up with for projected sales. Naturally, you want to get to that break-even point as soon as possible. If you have to take a year or longer, you may be in serious trouble. If yours is a slow-starting type of business, you may be able to go a year without a profit but you'll have to know where the money is coming from.

An accountant can help you discipline yourself to see just how much of a time gap you'll face trying to get to that break-even point and beyond. I reached my break-even point in a few months. This means I was able to make enough money for the business to pay for itself but I still wasn't able to draw down a salary. During the first year, my business made around $3,000 profit. That's not much money to live on. I had figured on not making much, if any, the first year and had savings stashed away to pay for living expenses. In the second year, the profit jumped three to four times and I was able to breathe a little easier. I still wasn't making as much money as I made before I broke with my organizational job. In the third year, profits took a nice jump to the point where I was making more than I was on my old job. I'm still not completely "clear" but I have enough momentum to be able to plan new ventures that might put me a comfortable distance away from the receding "failure zone."

When you're figuring prospective sales, an accountant can ask some embarrassing questions that you'd better find the answers for. How much will you make during the first weeks? How much during the first months? The first year? The accountant will ask for figures, market testing, contracts and the like to back up your estimates. Also, you'll have to find out if there are seasonal ups and downs in your business and take them into account. Sometimes summers are slow. Sometimes winters are slow.

Once you've figured your business costs and profit estimates, the accountant will then help figure out whether you can afford to have your business not make much of a profit for the first year or so. You need to buy time. Where will the money come from to buy this time? Let's say your annual living costs are $15,000. This is after you cut down to the bare essentials. To pay for part of this, let's further say you can get a moonlighting job that will bring in $10,000 a year. But your new business will just be at the break-even point at the end of the first year of operation. This means you'll have a $5,000 deficit to make up to pay for family living expenses. Do you have the money in savings? Or perhaps you can sell some securities, a car and a boat or even your house? Maybe you can get a loan or a gift from a member of your family? The money has to come from someplace and you shouldn't cut it as close as I've cut it for illustration purposes.

I figured my living costs conservatively and was even able to cut them further than my wife and I (and the accountant) originally thought was possible. I figured my business operating costs accurately, but I slipped up on figuring how long it would take a newspaper column to make the kind of money I needed. As a matter of fact, my overestimating the newspaper column's potential actually forced me sooner into new ventures. At one point I was nickel and diming them to death in order to pick up cash sales. I did lectures for money, any magazine assignments I could grab and finally was able to make a slow-starting radio program into a good money-maker.

You have to be careful when you're working with an accountant. You can be overcautious to the point of being a chronic pessimist. You have to make some sort of a gamble. If the accountant asks hard questions about where the money will come from, you have to answer the questions up to the point of taking a calculated risk. Try to have contingency plans in case your project starts slowly or reaches a peak below the amount of money you need. Moonlighting in your field is, perhaps, the quickest and easiest contingency plan—at least for service businesses.

If you need a loan, all these figures and estimates will be invaluable as part of your presentation to a bank or credit union. A good accountant can help make a proper presentation. The accountant knows the kinds of questions bankers ask. The presentation should be neatly done, with all the figures, a factual description of the business and your qualifications. Models of products, samples of services, copies of contracts or market studies—all these things should go into a good presentation. If you can make a presentation for a loan that satisfies your accountant and your banker, chances are your project will be a success. Banks are, by nature, conservative and don't like to bet on iffy ventures.

For those who are considering buying a business outright, a top-notch accountant is an absolute necessity. The accountant can answer that big question: 'Why is the owner of the business selling?' If the business is having trouble or is about to have trouble, the accountant can often spot the illness in the company's books. The accountant can also help you reach a fair purchase price to offer the owner. All too often, people who have owned a business over the years, put too much of a price on its "good will" or "name." If you need a loan to buy an already going business, the accountant can make an analysis based on past and current sales that will help sell the bank's loan officer.

When you're starting out, a good accountant can act as a counterfoil for your lawyer and other professionals. Lawyers may be good with the law but they're often not much with balance sheets and they usually don't know the day-in, day-out money you can save on the tax laws unless they're tax specialists. For example, a lawyer may well know that a Subchapter-S corporation is the structure you need for your business but might not know about a special little part of the tax laws called Section 1244. This section permits almost any small corporation owner the right to insert special language in the company's minutes of the first regular meeting which will make the government underwrite part of the losses if the business fails. If the business goes bust, you can deduct the money you lost from your regular income. It's an important point that a good accountant would pick up but many lawyers might miss.

Once you get started, your accountant can help you thread your way through an incredible maze of taxes and tax forms. At first, my accountant handled all these taxes and payments for me, but now, with the help of a part-time bookkeeper, my business does all the work except the annual federal income tax return. Let's take a look at some of the tax and other payments you'll have to make on a regular basis:

Federal Income Tax is based on records you've kept during the year. If you have a corporation, a CPA should do your tax filing. If you have a proprietorship, you might be able to handle it on your own income tax return through Schedule C, but even this is tricky.

State and Local withholding taxes are usually paid on a monthly or quarterly basis.

Federal Payroll Withholding Tax is usually paid by the fifteenth of every month in a special deposit made at your bank. If the withholding is less than $100, it can be paid in quarterly deposits. For those who are in the early days of opening a small business, this withholding tax can present some problems. The uninitiated forget that they have to pay this tax and, somehow, think that the money they have in the till is all theirs. If the money is spent to cover other business expenses, then there's a terrible crunch comes tax time.

Personal Property Tax is paid once a year to the local government. For service businesses like mine, it isn't much of a tax but for those running a store, the tax on inventory can be considerable.

Unemployment Compensation is paid to the local government on a quarterly basis and is used to cover employees if they are out of a job and need to draw unemployment checks.

Workmen's Compensation is more of an insurance premium than a tax but the law requires you to have it. This covers any accident an employee may have on the job. It's paid annually and sometimes is a lifesaver. A friend of ours was working on an assignment which required her to take a bus to a lake resort to get pictures and an interview. Her bus cracked up and she was hurled down the aisle between the seats with her face acting like the head of a missile. Her jaw was shattered and eight teeth were knocked out. Workmen's Compensation paid for nearly all of the $13,000 needed in plastic surgery and dental work to make her face look good again. Her regular medical insurance would never have covered that amount.

Although questions revolving around these taxes and insurance premiums often occupy most of your dialogue with an accountant during your first hectic days of operation, there are other questions that can cause all sorts of trouble if you don't get the answers from a pro. For example, whenever you spend money at home that could be considered a business expense, you should never put it down as a business deduction on your own income tax return. Always have your corporation reimburse your family funds for the amount. The Internal Revenue Service is apt to look with a jaundiced eye on business deductions in personal income tax returns. They don't seem to mind the deductions at all when they're down as part of your own business' monthly operating expenses. If you have a party and several guests are there for business reasons, have your company reimburse you. If you use your car for business purposes or entertain a potential customer at a restaurant, make note, keep receipts, and put it down in your monthly expense account.

I made a copy of my old company's standard monthly expense account form when I went out on my own. I blocked out my employer's name and inserted my own. A friend then cranked out a stack of copies, which I now use as my regular expense account. I was familiar with the form and it's an easy operation.

Lawyers and accountants will probably be your two mainstays when you plan and eventually launch a new business but they're not the only ones. There are others who can help and many of them have services that are free. Your banker or credit union manager can be most helpful and, if you have an account with them or are planning one, they can give background advice and in some cases can open some doors for you with prospective customers and suppliers.

How do you find a good banker? As you know, there are banks all over the place. But the best for you, perhaps, is the one in your neighborhood. Pick a bank that is small but is well established. Suburban or neighborhood banks are small enough so you can go right to the president or general manager for advice.

After you've selected your bank, see the president and briefly outline your plans for your business. Usually, the head of a small bank will want to give help in the hope that your business will grow and become an important commercial account. The banker can suggest names of bank customers who might be interested in your business and, of course, can help you with your list of names for prospective lawyers and accountants. Keep reporting progress to your bank chief. Some day all this groundwork may come in handy when you're looking for a loan. A small bank may only be able to participate in part of a major loan but the bank's name and the president's recommendation can be instrumental in getting more money from the big banks downtown. Unless you have some special connection, I'd steer clear of the big banks when you start out. You're better off with a big frog in the smaller pond of suburban or neighborhood banks. Convenience is also an important factor. It's ideal when you can practically walk next door to make deposits or have a chat with the head of the bank. If your business depends on sales around your community, don't underestimate the power a banker has to throw business your way through word-of-mouth advertising to bank customers and business colleagues.

There are also organizations that are specifically set up to help you start a small business, especially if you have limited resources or are in one of the minority groups. The Small Business Administration, run by the federal government, is perhaps the best known. As a government agency, SBA can provide all sorts of pamphlets, tear sheets and other background information on starting a small business. Some of them are jargonistic junk. Others aren't bad as idea stimulators or checklists aimed at gathering more information. You should drop by your local SBA office (found under U. S. Government in the phone book or under the same listing in the nearest major city). First, pick up a booklet called *Small Business Administration Publications.* It lists hundreds of publications by number which you can pick up while you are there or can order. Many are free. Others cost anywhere from twenty cents to a little over a dollar. Under the free ones, I noted: *How to Analyze Your Own Business; Expanding Sales Through Franchising,* and *Tips on Selection of Salesmen.* Under the "for sale" list, I noted: *Starting and Managing a Small Book-keeping Service* (thirty cents) and *Starting and Managing a Small Motel* (thirty cents). There are hundreds more.

On the pamphlet side, SBA is pretty good. But on actual business counseling or on providing loan money, don't count on SBA for too much. One management consultant friend says that anyone who goes into business with SBA as one of the major supporters is in trouble by definition. SBA won't give you a loan unless banks have refused to do so. And when banks refuse it's usually for a good reason—they think you'll fail. In some cases, when it's a minority operated business, the banks may well be overconservative, but still the SBA probably can't provide enough money for the business to succeed. SBA also has programs whereby certain government contracts are "set aside" for small businesses. This sounds good but it often turns out that you're just working for the government on very low priority, low profit contracts with the whole thing disguised as "free enterprise."

SBA has enlisted the aid of retired businessmen to form SCORE (Senior Corps of Retired Executives), sometimes irreverently referred to as the "Paunch Corps." Maybe, here and there, you might find a SCORE advisor who just happens to know quite a bit about the particular business you are setting up. But, as a rule, you're better off paying for advice from a recommended pro than you are getting it for nothing from SBA. You usually get what you pay for.

The Interracial Council for Business Opportunities (backed by the Rockefeller Brothers Foundation and the Department of Commerce) operates in ten cities and does a pretty fair job advising minority groups (primarily black or Spanish-speaking) on how to set up a small business. ICBO gets good management consultants, some of whom are on loan from major corporations. If you are in a minority, be sure you check out your area for organizations that are set up to help members of such groups start up small businesses. In my area, besides ICBO, there is also the Uptown Progress Committee and United Planning Organization, both of which can help get financial backing and professional counseling for minority entre-preneurs. Some chambers of commerce or local civic organizations have modest funds aimed at helping young people start penny-ante businesses and there are various organizations emerging to help women get professional job status.

Most of the time, programs aimed at helping small busi-nesses are concentrated in the cities but there's a sleeper out in the country—the Co-operative Extension Service. This multi-government organization is backed by federal, state and local governments and operates on a county or city level (you can find it under county or city government listings in the phone book). The extension service has training programs and a whole shelf of booklets that outline technical and financial as-sistance available to those who want to set up a business in rural areas. Drop by your local extension service office and get a list of the available publications.

Of particular interest are publications aimed at helping

those who want to start a recreation business out in the country. This includes ski slopes and lodges, lakes (boating, swimming, fishing), hunting and fishing lodges, golf courses, camping grounds and even "vacation farms" where city slickers pay to get a glimpse of farm life. You can even set up a "trout farm" to raise fish for city restaurants or for a fishing club. In many instances, trained agents will help select a site, stock your pond, build your dam or whatever—all for free. You have to put money into the deal but you can get extra financial assistance and professional help if you know how to mine the programs offered by the extension service and other agencies affiliated with federal and state agriculture departments. Some good booklets to pick up from extension service offices are: *So You're Planning a Vacation Farm Business, Rural Recreation—New Opportunities on Private Land, Trout Farming* (leaflet 552) and *Rural Recreation Enterprises for Profit* (Bulletin no. 277).

Some major banks around the country have special programs for small businesses. The Bank of America, for example, publishes a series of booklets called *Small Business Reporter.* Some titles: *Day Nurseries for Preschoolers, Handcraft Business, Marketing a New Product and Repair Service,* to name just a few. You can get more information by writing: Bank of America, Department 3120, P. O. Box 37000, San Francisco, Calif. 94137.

The Chase Manhattan Bank in New York has a subsidiary called Chase Manhattan Capital Corp. which is devoted exclusively to helping finance and advise small businesses. The president of Chase Manhattan Capital, Louis L. Allen, wrote the technical "bible" for small businesses. It's called *Starting and Succeeding in Your Own Small Business,* published by Grosset & Dunlap, Inc. ($5.95).

General Business Services, Inc., operates an "automated" bookkeeping and advisory service for small businesses through some 700 franchised offices around the country. GBS has some interesting booklets and can help with monthly bookkeeping problems once you get started. But I think you still have to get your own accountant and lawyer. For more information, write: General Business Services, Inc.; 7401 Wisconsin Ave.; Washington, D.C. 20014.

As you can see, there are all sorts of places where you can get free advice and paid professional help. Skillful use of these professional helpers can make it easier to get along with less full-time, paid experts in your own company. You buy consulting help only when you need it. Having a full-time partner to fill an expertise void in your business can be much more costly.

Then comes the day. You've marked it with a big X on your calendar. It's the day you make the break. You've announced that you are leaving your employer (be it office, plant or daily household chores) and you're ready to start your business. For a few days, things might seem a bit ominous. Your employer might go through a ritual such as the "exit interview" (Why are you leaving? Were you happy?). You might get a carry-over paycheck if your employer is nice. You might also be getting some money back that you'd put into a pension plan. These funds will come in handy. My employer, *Forbes* magazine, gave me considerable time off during the transitional stage so I could line up a new office and otherwise attend to my new business. I also got two months' extra pay (vacation time plus five extra weeks as a gift).

I can't complain. My company gave me a fairly easy time of it. This is why it's so important to keep on good terms with your employer and not just break off in a huff. I think my boss was so relieved that I wasn't going over to one of the opposition magazines that he was extra generous in the bonus and time off I was allowed. I tried to snag a retainer to continue writing some pieces for my old magazine, but no dice. That's where the generosity stopped. They didn't want any "hangers-on" and I guess it was just as well I didn't have to continue a relationship with my employer. Still, if you can grab any kind of contract, fee, project money or whatever from your old boss, so much the better. You'll need every cent you can get to keep your business going during the start-up stage.

Your first big decision after the breakaway date has been set will concern getting an office, small workshop or whatever cubicle you'll be needing for your work. You simply have to keep overhead down to the absolute minimum. You might have had a nice office where you worked before. But now you're going to have to make do with the lowest-priced place you can find.

Your home stands out as being the most economical place to start. After all, you're paying for the place anyway, why not work from home base? If you've set up a little "corner" office at home when the plan for your breakaway was hatching, you can easily convert it into a semi-permanent workshop. At first blush it sounds appealing. But permanent home offices, for some people, can have many drawbacks.

You have to have a place that's convenient for your customers, suppliers and others with whom you'll be doing business. If your home is out in the suburbs and most of your business is conducted downtown, then you're stuck. It's so difficult getting started, you shouldn't burden yourself and your customers with long trips in and out of town. If you can visit your customers easily enough from your own home, then that's fine. You can get away with it for a while. Try doing some business from your home to see how it works before you decide to make it permanent.

You might find that your children get in the way, especially if they're toddlers. It's unsettling to be talking with a customer on the phone and have a little one bawling in the back-

226

THE FINAL BREAK

ground. You might be able to get a room, a loft, a basement or garage converted into a fairly respectable home office where you can seal yourself off from the normal household clatter. Even if you can do this, you should sign up for some kind of answering service and get a separate telephone.

Speaking of telephones, you've just got to get one that's separate from the family phone, because otherwise it's almost impossible to keep accounts separate for tax purposes. You need a company phone. When you talk to the telephone company about your plans for a new business and a new phone you'll find that they are willing to help as long as you fork over a big deposit in advance. In my case, I had to pay a $100 deposit. No deposit, no telephone, even though you've had a home phone for years and have always paid your bills on time. Apparently, the phone company looks at the "failure rate" for small businesses and figures you might go bust and try to skip out with some unpaid phone bills. When you pay your deposit, make sure they agree to pay interest on it and agree to a reimbursement date. They're sometimes vague about this. Pin them down. After some haggling, I was given 6 per cent interest on my $100 and it was returned to me after one year (I had to remind them).

The home is the absolute lowest-cost place for your office and it can have some tax advantages too. You can declare your office or work space as a tax deduction. It's a bit complicated but your accountant can fix it up in no time. However, the home does have its drawbacks and, in most cases, you will enventually have to break out and get your own, private place to work.

The next step up from the low cost of working from your home is to bunk in with somebody else and use a corner of their office. This may cost something, but not very much, and it can have all sorts of advantages. I moved in with a friend, Dave Dear, who owns a chain of small newspapers. Three of his papers were among my first customers for the consumer column. Dave had a tiny office space and offered it to me for thirty dollars a month. I was able to get an answering service in our building for eight dollars a month. So my major, fixed office expenses were kept to thirty-eight dollars a month.

As I said, the place was tiny. When I later moved out into a bigger office, friends facetiously claimed "they put the brooms back in the closet when you left." It was a glorified broom closet but it cost very little and I was able to squeeze two small rented desks and a file cabinet inside. Both desks rented for fifteen dollars a month, "with option to buy." The option must have been a joke. Who would want to buy two old desks that had room for only a typewriter and some stuck drawers? Still, I kept my office overhead down to fifty-three dollars for the first month.

My biggest expense was the salary I paid an editorial assistant, who also acted as secretary, filing clerk and overall troubleshooter. Maybe I could have gotten away without hiring anyone right off, but, having worked for big organizations so long, I was insecure and felt the need for the company of paid help. There are many, many things to do when you're starting up. You have to get office supplies, you have to be around when the telephone people come by and you have to be there when they're delivering office furniture. Being new at the newspaper column business, it took me longer to get the information I needed. My assistant got a lot of the basic work done so I could be free to work up new and much-needed money-making projects.

Sharing an office with a friend was, perhaps, the smartest thing I ever did. It not only gave me a ridiculously low-priced place from which to work, it gave me the necessary comraderie and feeling of being backed up. Dave Dear would listen to my tales of woe. He would suggest sources of information. He would read some of my first columns and give good, critical opinions. In short, he greatly helped me bridge the gap between the security of working for a big organization and the initial loneliness of working for yourself. He was, and still is, one of my greatest morale boosters. Dave also has a hard head for business and keeps prodding me into developing new, income-earning projects.

Another friend who also has his own business claims to have done one better. He says he moved into a friend's office and didn't pay any rent. He even got the use of office furniture and a telephone (he paid his own long-distance calls). How did he get this deal? He paid his rent by doing some work for his friend. They both were reporting and writing in similar fields, so my friend could cover for his "landlord's" vacations. If you can get in with someone who can use your part-time services, so much the better. For just a little extra work, you get companionship, a free office and overhead is kept next to nothing.

After a while, I found that the "broom closet" I was renting for thirty dollars a month was just too small. I needed extra filing space and a place for visitors to sit down. I hated leaving Dave Dear's office because we enjoyed each other's company and were good listeners for each other's business problems. I eased the pain, however, by moving in with another friend, who had a much bigger office to rent. This new office was modest but seemed spacious by comparison to the one I was leaving. By this time, more money was coming in and my business looked like it had at least a fifty-fifty chance of succeeding. It was worth the risk to move up a notch. My new rent was eighty dollars a month, still not a large figure by today's standards. I had to buy new furniture and thought the time was ripe. I thought my business would at least last long enough to pay for two new desks and some chairs.

My new office was part of a complex of offices run by Peter Nagan, a friend who published his own newsletters and printed and published newsletters for other authors. I have my own separate space and entrance. Our businesses were compatible and we've even embarked on several joint ventures. One of them, a booklet on how to buy toys, sold more than eight thousand copies at twenty-five cents each. The booklet was reported, written, edited, designed, printed and mailed—all from our office. We're going ahead with some other booklets and, I think, we'll make money and enjoy each new venture. Both of my shared-office partners have been instrumental in lining up new business for me.

By sharing office space, you can form a sort of "capitalistic commune." You share expenses, keep overhead way down and bolster each other's businesses and spirits. Even though I make more money now, I don't think I'll ever move completely away from my friends' offices. When I've just learned that some newspaper has dropped my column and my face looks weary and worried, my friend pops his head in the door and says, "How about lunch?" We eat and talk. My troubles come out. He has some suggestions and reaffirms my faith. I do the same for him when two of his key printers quit just before a big job. I like office sharing. You might not. You can try it for a while and the least it will do is save you some money.

After getting some sort of place to work on your own, the next big crisis is: Hiring the first employee. It may sound like a small item, but, believe me, it looms big when you're the one that's paying for it. You're making a commitment to pay someone a relatively large chunk of your overall sales income. You don't take the task of hiring lightly. It's sort of like the trauma of taking on a partner, only you have less of a commitment and entanglement with a hired employee.

It's so crucial that you get every penny's worth out of each major expenditure; you have to get a good employee, one who can help make money and free you of many of the routine worries. How do you find good employees? There are always the employment agencies, but I tend to steer clear of them. I've seen friends go through a whole string of people before they could get the right one.

Personally, I think it's a good idea to hire part-time help if you can find it and have a person first work on projects. Then, if they turn out good work and you are compatible, you can hire them on a more permanent basis. I hired a part-time editorial assistant and she's turned into a full-time stalwart. Of course a lot depends on what kind of business you're setting up, but I've found that talented housewives, retired persons and university students can make excellent part-time employees if you give them proper direction and let them work on projects or on hours that suit their own needs.

In and around any urban area there's a wealth of housewives mostly going to waste. Many of them have had excellent training and can do marvelous work if you'll just give them the chance to prove themselves on their own hours. Most housewives can work during school hours but like to be home when the children get home. If you're willing to let them work from, say, 9:30 A.M. to 2:30 P.M., you can get excellent work done. I've found that housewives who are reporters and writers (or were before they were married) can get more work, and better work, done in five hours than many full-time employees can get done in eight. Because they officially work less hours, you can pay them less and they don't mind. They like the fact that you're paying them a combination of time and money. Often, you have to let them adjust their own schedule. One day a child has to be taken to the dentist. Another day, another child calls in with an injured arm or leg and the mother must dash home. The thing is, a talented housewife will make up the time lost on the job by taking work home or by coming in early or staying late the next day. Let a housewife come and go as she sees fit, and you've got yourself an excellent helper.

After my business began to expand, I called on my wife,

Vida, for help in the office. She was good at organizing, setting the books straight and seeing that all our bills and taxes got paid on time. She also pitched in on answering readers' mail and in researching questions for the column. One night she said: "You've just got to get a secretary . . . don't be a tight-wad . . . there's too much work piling up." I had one permanent employee, my wife was helping me and I dreaded the thought of having to hire someone else. I was a firm believer in the self-bosser's credo: Thou Shalt Keep Overhead at a Minimum.

What was really needed was someone to handle the increasing volume of filing and keep the books straight. There was a whole list of taxes to pay and forms to fill out each month. My wife was able to organize things so that all the filing, bill paying, bookkeeping and whatnot, could be done in one week at the end of the month. So I dipped into my next favorite employee pool—the senior citizens. Like housewives, there are many retired persons living in and around any given community who have many talents if people would just use them. The retirees are in desperate need of extra income and, more than that, they need the socializing and the feeling of being wanted that comes with an interesting part-time job. I called one of the "Over Sixty Employment Services" and described the kind of person I wanted. Right off the bat, I got a retired secretary who had worked for the Internal Revenue Service. How about that? Her name is Gerry Boudreau and she comes in the last week of every month. She's a great addition to my office and does more work in one week than a whole fleet of secretaries do in a month. And what's interesting is the fact that Gerry is learning skills on this job (taught by my accountant) that will enable her to pick up other clients and, in a sense, go into business for herself.

Finally, there's the student pool. I've found that you can get good work out of students if you package your projects properly. You have to let them work their own hours and have a fairly flexible deadline for project completion. They work under a fearful pressure-cooker system in school and cannot be counted on, as a rule, for steady work and regular hours. I have students researching answers to readers' questions, many of which form the basis of some of my columns. One high school student, working on her first summer job, came in to help straighten out the mess in our files. If you package the project, give a clear outline of what's to be done and work out a realistic deadline for job completion, a talented student can do excellent work. Look at what Ralph Nader has accomplished with his youthful army of "Nader's Raiders." You don't have to pay the students too much. They'll tell you the going rate. Usually, it averages from the minimum wage to around $2.50 per hour. What the students need as much as, or even more than the money are employment items for their résumés.

Every job completed for a student can be noted in a résumé. Samples of work, wherever possible, can be copied and included in the student's résumé. I feel like a proud parent because of some of the jobs my students have been able to get after working on my journalistic projects. One girl got a job with National Public Radio and has become a producer for a new show. Another girl, who worked on a TV project with me, now has her own educational TV program. Another girl, who helped with some research for my columns and helped with the initial research for this book, is now the editor of a newsletter in the recreation field. In each case, the students said the part-time work done through my office was instrumental in getting the job they wanted.

You can get much work done with these talented part-timers. But the time may come when you have to get a full-fledged, full-time, full-paid employee. Having worked with the part-timers, you've gained experience that will help pick, and properly supervise, a full-time helper. Chances are you might have to hire someone away from another full-time job. This is quite a responsibility on your part. You'd hate to hire someone away from a regular job and then find out later that the whole thing isn't working out. You'd feel you'd lured someone away and were responsible, to various degrees, for their well-being and livelihood.

The best way to handle hiring someone is to put the word out that you're in need of help. You'll get some names. Talk with prospective job seekers informally after work or at lunch. Say that someday in the future you might need some permanent help but right now you need someone to help on a moonlighting project. Outline a project. Make it a package deal with specific work to be done in a specific length of time. Work out an agreeable price for the package, then assign your prospective employee the task of getting the work done.

Arrange for some periodic check-ins or monitoring of the work as it progresses. You'll need to leave the door open for calls or visits to clear up possible problems or questions. During this moonlighting period, you'll find out what it's like to work with your prospective employee. You may not find out all you want to know during the first project but you can assign one or several more projects to get a good idea of how well you work together. If, after several projects, you feel the moonlighter won't work out on a permanent basis, then you can call it quits and nobody is hurt. You've gotten some work done at a reasonable price and the moonlighter has some extra cash and still has a regular job. If, on the other hand, you like the work that's been done and you get along well with the moon-lighter, you can work out an arrangement for permanent employment. You'll be getting a proven worker and the chances of selection error will be greatly reduced. The same goes for the moonlighter. He or she will be making a move to a proven employer and there will be few, if any, unpleasant surprises.

Hiring your second employee is much easier than the first.

You've been through the whole ordeal once and have experience. It takes nerve the first time, because you're committing a big hunk of your income. The second employee comes much easier and, besides, your first employee can help with the selection and testing process. Remember that old devil OVERHEAD. Don't get carried away by the ease of hiring second and third employees. Talk over every hiring move with your accountant to make sure you're not overextending your fixed costs. Only hire someone when your needs are busting out all over the place. Only hire after you've made enough extra income to be able to afford it. Make sure you know where the money is coming from. Don't hire people on iffy contracts or promises. Have steady income you can count on before you begin hiring. It's possible for part-timers to carry you through the first two crucial years or longer. After that, if your business is set, you may want to hire someone on a full-time basis.

Just a side note. Don't be a "broom grabber" with your employees. You know what a "broom grabber" is? This is a boss who walks into the office or plant and spots someone sweeping up the place. The boss runs over, grabs the broom and says: "No, no, this is the way you sweep." Don't keep grabbing someone else's broom. Check on the work from time to time to see how it's going but let your employees do their work in their own way and in their own time. Remember, you've selected them after a moonlight testing period and they're supposed to be good at what they're doing. Don't hover around. Spell out the work to be done, agree on realistic deadlines and let them do it without your hot breath on the back of their necks. Having someone on top of you too much was one of the reasons you left your old job, wasn't it? Keep this fact in mind when you deal with your own employees.

In dealing with outsiders, such as customers and suppliers, don't skimp on your lines of communications. Get good, respectable letterheads and envelopes. They needn't be fancy but should be carefully done by a professional designer and printer. Any brochures you do to promote sales should also be professionally done. They're your link with the outside and should reflect, somehow, your personality and the new spirit you've created with your business. The person that answers your telephone (yourself included) must realize that this, too, is an important link with the outside world. If you get an answering service, and I strongly advise it for those who are not in the office or plant all the time, the voice that answers should be cheery, polite and most informative when need be. My first answering service was inexpensive and served a purpose for the first few hectic, low-income days. But the voice that answered often sounded tired. It often took from six to eight rings to get the voice to answer. So I got a new service and "voice."

Your communications with the outside world should be neat and cheerful. You never know. A customer may make an important decision on whether to buy or not to buy on such a seemingly unimportant thing as a phone call, letter or flier describing your product or service. The voices that answer my phone and answer my mail have a lot of charm. Outsiders have remarked how pleasant it is to chat with my employees. I must admit that I sometimes don't practice what I preach. Some evenings after a horrible day when nothing seemed to go right, I get a phone call and grab the phone with a gruff "halloo." When the other person has to ask, "Am I bothering you?" I snap out of it and apologize for the rude telemanners.

Inside your office, out of sight from the outsider, you have to keep good records, good books and good files. It isn't easy and requires periodic discipline to weed out old papers and names from your files and telephone directory. Keep your "key name" file up to date. It pays every now and then to hire a student or students to come in for a weekend to help weed out and update your files. If you don't do this, you eventually build a file like the one I had at first. We called it "the cave." It was so dark and disorganized in there, we were almost afraid to look for things. This botches up your work day and makes supposedly simple tasks take much longer. Time is money and if you waste your time looking for things, you'll lose money. At one stage, when I shifted offices, I had a top-notch executive secretary come in as a moonlighting consultant to show me and my editorial assistant how to set up a good filing system. The secretary went through the whole office and outlined what we had to buy and how we had to set up our filing procedures. I had to have a good file because a writer depends heavily on good source material that can be quickly retrieved.

One simple suggestion, getting a "flip-card" desk-top telephone directory, has saved me countless hours. I used to waste a lot of time pawing through a bunch of cards in a box. They were hard to pull out and were hard to put back in the right place. Because I make a lot of long-distance phone calls, it was suggested that I have pre-cut tickets made of inexpensive paper so they could be put on a spindle. Each time I make a long-distance call, I note the date and the phone number for the spindle file. With the spindle, we've been able to catch several long-distance phone calls that weren't ours.

Everyone has different filing and office organization needs. At some stage of the game, it might not be a bad idea to hire a local secretary pro who has done a good job organizing somebody else's office, to come in and help sort out yours.

Remember, before you make any long-term commitment leasing an office or hiring a full-time employee, let your lawyer and accountant know about it. Your accountant may say that you can or cannot afford it and your lawyer may find some booby traps in an office lease. Both of these professionals might be able to spot certain tax benefits in advance of hiring an employee.

Much has been said about starting a new business. The Small Business Administration has a whole series of booklets on how to *start* every conceivable kind of business from a car wash on up to an aviation maintenance and repair operation. The emphasis is always on "starting" but not much is said about "keeping going." I guess it's because many of us believe that, if we could only start something, it will somehow work out. Once we get going, make the move, then the tough part is over.

This is partly true. Breaking away from the womblike protection of a paternalistic organization is hard. Making the decision that you're not going to continue in an organization and then putting your decision into action is, indeed, hard work—mentally and physically. But keeping going is also hard, especially after the first blush of success. When you're starting a new business from ground zero as I did, you can become overly impressed by the big percentage jumps in the first few months' income.

At first, many small businesses rise up fast. You can kid yourself that "all's well" and it will be clear sailing ahead. But, in most cases, you'll find that a leveling-off period comes along and then it's much harder to get new sales. You have to be prepared for this "slump" or leveling off. You have to have enough capital to break through the inevitable slack period, especially if it coincides with a national or regional recession. You may have started your business when the economy was roaring along at high speed. Then, after your first year, there comes the cutback. Business recedes. This can kill your business if you're not psychologically and financially prepared for it.

According to Brandeis University economist James Schulz:

"You have to take into account the fact that our economy runs in cycles. It's a fact of life. We haven't beaten the economic cycle problem and we're still going to have major recessions in the future. People go into some business just at the right time and things seem great. They add employees, they have a fixed-payment loan and otherwise overextend themselves. They become vulnerable to the first big cutback. Remember this rule—It's always going to get bad, but it's always going to get better."

If you can get over an economic downturn and survive until business is better, your overall chances of survival are greatly enhanced. Downturns usually last from a year to two years. You have to have a way of rolling with these economic punches. You should have a contingency plan. You should have things you can clip off your business and home expenses to save money in an emergency. Make a priority list. Remember the warning about the plane losing altitude. When business begins to fall off, you don't start throwing out the co-pilot . . . you throw out baggage, furniture, and other expendables. Make up a list of things you can do without in case things take a turn for the worse.

You may be able to use the original priority list you and your family made up when you first started out on your own. For example, I've had to weather a couple of business "recessions" and during the first one, which was the toughest, my wife and I considered selling our house and moving to a smaller place.

Over the years we had built up considerable equity in our house and could have made money on it. The cash we would have received plus the dramatic cutting of expenses could have bought more time to let the business grow out of the recession.

Fortunately, things began to pick up and we postponed our house-selling plan. But it's still there on the shelf in case of an emergency. Aside from the business recession, though, we learned that you often can't stick with your original business plan. You have to expand to new products, new services. At first, I mistakenly thought I could just write a newspaper column and do some public lecturing to make enough to live. I was rudely shaken out of that dream. Perhaps the economic recession of 1970–71 shook me up soon enough so I could start looking for new business outlets before it was too late.

At first, I would accept any speaking engagement, anywhere, to make a buck. My speaking jaunts took me into such places as the northwest corner of Missouri to speak to a college audience and into the Florida panhandle to speak to a small-town audience. I made some much needed money but, more important, I was able to build up my wavering confidence. I was forced out into the field and I picked up all sorts of new material for my column and for future business projects.

At one of my speaking dates, I was interviewed by a local radio reporter and learned about radio's sudden interest in the whole consumer-ecology field. When I got back home, I dusted off a "future" business presentation I had made up for consumer reporting on radio and TV. I even wrote a few scripts and taped a couple of sample broadcasts. A friend got wind of my radio ideas and at a business lunch brought it up with a man who had just been hired by an association to revitalize its communication with the public.

Out of this lunch came a proposal for me to come up with minute-and-a-half scripts on consumer subjects for radio. I passed the first test, just barely, and was given the go-ahead to write some more. I did twenty or thirty scripts and broadcast tapes and then had to sit back and wait an agonizingly long time for people to sell the consumer program idea to radio stations and to the bureaucratic powers at the association itself. I insisted that there would be no suggestions, no censorship, no interference whatsoever in what I wrote. I was to have complete control because the programs were being billed as "public service" broadcasts paid for by a grant from the association.

After several spluttering starts, the radio programs were launched and are now being used by more than a hundred stations around the country. After the entrée into radio, the next step was TV. We tried eight TV shows with consumer experts as panelists and the shows were moderately successful. I made some money, but not much. Television requires considerable work for much less pay than most casual viewers realize. You hear of names like Carol Burnett, Walter Cronkite and others making big money, but, believe me, there are many thousands of others in the television business who make very little for the grueling work they do. However, I learned about television and got paid for it. Perhaps some day I'll be able to use my experience with program production and actual participation on camera in some new field such as cable TV.

From the very beginning, when I saw that my newspaper column might not make it alone as a provider for my family's welfare, I began scrambling around writing free-lance magazine pieces for any and all who would pay enough for the time I had to spend. One editor of a New York financial magazine called and asked whether I knew of anyone to handle a tough, technical assignment on the U.S. export of capital funds. I said I'd do it. I knew absolutely nothing about the subject but I bluffed my way through on the hope that my list of friends and news sources would help me out. They did, and I was able to send a passable piece and get a $450 fee. I only spent two days on the assignment, so my schedule wasn't upset much and, of course, the money was poured in to help fill my own balance of payments gap. I picked up several more magazine assignments while my newspaper column and my radio show were slowly building.

I learned that I had to keep a very active "ideas for future projects" file. As busy as I was, trying to keep enough money coming in to stay afloat, I still had to take several days off each month to probe new business ideas. For example, I'd always figured that there were several kinds of "consumers." There was the general audience I was reaching with my column and the little radio shows and then there were audiences such as women, senior citizens and businessmen. They all had their special needs and special interests. Perhaps I could get custom-tailored information out to them.

After studying various publications that were read by these special interest groups, I went to see the editors of *Nation's Business* magazine, which is backed by the Chamber of Commerce and goes to around one million business and professional people. They had no personal consumer or personal finance column and I offered my services. I was told I would get a brief "trial." I was able to extend the brevity out into seven months and a good-sized total fee. Alas, after the seventh column, I was cut off.

But the experience opened the way for doing the same kind of "personal money memo" thing for other trade and business magazines. I'm now writing for *Woman's Day* magazine. I completely struck out on writing a column and special newsletter for senior citizens. After considerable effort and market testing, I came to the sad conclusion that the elderly in this country are in dire need of hard information on how to make do with the little money they get and how to protect themselves against fraudulent and misleading sales pitches. The elderly desperately need to have more information on how to protect themselves but they have very little money. And, it seems, nobody is willing to subsidize any plan that would give out tough, sometimes anti-advertiser, information for these people. Some three hundred souls sent in money for our newsletter but it wasn't enough to make it go. Several senior citizen organizations asked if they could get the information free.

When you're on your own you realize that the main thing you have to sell is your time, whether it's involved in putting out a product or service. I had to ration my time and was unable to do this much needed service for free. I periodically speak to groups of elder Americans on a no-fee or low-fee basis. Maybe some day I'll be able to put my experience of handling elders' money problems into some kind of consulting service for industry or government.

These are just some of the ideas I have filed in the "future" box. There are others that are aimed at writing and producing information booklets on such subjects as buying toys, buying food and buying medicine. I'm even considering trying to do consulting work with suburban weekly and daily newspapers to show how they can get much better consumer information out to their readers for very little, if any, increase in costs.

I keep clipping magazine and newspaper articles and ads that give me ideas. I write down ideas and have to keep a pad and pencil in my pocket and by my bed at all times. You never know when a good idea will roll around. Feeding your idea file is like feeding a backyard compost heap. After a while, some of the ideas get ripe and can be used. Others just die or are replaced with better material.

You have to know when to drop ideas too. If you keep pushing something and keep spending your time and your money too long on an unproductive project, you weaken your business. You have to keep revising your new project priority list. Then there are times when you have to stop all new projects and go back and revitalize some of the old ones.

All of this probing, revising and evaluating is part of growing. The big problem, you find, is knowing how fast to grow. After the initial shock of getting your business started, this expansion puzzle is one of the hardest things you'll have to face. Of course, if you expand too slowly, you'll run out of money and run the risk of having to slide back into the ranks of establishment jobs. So expand you must. If you expand too rapidly, you run the risk of overextending yourself and becoming a "workaholic"—compulsive twelve-hour-a-day, six-day-a-week work freak. You broke away from the establishment to avoid this kind of slavery. Don't let your own organization take over where the establishment left off.

A dear friend runs his own consulting business. It's highly "successful." It's too successful. He has a big organization now and his company devours more and more of his time and energy. He's back in the organizational world, but this time it's his own organization. You really aren't your own boss any more if your company drains so much of your energy you haven't time to enjoy yourself and your family. Another consultant I know scrupulously sticks to a schedule that gives him several months in Maine every year. He spends considerable time with his family and won't take on any extra clients if they demand more time than he's willing to give. He does enough business to feed everybody, enjoy life and otherwise be happy. More business he won't take.

If your business is growing too fast or you are pushing too hard, you have to ask yourself: Why? Of course, if you are in the initial stage of starting up a business, you're probably going to have to push like hell to give the thing enough of a shove so the momentum will keep you rolling. I know, I pushed so hard my wife had to tap me on the shoulder from time to time to say that I was wearing myself out and that my family was getting less attention than it did when I was in the establishment grind. I learned that I had to grow at a slower pace.

244 THE FINAL BREAK

You'll face some tough decisions on how fast or how slow your business should grow. How you tackle the decisions will be based a lot on your own personality. If you like managing things on the administrative side, you might have to hire others to handle the production or promotion work. If you like the day-to-day production (as I do), then you might have to hire people to do the administrative work and the selling. This doesn't mean you have to abandon your administrative or promotional duties, it just means that you concentrate on the things you like in your business and leave the rest to others. Stick with the things you like, even if it's personally delivering your product or service or hard physical work.

I heard about two men who formed a construction company and business eventually grew to the point where the company was making several million dollars a year. The men were rough and tough construction types who loved roaring back and forth moving dirt with bulldozers and other pieces of machinery. It gave them pleasure to be outdoors getting their hands dirty and sweating over some project. Over and over again, the company's board asked these men to stay in their sleek offices to administer the business. The two construction buffs never did, even though they lost some business. They had enough money to live the way they wanted and they were happy outdoors working on their own construction jobs. They hired administrators and only came by the office once a week to keep an eye on things.

It's a common mistake with some self-bossers, this obsession of wanting to make more and more money. Maybe the seed is sewn in the early, anxious days of getting started. You can become so preoccupied with having enough money to keep going that making money can become addictive. Once you've made enough to live well, you can't stop. Maybe the fear of sliding back was too firmly planted in your brain. You may feel you need piles of money to protect yourself against some future mishap. You need some money, but not piles of it. You should never sacrifice your original convictions about freedom, happiness and independence just to keep piling up money.

If you keep looking at the bottom line on your business balance sheet and think of little else, you may make good money for a while, but eventually your business may suffer. Take the example of a couple that bought their own small motel. A fundamental function of the motel-hotel business is taking care of people. When this couple kept their eyes glued on that profit and loss statement all the time, they began to forget about the "caring" side of the business. They cut away one personal touch after another because they couldn't see any immediate financial gain. They left the caring completely to the maids and waiters. This undermined the business and eventually customers began going to competing motels where "people cared."

I heard about a man who started a new restaurant. He knew the food business and was good at it. But he became so concerned about making a profit, he cut down the food portions. This upset the customers and his knowledge of food didn't come through. The size of the portion, he abruptly learned, was not where the money lies. He painstakingly had to go back to much slower growth and less profit to rebuild his good name. Actually, he discovered that he could give customers almost all they wanted to eat and still make money. He was able to sit and chat with customers. After a while his business began to grow again without his hand-wringing over cutting costs.

There's nothing wrong with cutting certain costs but you should never cut into things that involve the character and soul of your business. You should be personally involved with your customers so they can get to know you and trust you. You should stick to the things you like. You should get gratification out of your job every day. There are too many people who made it on their own and made it big, but aren't having any fun. They concentrated purely on the money side. Finally, when they did make a lot of money, they didn't know what to do with themselves.

To get the most enjoyment out of your business and to make sure you are keeping in touch with your customers, you have to measure your time and pace yourself. At first, you'll be spending a lot of time on certain initial projects because you're still unfamiliar with the work. For example, it used to take me nearly a whole week to think up, research and finally write two newspaper columns. I had to spend considerable time finding and evaluating information. Now I'm able to do my columns in around two days and still keep up the quality. With experience, the columns took less of my time.

I needed this extra time to investigate and experiment with new projects. As each project came along and a new routine was learned, I was able to fit it into my week. You shouldn't take on a new project until you have gone through a shakedown period with your first project. Once you've learned the routine and have a project going well, then you can trot out one of your "future hopefuls" for a try.

There will be times when, in order to get a new project started, you may have to take a calculated risk of working flat-out for several months before things settle down. If, after months of working on a new project, you still aren't able to settle back into a more comfortable routine, then you might have to give up the project and try another one. It's not easy to determine when to quit. Who knows whether a couple more months might do the trick? You have to give yourself some kind of a deadline and, when the deadline passes and you haven't been able to get your new project into some sort of sensible routine, you have to make a careful appraisal. Talk to others in your business. Do some hip-pocket market surveying on your own. Talk to customers and, perhaps, a hired professional marketing or management consultant.

You may decide to give yourself x number of months more for the project to prove itself. If it doesn't make it with an extended deadline, then drop it, write off your losses, and spend the time recharging those batteries with new ideas. I've dropped many a project after slaving away to get it started. I give each one a deadline and some minimum income figure that has to be made. In a way, it's sort of like doing your own market research. You try out your new product or service and if it can't make its own way within a specific trial period, then you have to let it go.

To give each project a chance, you have to do a lot of your own promotion. This involves selling yourself and your ideas. You have to learn to meet people who might help you get your name and product or service in newspapers and other places where people can see your name. Study your own, local papers, trade magazines and local TV talk shows. Analyze what you're doing and what might be interesting to a general audience. Wherever there's some human interest side to your business, see if you can write it up as an idea for some local newspaper, magazine or broadcaster.

Maybe, if you're not too handy with pen or typewriter, you can get a friend to help. Often, a personal account submitted to a local paper will get in faster than one that might have been fancied up by a public relations firm. Public relations firms may be called on later in the game but when you're starting out, your own enthusiasm and your own fresh ideas are usually much more attractive to an editor or broadcaster than those that have been polished by some public relations writer.

Those of us in the news business get so many pitches from public relations specialists that a heartfelt, personally conceived pitch from an actual owner of a new business comes as a refreshing change. Public relations people are most helpful when they can help answer questions or help steer news writers toward an interesting story. They're usually more effective with bigger, more complicated businesses whose owners can't spare the time to go around tooting their own horns.

When you're building a business, be your own public relations director. Let your personality and your enthusiasm come through directly to the professional news people who have to decide who gets in print (or on the air) and who doesn't. It won't cost much, just a little time to think out the story you're trying to sell. And don't forget the trade magazines and newsletters. They're always looking for interesting material about new businesses. Use your local library as a research laboratory for your own public relations work. See what kinds of stories are getting into print. See where your special service or product might be presented in a way that would be of interest to an editor or broadcaster.

You may eventually have to hire professional sales people and marketing experts to get your product out to customers but you should still promote yourself wherever possible. You've got to take time off at least once or twice a month to get your name and product out in the public eye. I have three professional agents selling my newspaper column, radio show and magazine and book ideas. Yet I'm always sending clippings or idea letters to people who can put my name in the public eye. You never know when a prospective customer might read about you or hear about you.

In your quest for getting your name out where the public can see it, don't forget your old customers. You can't take them for granted. Keep sending ideas to them so they can better use your service or product. Your old customers like to see your name in print or hear it on the air. Whenever something about your company is in the limelight, send your customers a little personal note drawing their attention to it.

You've got to hustle your own business. Maybe where you used to work they had paid professionals doing this hustling. Now you should learn to do it yourself.

If you handle your own public relations, you most certainly should handle your own employee relations and handle them with care. Don't bring the establishment's faults along with you when you start up your own business. Get to understand your employees' needs, both financial and psychological. Try to think of all the things you wanted as an employee but never got. For starters, listen to your employees. Find out what they want out of their job. As we've seen, employees these days want more than just a paycheck. They want to participate and be able to learn.

Wherever possible, make your professional advisors available to advise employees on their financial problems. One thing that's sadly lacking in most organizations is financial counseling for employees. The executives get all sorts of free counseling from lawyers and tax experts—but not the employees. Help your employees with this kind of counseling. Let your employees see how they can be paid with money or free time or a combination of both. Also, let them see how they can get a smaller paycheck now, if both husband and wife are working, and get part of their pay set aside in a deferred income plan. When two people in a family are working, the joint return tax bite can be tough. If your employee agrees to getting less pay now in order to build up deferred income, he or she can then use that income later when both partners aren't working. The deferred income can also be used by an employee to start a new business some day.

If you're really enlightened—and why not be?—you'll help your employees save money and learn skills that they can eventually use to start their own business. Remember, you can't force loyalty out of your employees. You've got to earn it. By helping them with financial and career planning, you'll earn their loyalty and you'll get far more creative and enthusiastic work than you would by trying to manipulate them with traditional carrot and stick (mostly stick) methods.

I've had several people slyly ask me: "Well, what if your employees want to start their own business? How would you like that?" I'd love it. I really believe in this and my beliefs are rubbing off on my employees. If they know I'll help them start up a business some day and if they know I trust and respect their need to do meaningful work, then they'll do much better helping me. Ruling by fear never pays off for the long pull.

I have no doubt in my mind that my assistant will be able to start her own little communications business wherever she goes with her Air Force husband. Step by step, I've given her more responsibility and more training. Of late, she has taken over the editing and design of some information booklets we're selling. She works with the printer and works with the promotion and mailing of the booklets. Wherever she goes, she'll be able to line up customers who will pay her to conceive, write, design and promote brochures, booklets and other information material.

Wherever possible, I try to share responsibilities and profits with employees. Wherever possible, I also try to give an employee extra training which will not only help me but which will help the employee become more independent. For example, my part-time bookkeeper is being trained by my accountant to do number codes on our checks so the final audit can be put on the accounting firm's computer. The bookkeeper is also learning to handle all tax forms and deposits except the final federal income tax return in April.

This not only cuts my costs because I don't have to rely so much on my accountant's help at the higher fee, but it also helps my bookkeeper build her own consulting business. She works for me now, out of retirement, for one week at the end of the month. With the knowledge she's gaining of how to manage the books and organize the files for my small office, she can offer this service to others. She can have my company and several others as "clients." This will make more money for her and will certainly make life more interesting. She'll have "portable professional skills," the goal most of us seek who want the independence that comes from having our own businesses.

With all this talk of the care and feeding of employees, don't overlook yourself. You are your company's most important employee. There is an added responsibility on your shoulders to take care of your physical and mental health. Working with an organization, you could afford to take sick leave for several days or several weeks. When you're on your own, especially in the formative stages of a new business, you can ill afford being ill.

Because of this new responsibility, I began to take better care of myself than I did when I was working for a company. If I worked extra hard for my company and my health suffered, I figured I could always call in sick after my specific task was finished. Now there's no place to call in sick. I can take several days off to combat some minor illness but I can't afford running myself into the ground.

I found that you have to get a good internist or general practice doctor and stick with him or her. Use your doctor to help solve health problems and help practice preventive medicine. Medical people have mixed opinions about the value of periodic physical exams or checkups. I find they are valuable, not so much for their detection of some hidden disease, but because they force you periodically to evaluate your own health. You get a chance to tell a' professional about your troubles. If you have a wise doctor you'll get sound psychological advice on how to pace yourself and how to take care of yourself. A good doctor will prescribe less medicine and rely more on basics, such as good diet, exercise and other healthy habits.

I'll never forget my doctor's advice. He said: "If people in business got more sex and more vacations, they'd be a lot better off." You have to be able to get away from your business to unwind. You need to keep strong ties with your family and you need to recharge yourself over and over again. A good doctor can pick at your conscience and make you take days off when you know you should but tend to feel guilty about it.

Dr. Irving Paige, a nationally known heart specialist at the Cleveland Clinic, says, "Most people don't know how to take vacations." He claims people tend to take "quickie vacations," and these won't do much good. When you're jaded from hard work, you need a vacation of at least two weeks and preferably three. Dr. Paige says, "It takes from a week to ten days just to peel the layers of fatigue off your mind and body before your vacation can begin the regeneration job it was designed to do."

In my first year of operation, I just couldn't take three weeks off. I took as many mini-vacations with my wife and two boys as I could. We took long weekends in the mountains camping and we took a week off in winter to go skiing and skating. These little vacations did a lot to keep family ties well laced while the pressure of my new business kept me pinned down at my office longer.

After the first year, however, when there was a little light at the end of tunnel, we took off for a full three weeks' trip to Nantucket and Lake Champlain. We didn't spend much money and I got a good rest. My idea machine was raring to go when I got back. I felt refreshed and was able to keep building my business. Now we are back on a good vacation schedule and I'm able to take five weeks off a year, usually in two chunks (one winter, one summer).

Still, every time one of my customers drops off or some other bad news comes in, I tend to "hunker down" and work harder. Fortunately, my wife and my boys keep me from being too much of a work worrier. They have an open communication line to my office and often use it. "Drop what you're doing right now and come home." That's the word I get and I usually obey.

There are times when you might want to take on a big proj-

ect and you know it will strain your every fiber. But you know
the project will only last so many weeks or so many months.
In this kind of situation your doctor can bolster your confidence
with a good medical report and you can present a fair proposi-
tion to your family. You explain that you may have to work
flat out for a certain fixed period of time but when the project
is over, you'll make up for it with a vacation dividend. And
you explain that you won't make a practice of these concerted
work pushes without compensating time off with them.

Work on this book has put a strain on me. But I knew it
would. I talked it over with my wife and later with my two
boys. I told them it would take x number of months and that I
would have to work six days a week all day on to 7 P.M. I explained that at least half of each week I'd be working at home.
That seemed to cheer them up. I only come out of my home
office "cave" every two hours or so to drink some juice and
fraternize. They don't seem to mind too much. Apparently,
"it's nice having Daddy home," even if he's grouchy sometimes.
When the children come home from school, I stop and listen
to their day's adventures. When my wife calls at 7 P.M., even if
I'm in the middle of a paragraph, I stop. Enough's enough.

I have to go to my office and work like an old-fashioned,
revved-up version of a Charlie Chaplin movie. In less than
three days, I have to get all my column, magazine and radio
work done. Then I devote Thursday, Friday and Saturday exclusively to the book. Whenever possible, I carve another day
away from my office time to add to the book. There is a
strain. I can feel it. My family can feel it. But it's going to be
for a limited time. You have to set specific goals for yourself
and not be lured into work for work's sake.

Besides the longer and more frequent vacations, my doctor
recommended losing some weight. And he suggested I get in
much more walking and swimming. I now walk everywhere. I
get off the bus at least fifteen blocks from my office and walk

at a fast pace. In my office building, I use the stairway instead of the elevator. Harvard nutritionist Dr. Jean Mayer claims building stairways can "serve as a busy man's gymnasium." I was told by my doctor to take it easy the first week or so until I became conditioned. Now I can bounce up six floors without puffing.

As for swimming, it's harder to come by. In the summer, you can usually find a place to swim, but in winter it's more difficult. I've found a local hotel that has an indoor pool which I can join, as a club member, for a twenty-dollar monthly fee. Three nights a week, I take off from work a little early and try to swim a set number of laps. My wife is a part-time student at American University and she has the use of the university pool. If you check around, you might be able to find a local high school, university or "Y" pool that's open year 'round.

Whatever your exercise, pick something that you can stick with. Jogging is great for some people, but it has a high number of dropouts. Programmed walking to and from work can provide more consistent exercise. Dr. Paige says bike riding is also good. So is riding one of those stationary bikes if you can read a book while doing it.

I've found that most people who have their own small businesses seem to run a little harder, stay a little thinner, drink less and smoke less. Oh, you can find some who are florid-faced, wheezing, too fat, drink too much and smoke too much, but in general most self-bossers tend to take care of themselves. Maybe it's because they realize that they are the most important asset on their company's books. They've invested so much time and money in their business, they want to protect their investment. Then, maybe it's because they're happier with life and they don't feel the need to overindulge as a means of escape.

As your business grows and you grow older, there may come a time when you want to slow down. You can accept less business and just do enough to keep yourself happy and keep the bills paid at home. Or you might want to sell out. I know several people who have built businesses and then sold them out for a handsome sum. Often they can get enough for their business to put into a retirement fund that will carry them through old age without financial worries.

Sometimes, people sell their business when it gets a certain size and then go back to start up another business. If you're good at it, this can be enormously rewarding, because many major corporations don't have much inventiveness of their own. They have to go out and buy little companies that have new ideas and new products. I know one fellow who invented a programmed-learning method of teaching. He built his company to where it was turning a good profit and then sold out to Litton Industries. He made plenty of money and went back to teaching for a while. Later on, he was back inventing some other teaching device to sell to another giant corporation.

One of the best things to sell these days is a small but profitable business. Buyers or investors have something they can see. They have records to analyze. Many big companies regularly buy up going little businesses as part of their diversification. There are merger brokers who are constantly looking for businesses to buy for their clients. Your accountant or lawyer may know some merger and acquisition firms and can quietly list your company as being "for sale."

Of course, your business has to be big enough to be worth purchasing. But it doesn't have to be too big. I know of one man who started his own newsletter and was later bought out by a large publishing house. He's now back starting another newsletter and has a good chunk of money stashed away from the sale of his first newsletter.

At some stage in your development, your lawyer and accountant may suggest converting your company into a regular corporate structure where stock can be issued. You can sell your stock on a local exchange and then you're in a position to sell your company through an exchange of stock with a much bigger company.

In many instances, the acquiring company will give you a combination of cash and stock in their company. They may be able to write a contract whereby you will continue to be paid a fee for a certain number of years as a "consultant." You continue to have your name associated with your company after it's acquired and you continue to get a handsome salary.

Building your company up to be a salable asset has other advantages too. It means that, if you die, your family will be able to inherit something of value. You've been able to build up an equity that can be sold. The company no longer depends 100 per cent on your presence and your daily supervision.

Whether you want your company to be other than an intimate part of your own personality is another matter. It depends on your goals and what makes you happy. For many, just running their own business until they drop is satisfaction enough. They save on the side for their family, and when they go—the business goes. For others, there's a need to build something more permanent, something their family and employees can continue to rely on when they're gone.

As you can see, we've come a long way. You no longer are worrying about whether you're going to make it or not. You've elevated your class of worries from such questions as: Will I fail? Now you ask more collected questions, such as: Should I sell out or should I take on a junior partner so I can take it easier and travel more? You've taken a quantum jump. These are the happy man's pensive ponderings and not the nagging nightmares you endured when you were working for some establishment organization.

It's because you're in control. You make the decision when, and if, you should slow down. You decide when you can take a vacation and whether you deserve and can afford a raise or not. These crucial, life decisions are not in the hands of some boss who may not have your best interests at heart. These decisions are, at long last, in your hands because—you're the boss.

Epilogue
CAPITALIST
COMMUNES
VS.
THE ESTABLISHMENT

During the research interviews for this book, I ran up against the same question over and over. It more often came from an establishment-oriented person, but sometimes it even came from those who have broken out of the establishment. The question asked was: What if everybody wanted to start up 'Me, Incorporated' and be on their own? At first I just shrugged and figured it was one of those absurd, argumentative questions where the asker doesn't really want the answer. But, as I thought about it, I began to sense that the people who wanted to know what would happen if everybody became independent of an organization were just wondering how it would all work. They are fearful that our whole system might slide back into some sort of anarchy and that our great production lines, communications systems and other institutions would grind to a halt. They sense important changes in the works and they fear these changes.

To get rid of the literal question "what if?" I reply that nobody runs out and does anything at once. If they did, of course, there would be chaos. If everybody flushed the toilet at the same time in any given city it would probably destroy the waterworks, the sanitation works and a few other works.

Same goes if everybody picked the telephone up at the same time. It would destroy the telephone system.

But, fortunately, nobody does everything on cue. Only a relatively small percentage of our population will be going off on their own business over the next few years. I believe it will be an increasing percentage, but you're not going to see everybody slamming the door on establishment jobs to hang up their own shingles. The move will be steady, but gradual. After all, it takes time, guts and money to wean yourself from an establishment job. Most people have to work on the project for several years before they can pull it off. Only a very few can make the quick jump.

The next question, I suppose, is: Will this exodus from establishment jobs eventually bring down our way of doing business and governing ourselves? Not really. I think it will change things. I don't think it will bring anything crashing down. And, I might add, I think it's going to change things for the better— much the better. I think the search for more freedom by employees will revitalize many organizations. It will either revitalize them or they'll eventually perish. It's going to force organizations to make much better use of employees' talents. It's going to force organizations to be more dynamic, more flexible and more honest with those who work for them. Organizations' goals are going to have to mesh much more with individuals' goals. In the long run, I think organizations will get more work, better work and more creative work out of their employees with lower overall cost.

The drifting away of talent will force organizations to be more creative with the use of people. Too many establishment organizations now feel that they can "buy" loyalty from employees. If they give you enough money and/or fringe benefits, they feel that you are enthusiastically supposed to do what you're told to do. When this "buying off" deal fails to get 100 per cent enthusiasm and loyalty, some organization chiefs become angry and grudgingly feel they have to keep raising the ante. They don't realize that you want your time and freedom as much, if not more, than you want money. What good is the money if you have to do the same kind of job over and over without time off to do what you want to do?

Organizations will have to adapt to this freedom movement. If they do adapt, they'll find that they can have a much better working relationship with employees and they can get much more creative work out of them. Why? Because employees who are paid in time and freedom, as well as money, aren't working from fear. They are getting back as much as they're giving to an organization. Their freedom to spend considerable time away from their salaried job, helps build their confidence and helps build a portable skill or sideline business that can supplement income and allow them to continue to grow.

Some companies see the handwriting on the wall and are just now beginning to offer employees more freedom to do other kinds of work. I mentioned that Xerox is giving a few employees a year's sabbatical to work on a challenging project in the social fields. IBM is also doing this. Polaroid is giving some of its employees "multiple assignments" where they can do several kinds of jobs on a rotation basis. TRW Systems is offering a 4-40 program, whereby you work four days a week but still do your forty hours. A select few are even being allowed to have completely flexible hours. They can work on any schedule as long as they get their forty hours in.

This flexibility of hours is called the "Flexitron system" and it originated in Great Britain. In some cases, you're required to work a set four hours in any given day and then can work the other four hours whenever you want. In other cases, you can work any combination of hours you want. This gives a great deal of flexibility to someone who is trying to set up their own business. It makes "creative moonlighting" much easier. You can take mornings off and work on your own business and give the later hours to your organization. Or you can work several long days and take off the rest of the week.

These, perhaps, are the first primitive, groping steps being taken by organizations to cope with the worker's new order of priorities. The rising disaffection and drifting away of employees is of great concern to many organizations. At first, some organizations try to fight it and blame everything on the "hippy youth" movement or the "general deterioration of the country." The only thing that's deteriorating is the old way of organizational life which claimed that a person had to devote all their time to the same boss—or else.

Flexibility with working hours aimed at giving employees more time off to do what they want, is part of the move by some organizations to develop a strategy to keep bright and interesting people. Here and there, organizations are beginning to offer employees contracts tailored to individual needs as much, if not more, than the organization's needs. If you want a bright person to stay, you've got to pay in the new currency —freedom and flexibility. The bright ones aren't so concerned about money. They feel they can make all the money they need—if they have enough of their own time.

In order to attract young people, you'll probably see more organizations offering special three-year contracts similar to, but probably more generous than, the "hitches" offered by the military. A young graduate signs up with XYZ Corp. for three years and everything is spelled out. The recruit knows just what kind of training will be offered and how this training can be used on the outside. A money package will be offered whereby some deferred income might be waiting at the end of the three-year contract period so it could be used as a stake to start an individual business or as travel money to move to another interesting job. Many organizations are finding that young people leave after three years anyway, so why not formalize it and make the best of it? Give them a chance to "re-enlist" for another three-year hitch with increased educational benefits and, possibly, a continuation of the deferred income package which would be bigger and better after six years' moldering with interest. At each contract point, the individual could have a chance of pulling out or signing on for another hitch with specifically detailed educational and financial benefits.

This way, a person could work with enthusiasm for an organization, because it would be part of a learning process. It would be much like the "paid graduate school" I mentioned earlier in the book. You could shop around and pick up the skills you needed to be in business for yourself.

Organizations have other problems than just attracting young tigers out of college or high school. They have to retain older and wiser heads. How can you keep good people long enough so that your organization will have some continuity, some institutional base? You have to give older people more time off. You have to offer such things as "joint appointments," which permit an employee to use the organization as an operational base for a consulting business or some other sideline. The employee works so many days of the month or week and then has the rest of the time off. He or she can even use their organization office as a base to take calls and arrange outside business appointments. Some organizations are experimenting with the idea of giving contracts to talented people that require only eight or nine months' work out of the year. The other three months can be taken off much in the manner of the summer vacation teachers and professors get.

Still others are helping certain key employees set up their own business so the organization can become one of the employees' "major clients." The relationship changes from employer-employee to client-professional. Organizations should also be able to benefit from the new freedom. According to management consultant Richard Beckhard, who teaches manpower development at M.I.T.'s Sloane School of Business: "Organizations who allow employees more time of their own will benefit from the fact that most employees will bring back fresh ideas and enthusiasm from the world outside of the organization." An employee who has a business sideline outside of the organization is dealing with all sorts of other people and other problems. This can bring in fresh ideas and fresh approaches to problems inside the organization. Also, the individual will be far more self-confident not having to depend too heavily on the organization and will be able to give more objective criticism without the old fear of falling into disfavor.

According to Beckhard, some companies are beginning to offer multiple benefit packages to employees. For example, an employee can agree to work for a specific period and then get a deferred income payment as a sort of short-term pension. Let's say you feel you want to work for the XYZ Corp. for no more than ten years. All your education and job opportunities have been spelled out and you think that, after ten years, you will have gained enough training in professional skills to be able to set up your own business. You will get hitherto untaxed, deferred income when you "retire" and this income can be used to help tide you over while your own business is building. You may get something like half or three-quarters base pay for anywhere from two to five years. You perhaps take a little less pay during your ten-year "growth period" and you get a good capital investment stake at the end.

Organizations are finding that, in order to get a talented person to stay ten years, they have to pay a lot in the "freedom currency." Robert Townsend, in his book *Up the Organization,* says most talented managers shouldn't stay with any organization more than five years. I think the period should be cut to three years. You can usually learn all there is to know in three years with the average organization. If they give you multiple assignments and allow you to work two different jobs in the organization (salesman and photographer or engineer and lawyer), then you can stretch the "learning period" out to five or more years. If, after three years, you feel you've stopped growing in an organization, then you've got to leave or they have to offer something new in the form of education—something that can be counted as a "portable skill" you can use on your own on the outside.

Organizations will have to become much more involved as education enterprises. Some are already spending plenty on training programs for employees. But this process will have to expand if an organization expects to attract and keep good people for at least five to ten years. Organizations can't rely on universities to keep up with what's going on. All too often, the universities don't offer enough work-study programs that involve the real world.

Establishment organizations will have to come to the point of offering prospective employees training in certain skills even if they know the employees will eventually leave to go out on their own or move to another job that offers more training in different skills.

"Look at the Plaza Hotel in New York," says Beckhard. "It has trained countless cooks who have gone out to run their own restaurants or be number one in another major hotel." The Plaza knows that many of its own trained cooks will leave but the management apparently feels that the years the hotel gets from the cooks while they're working and learning at the Plaza kitchen are worth it. Because it has such a good training program, the Plaza is able to attract some of the best prospective chefs. And, while they're working at the hotel, they give their all. They give super work because they know that "Plaza graduates" are almost guaranteed a business of their own later on if they want it. So they work extra hard and put all their culinary creativity to play. They're building a skill and reputation that will be like money in the bank later on.

Mind you, I'm talking about just a few organizations. As you probably realize, the traditionalists who talk about loyalty to the organization and revere organizational bureaucracy are still the majority. They fear the whole concept of paying people with freedom and time off. This means less raw control over an employee. Some organization bureaucrats have operated so long on the threat of firing or shelving an employee who doesn't follow orders that the job freedom movement comes as a threat to their whole way of life. They don't know how to motivate people except with a bribe or a brickbat.

You're going to see a head-on clash between the new-freedom type of employee and the loyal bureaucrats. It's curious, but most of the resistance to paying people in freedom and time, as well as money, usually doesn't come from top executives. It comes from those down the line who have based their whole working life on climbing the ladder and using the political, organizational ploy to get what they want.

You see this, for example, in universities. There is often considerable jealousy and animosity found among full-tenure professors who resent the new breed of part-time or associate professors who have their own outside consulting firms or other professional businesses. Perhaps they resent the fact that the "outsiders" often make more money, have better professional standing and attract much more attention from students who are eager to learn more about the outside world. These outsiders who don't have to rely on the university for their whole life and livelihood often bring a breath of fresh air into our somewhat stagnant academia. They can bring in real problems that happen to a real client. They can criticize outdated textbooks with contrary facts they've picked up as they hustle business rounds on the outside. I'm not suggesting that we abandon our system of academic bureaucracy completely. I'm just saying that the job freedom movement has done much to stimulate teaching in every college and university that dares to give outsiders teaching jobs with enough pay to attract the best people. Of course, when a professor has an outside job that completely takes over his or her time and little or no time can be devoted to the students, then that's an abuse of freedom.

A university can offer a talented professional a base of operations and the professional can have the "best of both worlds" by commuting back and forth between a business on the outside and classes or research on the inside. I know of one professor who steadfastly refuses acceptance of a full professorship and tenure because he doesn't want to be bogged down in the university's bureaucracy. He doesn't want to spend the time that's required of a full professor. He does his one class a week, enjoys it, uses the university as a base and that's it. His own outside business usually keeps him busy during the rest of the week but he still finds time to talk with students while they tag along as he works on a project. Students who are let in on his work tend to learn faster and with more enthusiasm.

The new freedom is also seeping into the military. When the President and Congress decided that we were going to have an all-volunteer force that didn't have to depend on the draft except in all-out war, the military establishment suddenly found itself in the position of having to compete with the outside world for talented employees.

Much better pay scales were installed and that helped. But the military also found that money wasn't enough. Once they got some good people into service and gave them further training in special skills, such as various types of law, nuclear engineering, electronics and other much needed disciplines, they then had to be able to retain these people long enough to get some use out of them.

After a hitch is up, of course, a military person can resign. In order to get certain skilled officers to "sign over" for another hitch, the armed forces have proposed offering up to $4,000 a year bonus for every year of a contract up to six years. This means an officer could get a total of $24,000 on top of regular pay and other benefits. This money could be used very nicely later on to set up an individual business.

If an officer skilled in nuclear engineering, signs up for an additional six years, he can invest the $4,000 bonus he gets each year and live off his regular salary. At the end of the six-year period, his annual bonuses, if invested, will probably total a figure in excess of $30,000—a nice sum to tide him over while he sets up his nuclear engineering consulting firm. During military service, if he was smart, he probably got extra training and the use of equipment that might have been impossible for him to get on the outside.

The new, all-volunteer armed forces should not be overlooked as a possible place to learn a profession and pile up investment capital for going into a small business. Aside from the special bonus system designed to help retain critical skills, the military has the traditional twenty-years-and-out pension plan. You join the military at, say, age twenty-two and get out at age forty-two with a monthly pension check worth half your base pay until you die. When you "retire" you can set up your own business and still have the security of that monthly retirement check. You and your family also get free medical care for the rest of your life. It's true, you have to stay twenty years in one organization, and that may sound grim. But, for those who have ambition and talent but not much money, it's possible to make a pre-enlistment contract that spells out just what kind of valuable training you're going to get.

When you "retire" from the military at age forty-two or so, the term seems ridiculous. Everybody knows you're not really going to retire. You're going to work on another job or start your own business. I think we ought to consider doing away with the word "retire." People have been retiring from organizations at such an early age that the word "retirement" has become outmoded. Perhaps "commencement" would be better. Unless you are really sick or exhausted, you shouldn't ever retire. You should be able to work as long as you want. In a sense, I "retired" from my company when I was forty-two. I had a little money and could have rested for a while or worked half time and lived in an apartment. But I didn't retire. I couldn't afford it. Few people can these days—even with a small pension and Social Security. I looked at it as a "commencement."

The stigma of the "job hopper" will fade fast as the new freedom takes hold. We used to think that anybody who changed careers or jobs five or six times during a lifetime was some kind of a kook or "disturbed person." Part of this stigma attached to changing careers no doubt was put forth by entrenched organizations that felt the "threat" of mobility had to be quashed wherever it reared its anti-establishment head.

No more. Changing careers will become the smart thing to do. In the not too distant future, we might find the situation reversed, with a stigma aimed at the "loyal" employee who sticks at the same task for most of a lifetime. A person who only masters one job in one field might become suspect of being a dullard with too narrow a mind to cope with today's rapidly changing scene. It's entirely possible that a person could stay with an organization for a fairly long time and still not be a dullard. This will be especially true if the one-organization type gets more free time to set up an individual business so that the parent organization eventually becomes just one of his or her clients. We're at the stage right now where having one career isn't enough. We'll need to be handling at least two careers simultaneously and perhaps even three.

I know a fellow who works for a moderately enlightened technical company on the West Coast. To keep certain key people (and the list is getting longer every year), his company lets him take off one or two days each week to work on his own business. He does consulting work and gives golf lessons. So, in a sense, he has three businesses going. Eventually, he'll only be working at his company's offices one or two days a week. You don't see much of this type of enlightenment yet, but I predict it will gather considerable popularity over the next five to ten years. As this occurs, executives will have to manage much more complicated, dynamic organizations. There will be many more individual relationships with employees. In some advanced cases, you may even see an organization become a sort of base of operations for many of its employees, who are working their own businesses on the side. Employees will be giving a certain amount of their time and talent to the organization and in return they'll be getting income plus the use of the organization's training, equipment, group services (insurance, medical care).

Perhaps ten years or more down the road we'll see some organizations turning into what I call "capitalist communes." A true capitalist commune will be a place where people can enjoy the benefits of an organization without all its faults. Workers give so much of their time to the organization for a fixed fee and the use of the organization's training and other facilities. They'll be using group buying power to get insurance, legal aid, discount vacation travel and special rates on the use or purchase of supplies and equipment. The organization will be getting talented people for set periods of time and both sides —employees and employer—will be working much more as equals with vested interests in each other's welfare. Of course, this will come slowly with only the most advanced organizations progressing fairly quickly. And, I think, these kinds of capitalist commune arrangements will come much faster for those who are professionals or have some highly needed skills. Still, for lesser skilled workers, there will be more free time to build up outside interests. The four-day week is a fact of life for many employees and this trend will continue.

You'll see the move toward capitalist communes coming from directions other than production- or service-oriented organizations. I think professional and trade associations will become "unions" for many individuals working on their own. For dues, association members will get group buying power and even group bargaining power. Until fairly recently, all too many of our trade associations were either just convention planners or lobbyists against specific legislation. They did little for individual members and often became self-perpetuating bureaucratic bogs. Now things are changing. More and more associations are offering members the advantages of group purchasing power and group protection.

We're coming to the stage where you will be able to enjoy running all or most of your work life and still have the protection of an association, company or some other organization. The association or company organization will need you (either your money or your talent or both) and you will need the protective services of the association or organization. Unions will also have to get with it or lose members. You'll probably see more unions reaching out to enlist more white collar and professional people. In order to do so, the unions will have to offer sophisticated group protection, group buying power and individual financial counseling to their members. A union will not be able to attract higher echelon workers with the old wage-benefit negotiating routine. Unions may find that they have to have something specific to offer members who go out on their own and aren't working for a big organization. Some craft unions do this now. They set minimum fees for union members who work on their own. But they'll have to do more. They'll have to offer sophisticated legal, financial and technical counseling to members who work their own businesses.

Somewhere along the line unions, associations and large

companies might find themselves, like trains, passing each other in the night. When a union member gets a business that's big enough to have employees, can both employer and employee belong to the same union? That sort of shoots down the collective bargaining principle right there. It may be possible to put some sort of size limit on a union member's own organization. Maybe we'll have to shift back and forth among various types of capitalist communes as our careers change.

You can even see the capitalist commune movement taking shape in the housing field. Not too long ago we had the choice of renting an apartment or house (no maintenance, no capital investment) or the investment value of buying a home. Renting an apartment gives away some of our freedom to the landlord, who holds the threat of being able to kick us out, and we also don't have an investment or equity in a rented place. But owning a home has its problems too. Many home owners find that the purchase price is just the beginning. There are all kinds of other bills and much maintenance to do. Maintenance costs run high and keeping the place up is a lot of work.

Now comes the condominium boom. With a condominium you can own your place and still have some of the convenience of a rented apartment. As a rule, down payments for a condominium town house or apartment aren't too high and monthly loan payments and maintenance fees come out about the same as a rented place. With a condominium home owners get all sorts of group buying power. They get maintenance work done through a group contract at a cost much less than that paid by an individual home owner. And some of the newer condominiums have HOA's (home owner associations) with group contracts for appliance and other repairs, group prices for insurance, travel and even equipment purchases. Owners get the protection of the group and the economics of

group buying and they get the freedom of having their own
home without the fear of a rent rise or an eviction.

You can see the capitalist commune thing, then, working in
the job area and the housing area. It makes sense. You want
the freedom that comes from more control over your own
time and income and yet you want the protection—when and
if you need it—of an organization.

You'll see all sorts of communes forming. Many won't be as
big and as formal as a union, company, association or even a
condominium. You may well see the advent of the specialized
building for those who are in business for themselves. It may
work much in the manner of the special medical buildings
we now see for doctors and dentists. Individuals may get
together in limited "share the costs" partnerships similar to legal
and medical partnerships. They needn't share each other's
profits—just the costs. A special building that offers group purchasing power to its clients may not be too far away. With it
you could buy office supplies, use special meeting rooms
(with projection and sound equipment), get legal advice, travel
service—everything at special members' rates.

As these smaller units take shape and as more people start
up their own business, what's going to happen to the giant
corporations? Will they be drastically affected by all this?
They'll certainly have to offer better employment contracts,
complete with payments in free time as well as money. But,
more important, these giants will discover that the increasing
number of small businesses set up by those freed from organizational ties will eventually provide something they desperately
need—new ideas.

It's a sad commentary, but giants such as the major auto
companies have to probe around among small, self-started
companies to find new products or technical know-how. Their
own organizations have become too muscle-bound, too bogged
in bureaucracy to adapt to new ideas. The little outfits that

were formed by people who left big organizations will be able to invent and market products and know-how desperately needed by the overextended giants. Remember the dinosaurs? They were enormous and had enormous power. But their brains were small. When something was biting their tail, they didn't feel it right away. They were clumsy. They were too big and too extended to adapt to the changing world and, eventually, they perished.

I'm not saying our giant corporations and other organizations will perish but I think they'll change. They will need the little self-started businesses to provide a constant flow of ideas and engineering. They'll be able to buy out or lease services and products from these small companies. We might well see a sort of "trickle up" method of technology. In the past, we heard about the "trickle down" theory, which claimed that giant organizations had the capital and the brains to develop new technology which "trickled down" to the rest of the community.

Now things are beginning to turn the other way. The little ones are developing the new technology, new products and services. The big ones often just sit there and buy it up. They've been reduced to producing and marketing. Thinking is becoming less and less of a function for some major corporations.

You can see this "trickle up" process of technology dissemination at work in the newspaper business. Technological innovation is not coming down through the big newspapers in the cities. It's trickling up into the industry from the small suburban newspapers. The little papers are much more flexible and are not weighted down with enormous capital expenditures in huge, outdated presses. The little papers also are not tied to expensive labor contracts and are not enmeshed in the traffic congestion downtown. They can move around where the market moves and aren't caught in the urban bog.

Although we will have macro-organizations with us for a long time, they will have their weaknesses. It's these weaknesses that micro-businesses will be exploiting with increasing effectiveness. You won't be seeing little businesses making an inroad into the big production industries, such as the auto industry, steel industry and oil industry. These will continue to get bigger, become more automated, use relatively less workers and become more like public utilities. As these industries get bigger and, therefore, become more entangled with the public welfare, they can't help but be slowly turned into public utilities. The auto industry is a good example. It is so concentrated, so monopolistic, that Congress and government agencies are confining auto makers with more and more rules and regulations. First, it was safety equipment. Next it was pollution-controlled engines and now we're seeing price controls. Controls on production and controls on prices. If that doesn't sound like a public utility—what does?

Micro-businesses will probably not go into major production ventures. The whole area of service is where micro-businesses will flourish. We're fast becoming a service economy with production of goods sliding further back in importance. The word "service" used to have a stigma to it. It conjured up images of "maids and butlers." No more. The service field is where it's at. Service businesses can prosper when they're relatively small because they're more flexible, more adaptable, to customer and client needs. Micro-businesses can prosper in the production area only where a lot of custom work or individual skill is required. The more mass production needed for a product, the less attractive it becomes for a micro-business.

You might well see service businesses competing with sales of mass-produced products. For example, you might find more rented or leased vehicles replacing the purchase of new cars for individuals. You might find private transportation services taking over commuters' cars so a family would need one car instead of two or three. You may well see leasing of "entertainment equipment" replacing individual purchases of TV sets, stereos and the like. The emphasis would be on continuous trouble-free TV viewing or music listening instead of individual brand qualities. Leasing an entertainment console would put the emphasis on maintenance and repairs and not on sales. Everywhere you look, the maintenance and repair business will be booming and small businesses will be best suited to cash in on it.

The influx of more small businesses into the service field, I think, will be the salvation of our economy. The dinosaurs of production will have to feed off the ideas and inventions the little businesses create. Without this bubbling up of ideas, innovation and new products coming from small enterprises, which are usually more in touch with people's needs, the giants might wither and die. Their very size keeps them from thinking up new ideas. The bigger they get, the more conservative they get. Don't rock the boat, they say. New ideas are forced on them from below. Look at the Wankel engine. It was developed and designed by a comparative micro-company in Germany. General Motors and others finally had to lease the right to use the engine because it was forced on them. They were using a much less efficient engine and were stuck with it because it's easier just to keep going with what you've got. Invention and innovation aren't much rewarded in big organizations. New ideas are often shelved because they require top management to think, take risks and to invest money. Sticking with what you've got is cheaper in the short run and, of course, doesn't tax your brain. Remember those dinosaurs in prehistoric times? They were enormous, they were powerful but they only had brains the size of a golf ball. Big, dumb and powerful. To push the image even further, relatively tiny organisms in prehistoric times were quick to adapt to changes in the environment and eventually one of the smallest and quickest, a shrewlike animal, evolved into homo sapiens. It's interesting to note that this shrewlike animal used to dart in, puncture holes in the dinosaurs' eggs and eat the contents. Enough said.

I've been concentrating on what would happen to our institutions if more of us went out on our own at a much earlier stage than the formal retirement at sixty-five. But what about individuals? What will happen to the individual worker as the evolutionary pendulum swings back a bit from bigness to an emphasis on the flexibility of smallness?

It won't come overnight, of course, but I think you're going to see more individuals who are self-contained and better able to take care of themselves. As the need to depend on traditional, establishment organizations for jobs diminishes, you'll see an earlier self-protection, self-starting awareness among individual workers. Retirement won't come so much as a shock because, in a sense, there will be no "sudden" retirement. There may be stopping of work because of a disability or there may be slowing down of work to enjoy other interests but the sudden chop-off at age sixty-five, as we know it today, will be phased out. People will "retire" or "commence" at much earlier ages in order to go into other lines of work. It will be more common to see people with several careers, so that when one diminshes or stops, the other (or others) continue.

You'll see people working much longer into later years. If they're not forced to retire at age sixty-five, most people won't. More people will have more access to money in later years. This will help take the burden off the government to be the sole supplier of income for a good number of people in their old age. Social Security, Medicare and other benefits will still be there but they'll serve much more as a supplement for healthy elders who want to continue being active. Those who are sick or disabled and can do little or no work are the ones who should receive major government benefits. Perhaps the disabled ones will receive a package of government and private benefits (amassed through association and other organizational pension plans). The system as we see it today is extremely inefficient and wasteful. We kick people out of work when they're sixty-five (and earlier) and force them onto public funds. If they could work longer, they'd be better off financially and psychologically and the public funds could be concentrated on protecting the sick and disabled.

As the concept of paying with free time as well as money catches on, individual employees will become much more productive and creative. They will be working in much less of a fear atmosphere and will have more enthusiasm because, in part at least, they'll be working for themselves. Employers will find that they can get more productivity out of a "free" person who only works twenty-five hours a week than they can from a "captive" who must put in the regular forty hours plus. With the new freedom, employees will be able to grow much more as people as they learn how to handle intellectual freedom and portable skills. Work organizations may evolve into partnership deals whereby an employee can spend part time on the job with continuing education in new skills and part time on his or her own project, using the newly acquired skills.

Experiments have shown that where workers are given the training, equipment, freedom and responsibility of managing their own work, productivity tends to go up. There will be less reason to goof off on a job, because your own self-interest will be at stake. There will be less infighting and competition within work organizations, because the concept of "climbing the ladder" will diminish as freedom to move in and out of an organization increases. The in-and-outers at first may clash with bureaucrats who chose to remain tied to the same job. But even this rivalry should diminish in the more enlightened organizations. Competition will be channeled outside the organization and into the marketplace, where it belongs, and there will be less destructive competition inside organizations.

It will take time, but as this "pay with freedom" movement gathers force, individuals will have much more say over the major decisions in their lives. They will be more in control of how they spend their time. They will have more control over their source, or sources, of income. They will have much more control over where they live. You'll see less and less shunting of whole families around the country at the whim of some company. People just won't put up with it when they are less dependent on an organization for their entire livelihood. If a company wants to move somebody, it will have to convince the employee that the move will be beneficial in learning a new skill which can eventually be used in an outside career. Employees will be able to resist accepting "marching orders" for fear of losing their jobs.

This ideal situation, of course, has not yet arrived. But it's in the embryonic stage. The more people that up and leave an organization because it isn't fulfilling their need for more freedom, the faster the movement will grow. As organizations discover that they cannot attract and retain talented, creative people, then they will have to offer more package deals to give an individual more freedom. There are organizations doing this right now. Not many. But, according to some of the best management consultants in the country, the number of enlightened organizations should grow rapidly. The more we are able to break away from unimaginative organizations and make it on our own, the faster things will go toward better work relationships for everybody. The less dependent an individual is on any given organization, the more bargaining power this individual has.

Alexis de Tocqueville, a Frenchman who extensively toured

the United States back in the early 1800's, wrote a classic book called *Democracy in America*. I suggest you get it out, dust it off and read it. De Tocqueville saw the dynamic power that was growing in a country that gave individuals equal rights. He said Americans believe that "man is endowed with an indefinite faculty for improvement. His reverses teach him that none have discovered absolute good; his successes stimulate him to the never ending pursuit of it."

This individualism, this struggle to better one's lot greatly impressed De Tocqueville. He saw the energy and vivacity it gave our country. But he saw some possible trouble down the line. He was concerned about the rise of manufacturing and mass production as a "new aristocracy" that could "spring from the bosom of democracy." With uncanny foresight, De Tocqueville wrote:

> When a workman is unceasingly and exclusively engaged in the fabrication of one thing, he ultimately does his work with singular dexterity; but at the same time he loses the general faculty of applying his mind to the direction of the work. He every day becomes more adroit and less industrious; so that it may be said of him that in proportion as the workman improves, the man is degraded. What can be expected of a man who has spent twenty years of his life in making heads for pins? . . .
>
> In proportion as the principle of the division of labor is more extensively applied, the workman becomes more weak, more narrow-minded, and more dependent . . . The art advances, the artisan recedes . . .
>
> The manufacturing aristocracy of our age first impoverishes and debases the men who serve it and then abandons them to be supported by the charity of the public . . . The friends of democracy should keep their eyes anxiously fixed in this direction; for if ever a permanent

inequity of conditions and aristocracy again penetrates into the world, it may be predicted that this is the gate by which they will enter.

De Tocqueville's "friends of democracy" might well worry when they see corporations in this country get to such a size that they have a net worth and capital flow far greater than most countries. Some of the corporate giants are almost countries in and of themselves. Some employees might well feel that the heads of the companies and corporations are, indeed, an aristocracy that forces them to do dull, meaningless work without their having much, if any, say about it.

De Tocqueville saw the rise of the "manufactures" as a threat but didn't see the rise of unions and government regulatory power as a counterbalance to the threat. In spite of, or perhaps because of, the rise of unions and government regulation, corporations still got bigger. The newest counterbalance to their power is the rise of "personal nationalism" or individualism. Individuals are following the same pattern that some small countries have been following of late. They want to become less dependent on organizations or "power blocs." They want to go their own way, in their own fashion and in their own time.

Writing in *Harper's* magazine, historian and former White House aide Arthur Schlesinger, Jr., said:

> Washington supposed that what was then known as the Free World should reshape itself on the American model, while Moscow supposed that the Communist World should reshape itself on the Russian model.
>
> But the world itself did not sit still; it began to change. And the most basic change of all was the rise of a new force in revolt against the reign of the Superpowers . . . That force was nationalism; and the rise of nationalism meant growing opposition to the United States

in the Western bloc, growing opposition to the Soviet Union in the Communist bloc, and growing opposition to both America and Russia in the Third World.

Nationalism means . . . the determination to assert national identity, national dignity, and freedom of action.

The rise of nationalism is an expression of the desire for freedom on a macro-scale, while the rise of individualism, as expressed in job disaffection, is an expression of the desire for more freedom on a micro-scale. It's all part of the same urge to be less dependent on the establishment and more able to make one's own decisions without fear of reprisal. The smaller countries want to be their own bosses. You want to be your own boss.

You may make it after considerable struggling, plotting, planning, fearing and fighting. Then, you may not make it. If you believe in the concept of eventually making your own way in life, and give it a good, all-out try, you'll still be better off for having believed and having tried. Your try at scaling the mountain may fail but, by trying, you may make it easier for the next person. And who knows? The next person may be your own son or daughter.

CHECKLIST:
Selected Reading and Sources of Help

DECIDING TO LEAVE:

Frankl, Viktor E. *Man's Search for Meaning: An Introduction to Logotherapy.* New York: Washington Square Press, Inc.

Levinson, Harry. *Executive Stress.* New York: Harper & Row.

Viscott, David S. *Feel Free.* New York: Peter H. Wyden, Inc.

FINDING MONEY:

Need a Lift. American Legion.

Columbia Books, Inc. *National Trade and Professional Associations of the United States.* Suite 300, 917-15 Street, N.W.; Washington, D.C. ($15.).

Fortune magazine, May issue.

Internal Revenue Service.

Standard & Poor's stock reports.

U. S. Department of Health, Education and Welfare. *Financial Aid for Higher Education.*

National Association of Investment Clubs; P. O. Box 220; Royal Oak, Michigan 48068.

DEVELOPING IDEAS:

Arthur, Julietta. *Retire to Action*. New York: Abingdon Press.

Goldman, Fran, and Renee Taft. *Best of Both Worlds*. Distaffers, Inc.; Suite 1130 Western Savings Fund Building; Philadelphia, Pennsylvania 19107.

Osborn, Alex. *Applied Imagination*. Paperback edition. New York: Charles Scribner's Sons.

Pitkin, Walter. *Life Begins at Fifty*. New York: Simon & Schuster, Inc.

Seabury, David. *The Art of Selfishness: How to deal with the tyrants and tyrannies in your life*. New York: Julian Messner.

Selye, Hans, *The Stress of Life*. New York: McGraw-Hill Book Co., Inc.

Snelling, Robert. *The Opportunity Explosion*. New York: The Macmillan Co.

Also useful here: *Executive Stress, Man's Search for Meaning* and *Feel Free*.

PROTECTING YOUR PRODUCT:

Jones, Stacy V. *The Inventor's Patent Handbook*. New York: The Dial Press, Inc.

————. *You Ought to Patent That*.

General Informal on Copyright. Copyright Office, Library of Congress; Washington, D.C. 20540.

General Information Concerning Patents; An Information Aid for Inventors; General Information Concerning Trademarks. U.S. Department of Commerce.

FRANCHISING:

Thomas' Register. New York: Thomas Publishing Co.

Brown, Harold. *Franchising, Trap for the Trusting*. Boston: Little, Brown & Company.

Dias, Robert M.; Gernick, Stanley I. *Franchising—The Investor's Complete Handbook*. New York: Hastings House.

Kursh, Harry. *The Franchise Boom*. Englewood Cliffs, New Jersey: Prentice-Hall, Inc.

Murphy, Thomas H. *The Franchise Directory*, and monthly magazine. *The Franchise Journal;* P. O. Box 6360; Denver, Colorado 80206.

WHERE TO LEARN SKILLS:

Agency Sales magazine. Manufacturers Agents National Association; 3130 Wilshire Boulevard, Suite 503; Los Angeles, California 90010 ($10.).

Occupational Outlook Handbook. U. S. Department of Labor.

WORKING WIVES:

Direct Mail Advertising Association (mail-order business); 921 National Press Building; Washington, D.C. 20004.

Direct Selling Association (party-plan franchisors); 1730 M Street, N.W.; Washington, D.C. 20036.

288 CHECKLIST

Some Ways of Distinguishing a Good School or Center for Young Children. National Association for the Education of Young Children; 1834 Connecticut Avenue, N.W.; Washington, D.C. 20009.

Code of Standards. National Committee on Household Employment; 1725 K Street, N.W., Washington, D.C. 20006.

Also useful here: *Best of Both Worlds.*

WHEN RETIRED:

Back to Work After Retirement. U. S. Department of Labor; Manpower Administration; Washington, D.C. 20210.

Mature Temps; 521 Fifth Avenue; New York, New York 10017.

Also useful here: *Retire to Action, Man's Search for Meaning* and *The Opportunity Explosion.*

PROFESSIONAL SERVICES:

Martindale-Hubbell Law Directory

Setting Up Your Small Business:

Allen, Louis L. *Starting and Succeeding in Your Own Small Business.* New York: Grosset & Dunlap, Inc.

Small Business Reporter series (*Day Nurseries for Preschoolers, Handcraft Business, Marketing a New Product* and others). Bank of America, Department 3120, P. O. Box 37000, San Francisco, California 94137.

Small Business Administration Publications (*How to Analyze Your Own Business, Expanding Sales Through Franchising, Tips on Selection of Salesmen, Starting and Managing a Small Motel* and others). Small Business Administration, under U. S. Government listing of local phone book. (Also: SCORE, Senior Corps of Retired Executives.)

Co-operative Extension Service booklets, under county or city government listing.

Interracial Council for Business Opportunities is found in ten cities.

General Business Services, Inc. (booklets and advisory services); 7401 Wisconsin Avenue, Washington, D.C. 20014.

INDEX

Academic bureaucracy, 268–69
Accountants, 210–18, 236
  first talks with, 212–16
Agency Sales (magazine), 154
Ages and stages, 119–91
  middle age, 137–56
  senior shock, 175–91
  working housewives, 157–74
  young person, 121–36
Allen, Louis L., 222
American Federation of Television and Radio Artists (AFTRA), 40
American Individual Merchants (AIM), 42–43
American Legion, 34
American Machine and Foundry Company, 106
American Orchid Society, 41
American Pharmaceutical Association, 128
American Red Cross, 183, 191
American University, 49, 254
American Woman's Society of Certified Public Accountants, 41
Amway Company, 168

Anger, constructive uses of, 138–39
Anti-establishment violence, 123
Applied Imagination (Osborn), 59
Archives of Internal Medicine, 177
Art and Antique Dealers League of America, Inc., 41
Art of Selfishness, The: How to deal with the tyrants and tyrannies in your life (Seabury), 64
Arthur, Julietta K., 65, 190
Art work, copyrights for, 103
Associations, 273–74
  fringe benefits, 39–43
  newsletters, 133
Automobile companies, 275–76, 277
Automobiles, 32–33
  buying, 33
  cost of keeping, 32
Avon Company, 168

Back to Work After Retirement, 191
Ballet and opera, copyrights for, 103

Bank account, opening, 52–54, 61

Bank of America, 222

Bankers, how to find, 218–19

Barton, Clara, 191

Bavarian Alpine Inns, 109

Baxter, Emogene, 180–82, 183

Beckhard, Richard, 13, 140–41, 265–66, 267

Best of Both Worlds (Goldman and Taft), 65, 161, 167

Blue Cross and Blue Shield, 40, 43, 44

Bogdonoff, Dr. Morton, 177–78

Bookkeeping skills, 180

Boston University, 10, 16

Boudreau, Gerry, 180

Brandeis University, 10, 46, 176, 238

Break-even point, 213–14

Brookings Institution, 175

Broom grabbers, 234

Brown, Bill, 83–85, 91, 93

Brown, Harold, 116

Buchwald, Art, 18, 134

Bureau of Public Roads, 31–32

Burnett, Carol, 240

Businesses, legal structure of, 206–9

Business Week (magazine), 79, 135, 145, 176

Butler, Dr. Robert, 179–80

Campos, Roberto, 19

Candle Manufacturers Association, 41

Capitalist communes, establishment and, 261–84

  academic bureaucracy, 268–69

  "buying off" deals, 262–63

  contracts (organization), 264–65

  educational enterprises, 267

  flexibility, 263–64

  the housing field, 274–75

  loyalty, 268, 271

  meaning of, 272

  the military, 269–70

  movement toward communes, 272–84

  percentages of new businesses, 262

  retirement, 270–71, 279

  sideline business, 265–66

  unions and associations, 273–74

  "what if?" question, 261–62

Carpentry, part-time, 184

Carter, Alice, 160–61, 163

Catalogs, copyrights for, 103

Certificates of deposit, 37

Certified public accountant (CPA), 211

Cervantes, Miguel de, 191

Changing Times (magazine), 191

Chase Manhattan Bank, 222

Chase Manhattan Capital Corporation, 222

Checklist (selected reading and sources of help), 285–89

Chicken Delight, 110–11

Civic Center and Clearinghouse (Boston), 181

Cleveland Clinic, 252

Cleveland *Plain Dealer*, 78, 134–35, 176

Code of Standards, 174

Cohen, Jerry S., 113–14, 115

Cole, Alan Y., 196–97, 198

Colleges, financial aid for, 34

Colonel Sanders' Kentucky Fried Chicken, 108

Community Chest, 77

Community colleges, 125–26

  advantages of, 34–35

Community Service, 77

Condominium boom, 274

Confidence, 24

Contracts, types of, 195

Control Data Corporation, 99

Co-operative Extension Service, 185, 221–22
Copley Newspaper News Service, 79
Copy editing, 186
Copyrights, 103–5
Corporate structure, 255–56
  advantages of, 207
  lawyers, 200
  tax benefits, 208
  types of, 206–9
Council of Social Agencies, 77
Creative moonlighting, 69–79, 263–64
  aimless type of, 75–76
  in confidence, 73
  free time and, 74–75
  getting started, 70
  as goal defining, 76
  and keeping quiet, 73
  to learn and probe, 73–74
  magazine writing, 78–79
  making a list, 69–70
  money and, 75–76
  newsletter, 73–74
  in small businesses, 73
  temporary employment, 70–73
  volunteer work, 76–78
Cronkite, Walter, 240
Cutbacks, government spending, 9

Day Nurseries for Preschoolers, 222
Dear, Dave, 226–28
Democracy in America (Tocqueville), 282–83
Department of Commerce, 103, 105, 221
Department of Health, Education, and Welfare, 126
Department of Labor, 131, 157, 169, 191
Dependency, degree of, 16
Derry, Mr. and Mrs. Jerry, 111–13, 115

Dias, Robert M., 116
Direction, change of, from up to out, 21–27
Direct Mail Advertising Association (DMAA), 41–42, 44
Direct Selling Association, 168, 169
Disability insurance, 40, 42
Distaff Staffers (employment agency), 65, 205
Don Quixote (Cervantes), 191
Double pay standards, 157–58

Economic Status and Opportunities Division (Department of Labor), 169
Education:
  academic bureaucracy, 268–69
  community college, 34–35, 125–26
  financial aid for, 34
  real-life work and, 122–23, 125
  scholarships and grants, 33–34
  senior citizen, 181
  technology and, 10
  work-study programs, 35, 125–26
Employees, training of, 22
Establishment, the, 1, 28
  kinds of, 23
  reason for leaving, 9
  young person and, 123–32
  See also Leaving the organization
Executive Stress (Levinson), 11, 16, 64
Exercise, importance of, 254
Expanding Sales Through Franchising, 220
Expense accounts, 12, 55
Experience, middle age, 155

Failure, fear of, 16
Family affair ideas, 91–92

Family lawyer, 195–209
  how to find, 198–200
  for legal structure of business,
    206–9
  reason for, 195–96
Faust (Goethe), 191
Fears and excuses, 11–20
Federal income tax, 217
Federal payroll withholding tax,
  217
Federal Trade Commission (FTC),
  109
Feel Free (Viscott), 16–17, 26,
  64–65
File drawer for ideas, 23–24, 56–
  57
Final break, the, 193–257
  getting started, 224–36
    dealing with outsiders, 234–35
    hiring first employee, 229–33
    hiring second employee, 233–
      34
  office space, 225–29
    records and books, 235–36
    salary expenses, 227
    time is money, 236
  keeping going and, 237–57
    building company as salable
      asset, 255–56
    doctor's advice, 251–52
    economic cycles, 238–39
    employee relations, 249–51
    file for future project ideas,
      241
    how fast to grow, 243–44
    leveling-off period, 237–38
    money obsessions, 244–46
    new projects, 246–47
    public relations, 249–51
    slowing down, 254–55
    vacations, 252–53
  professional help, 195–223
    accountants, 210–18
    bankers, 218–19
    free advice, 210–11

    lawyers, 195–209
    miscellaneous, 219–21
    reading material, 221–22
*Financial Aid for Higher Educa-
  tion,* 34
Fisher, Eugene, 212
Fixed costs, 212
Flexitron system, 263
Foot-in-the-door   (employment
  technique), 159, 161, 167
Forbes (magazine), 81, 83, 135,
  142, 176, 224
Fortune (magazine), 37
Forty-Plus (employment service),
  143
Four-day work week, 130
Franchise Boom, The (Kursh),
  116
Franchise Directory, The, 116
Franchise Journal, The, 116–17
Franchising business, 107–17
  checklist, 287
  compared to buying local busi-
    ness, 115–16
  hard-sell schemes, 108–9
  investigating, 107–8, 114–15
  leasing arrangements, 115
  mediocre or fraudulent, 108–11
  pitches, 107–8
  reading material, 116–17
*Franchising—The Investor's Com-
  plete Handbook* (Dias and
  Gernick), 116
*Franchising, Trap for the Trust-
  ing* (Brown), 116
Frankie Greene Studios, 85–87
Frankl, Dr. Viktor E., 19, 64, 156,
  191
Fraser, Douglas, 122
Free advice, 210–11
Fringe benefits, 39–51, 262
  buddy system, 45–46
  life insurance, 46
  medical coverage, 40, 42, 43–46

office overhead protection, 45–46

pension plans, 49–51

profit-sharing, 51

term insurance, 46–49

trade associations, 39–43

wife insurance, 49

Games, copyrights for, 103

Games bosses play, 21

General Business Services, 222–23

General Eclectics, 127–29

General Information Concerning Patents, 105

General Information Concerning Trademarks, 105

General Information on Copyright, 105

General Motors, 3, 81, 278

Georgetown University, 127

George Washington University, 4, 181

Germany, 278

Gernick, Stanley I., 116

Gerontologists, 177

Getting started, 224–36

  dealing with outsiders, 234–35

  hiring first employee, 229–33

  hiring second employee, 233–34

  office space, 225–29

  records and books, 235–36

  salary expenses, 227

  and time is money, 236

Gitomer, Ralph, 127–29

Goethe, Johann Wolfgang von, 191

Goldman, Frances, 65, 159, 161, 165, 167, 205–6

Goodwill Industries, 166

Goss, Mr. and Mrs. Pat, 94

"Go-to-hell" savings fund, 17

Great Britain, 263

Greene, Lute, 86

Haines, George, 43

Handcraft Business, 222

Happiness, meaning of, 19

Harper's (magazine), 283–84

Hartig, Al, 88–90

Hartig, Betty, 88, 89

Harvard University, 10, 121

Havermeyer, Mr. and Mrs. Henry Mitchell, 148–50, 151

Head, Howard, 106

Head Skis, 106

Health and Welfare Council, 77

Hobbies, after retirement, 182

Holiday Inns, 108

Holt, Frank, 143

Home health aides, 183–84

Home office, 54, 62–63, 225–26

Home owner associations (HOAs), 274–75

Housewives. *See* Working housewives

How to Analyze Your Own Business, 220

Human obsolescence, problem of, 10

Ideas, 23–27

  checklist for developing, 286

  consumer cause, 81–83

  consumer column, 93–94

  family affair, 91–92

  getting, 22–23

  keeping cool about, 25–26

  keeping files for, 23–24, 56–57

    future projects, 241–42

  necessity of, 52

  and patents, 96–106

  personal interest push, 83–89

  personal touch, 80, 93

  presentation of, 24–25

  putting money into, 24–25

  starting up, 52–66

    bank account, 52–54, 61

    expense account, 55

    file drawer, 56–57

    getting answers for, 59–60

    home address, 54

home office, 62–63
letterheads and envelopes, 54
note pad and, 57–58
reading list, 64–65
sales, 60–62
tax deductions and, 55–56, 62
telephone number, 54
strong personal interest, 90–91
telling your spouse, 26–27
that work, 80–95
and those that don't, 95
think small, 92–93
writing down, 24, 58–59, 60
Information Aid for Inventors, An,
105
Internal Revenue Service (IRS),
55–56, 171, 172
International Business Machines
(IBM), 263
International Franchise Association, 117
Interracial Council for Business
Opportunities (ICBO), 221
"Inventor's aid" company, 98
Inventor's Patent Handbook, The
(Jones), 105
"Investigate Before Investing" (International Franchise Asso-
ciation), 117

Jackson, Robert H., 196
Jegolsky, Tom and Dorothy, 150–
51
Jones, Mary Gardiner, 109
Jones, Stacy V., 105
Journalism, for young person, 132–
36
Junior Catering business, 129

Keeping going, 237–57
building company as salable asset, 255–56
doctor's advice and, 251–52
economic cycles and, 238–39
employee relations, 249–51

file for future project ideas, 241
and how fast to grow, 243–44
leveling-off period, 237–38
money obsessions, 244–46
new projects, 246–47
public relations, 249–51
slowing down, 254–55
vacations and, 252–53
Kelly Girl, 71
Kelly Service, 112
Keogh pension system, 51
King, Martin Luther, 83
Kursh, Harry, 116

Lansing Community College, 125–
26
Lawyers, 195–209, 236
accountants and, 216–17, 218,
219
fees, 202, 203
general practice or specialist, 197
"issue" or "people" oriented, 199
Leaving the organization, 9–14
checklist (sources of help), 285
economic and technological reasons for, 9–11
fears and excuses, 15–20
out, not up, 21–27
psychological reason for, 11–13
retirement, 14
sabbaticals, 130–31, 263
Letterheads and envelopes, 54
Levinson, Dr. Harry, 10, 11, 12,
16, 18, 64, 123, 138
Liability insurance, 81
Life (magazine), 79
Life Begins at Fifty (Pitkin), 94–
95
Life insurance, 40, 42, 46
Lifetime Living (magazine), 79
Loans, 215–16
Local withholding taxes, 217
Logotherapy, 191
Los Angeles *Times,* 121–22, 142
Los Angeles Times Syndicate, 83

McDonald's (franchise), 108
McGraw-Hill Company, 145
McKenna, Margaret S., 121–22
Magazine writing, 78–79
Mail-order business, 77, 90, 91
    hucksters, 95
"Make money at home" schemes,
    95
Malcolm X, 83
Management consultants, 246
Manpower (employment service),
    71, 72
*Man's Search for Meaning: An In-
    troduction to Logo-therapy*
    (Frankl), 19, 64, 191
Manufacturers Agents National
    Association (MANA), 154
Manufacturers' representatives,
    153–54
Maps, copyrights for, 103
*Marketing a New Product and Re-
    pair Service,* 222
Martindale-Hubbell Law Directory,
    199–200
Massachusetts Institute of Tech-
    nology (M.I.T.), 13, 140,
    266
Mathews, Frankie Greene, 85–87,
    91, 93
Mature Temps (employment
    agency), 181
Mayer, Dr. Jean, 254
Medical insurance, 40, 42, 43–46
Medicare, 279
Middle age, 137–56
    anger and conflict, 138–39
    being fired, 142–46
        for the better (case histories),
            146–51
    being frustrated, 137–42
    capital, 155
    contacts, 155–56
    direction and aims, 140–41
    employer contempt, 138
    experience, 155

moonlighting, 139–40, 141, 155
    pluses, 155–56
    self-inventory, 141
Military establishment, 269–70
"Mind Your Money" (radio pro-
    gram), 40
Mini-Gifts, Inc., 108–9
Mitchell's Book Corner, 150–51
Money, 5, 23, 262
    creative moonlighting, 75–76
    fears and excuses, 15
    finding, checklist for, 285–86
    new business and, 28–38
        children's education, 33–35
        cost-cutting expenses, 29–33
        essential expenditures, 35–36
        food costs, 29–30
        housing and transportation
            costs, 31–33
        investing, 36–38
        moonlighting for, 36
        putting into ideas, 24–25
        saving, by using family lawyer,
            197–209
Monopoly (game), 104
Monthly Investment Plans, 37
Moonlighting business, 2, 15, 28–
    29, 36, 53, 114, 116, 178,
    211, 215
    middle-age, 139–40, 141, 155
    what to do, 69–79
    See also Creative moonlighting
Movies, copyrights for, 103
Murphy, Thomas H., 117
Music, copyrights for, 103–4

Nader, Ralph, 3, 81, 94, 116
Nader's Raiders, 232
Nagan, Peter, 11–12, 17–18, 58,
    211–12, 228–29
Nantucket Kite Man, 88–90
National Aeronautics and Space
    Administration (NASA),
    127, 128

National Association for the Education of Young Children, 174

National Association of Investment Clubs, 37–38

National Association of Temporary Services (NATS), 70–71

National Automobile Dealers Association, 114

National Bureau of Standards, 98

National Committee on Household Employment, 174

National Congress of Petroleum Retailers, 113

Nationalism, rise of, 284

National Trade and Professional Associations of the United States, 41, 64

Nation's Business (magazine), 241

Need a Lift (American Legion), 34

New businesses:
  ages and stages, 119–91
  establishment vs. capitalist communes, 261–84
  finding money for, 28–38
  fringe benefits, 39–51
  getting started, 224–36
  ideas, starting up, 52–66
  keeping going, 237–57
  leaving organization and, 9–27
  professional help, 195–223

"New Horizons" (education course), 181

Newsletters, 133–34

Newsletter Services, Inc., 11

Newsweek (magazine), 133

New York *Times,* 105, 133

Nietzsche, Friedrich, 64

Note pad for ideas, 57–58

Novak, Robert, 18

Occupational Outlook Handbook, 131

Office of Invention and Innovation (National Bureau of Standards), 98

Opportunity, Inc., 181

Opportunity Explosion, The (Snelling), 65, 190–91

Orange Coast Community College, 126

Organization. *See* Establishment, the; Leaving the organization

Osborn, Alex, 59

Overseas Press Club of America, 40

Over 60 Counselling and Employment Service, 180–81, 183, 184

Paige, Dr. Irving, 252

Para-medical aides, 183–84

Partime (employment service), 71, 72

Partnerships, 201–2, 206

Part-time jobs, 19–20, 71–72, 123, 230–32
  housewife, 158–69
  senior citizens, 186–87

Patent brokers, 100

Patent lawyers, 97, 103

Patent Office Search Center, 97

Patents, 96–106
  and copyrights, 103–5
  costs and fees, 97, 98, 102–3
  ins and outs of, 96–98
  number filed per year, 98
  "pending," 100
  planning stage to marketing of, 98–101
  protection, 102–5, 286–87
  time length of, 102–3

Payne, Elaine, 87–88

Payne, Frank, 87–88, 101–2

Payne, Grayford, 88

Payne, Seth, 88

Pechman, Joseph A., 175

Pension plans, 49–51
 myth of, 176
 senior shock, 175–76
 tax loopholes, 50–51
Personal interests push ideas, 83–89
Personal property tax, 217
Personal touch, ideas and, 80, 93
Philco Corporation, 99
Photographs, copyrights for, 103
Pitkin, Walter, 94–95
Plaza Hotel (New York City), 267
Polaroid Company, 130–31, 263
Portable skills, building, 126–27, 162
Post, John C., 43, 46, 48
Preventive law, 198, 206
Professional help, 195–223, 246–49
 accountants, 210–18
 bankers, 218–19
 checklist, 288–89
 counsultants, 246
 free advice, 210–11
 lawyers, 195–209
 miscellaneous, 219–21
 reading material, 221–22
Profit, business, 214–15
Profit-sharing plan, 51
Project Head Start, 86
Promotions, organization, 21, 23
Public relations specialists, 247–49
Public Workers and Public Unions (Zagoria), 12

Radio Corporation of America (RCA), 99
Rainbow, Jack, 98–100, 101, 106
Rainbow Engineering, 98, 99
Raises, 12
Recession of 1970–71, 239
Retire to Action (Arthur), 65, 190
Retirement, 14, 177–78, 279
 checklist, 288
Rockefeller Brothers Foundation, 221

Rural Recreation—New Opportunities on Private Land, 222
Rural Recreation Enterprises for Profit, 222

Sabbaticals, company, 130–31, 263
Saint Joan (Shaw), 191
Savings accounts, 28, 37
Savings bonds, 37
Schlesinger, Arthur, Jr., 283–84
Scholarships and grants, 33–34
Schulz, Dr. James, 10, 46, 176, 238
Scott, Howard, 70–71
Seabury, David, 64
Securities, investing in, 28, 37–38
Securities and Exchange Commission, 80
Security, false sense of, 9–11
Seefeldt, Dr. Carol, 173–74
Self-inventory, middle age, 141
Selling your idea, 60–62
Selye, Dr. Hans, 59
Senior Corps of Retired Executives (SCORE), 220–21
Senior shock, 175–91
 meaning of, 175
 moonlighting, 178
 and new training, 179–87
  educational courses, 181
  part-time jobs, 186–87
  volunteer work, 179, 181
 pension plans, 175–76
 reading materials, 190–91
 retirement syndrome, 177–78
 Social Security, 175, 176–78, 180, 187–89, 190
Sensitivity Games, Inc., 16
Service businesses, mass-produced products and, 277–78
Shaw, George Bernard, 191
Shepard, Tom, 146–48, 151
Skills, learning, checklist for, 287
Sloan School of Management (Massachusetts Institute of Technology), 13, 266

Small Business Administration (SBA), 219–20, 237
Small Business Administration Publications, 220
Small Business Reporter, 222
Smithsonian Institution, 86
Snelling, Robert, 65, 190–91
Social Security, 14, 49, 175, 176–78, 180, 187–89, 190, 271, 279
Sole proprietorship, 206
Some Ways of Distinguishing a Good School or Center for Young Children, 174
So You're Planning a Vacation Farm Business, 222
Space Anti-Fogger, 128
Spra-Kleen, 88
Standard & Poor's, 37
Starting and Managing a Small Book-keeping Service, 220
Starting and Managing a Small Motel, 220
Starting and Succeeding in Your Own Small Business, 222
State withholding taxes, 217
Stationery, 54
Stocks, buying, 37–38
Striedl, Isabelle S., 169–70
Stress of Life, The (Selye), 59
Strong personal interest ideas, 90–91
Subchapter-S corporation, 207–8

Taft, Renee, 161, 205–6
Taxes, 217–18
  deductions, 55–56, 62, 171–73
  laws, 195–96
Technology:
  education and, 10
  "trickle up" process of, 276
Telephone answering service, 227, 235
Telephone number, 54
Temporary employment, 70–73

Tension, 19
Term insurance, 46–49
Think small ideas, 92–93
Thomas' Register, 105–6
Tips on Selection of Salesmen, 220
Tocqueville, Alexis de, 281–83
Townsend, Robert, 266–67
Trade associations, 39–43
Trademarks, 102–3, 104
Trout Farming, 222
TRW Systems, 263

Unemployment compensation, 217
Uniform Commercial Code, 168
Unions, 273–74
United Appeal, 77
United Auto Workers Union, 122
United Funds, 77
United Givers, 179, 183
United Planning Organization, 221
U. S. Senate Special Committee on Aging, 179–80
U. S. Training and Employment Services, 179
United Way, 77
Univac Corporation, 99
Universities, financial aid for, 34
University of Illinois, 177
University of Maryland Early Childhood Education Center, 173
University of Missouri School of Journalism, 83
University of Vienna, 19
Unknown, the, fear of, 16
Up the Organization (Townsend), 266–67
Uptown Progress Committee, 221

Vacations, importance of, 252–53
Variable costs, 212–13
Viscott, Dr. David S., 16–17, 26, 64–65
Volunteer jobs, 76–78, 124
  housewife, 165–66

senior citizens, 179, 181
for young person, 124

Wankel engine, 278
Weaver, Paul, 92
Weaver, Vida, 96–97, 230–31
Weaver Communications, Inc., 4, 32, 53
Weaver Reports, 2, 3, 17, 53, 79
Western Girl (employment service), 111, 112
Wife insurance, 49
Williams, Martha, 170, 171
Woman's Day (magazine), 241
Working housewives, 157–74, 205–6
checklist, 287–88
getting sales experience, 168–69
handling husband and family, 170–71
household duties and, 170–71
job résumé, 167–68
mechanical or repair jobs, 169–70
number of employed mothers, 158
outside help for home, 171–72
part-time jobs, 158–69
family business, 163–64
"on-your-own" experience, 164–65
sales, 168–69

setting a goal, 162
success steps for, 166
volunteer work, 165–66
salary discrimination, 157–58
setting specific hours, 170
tax deductions, 171–73
Workmen's Compensation, 180, 217–18
Work-study programs, 35, 125–26
Written work, copyrights for, 103, 104–5

Xerox Corporation, 130, 263

Yellow Pages, 66, 70, 186, 200
Young person, 121–36
establishment and, 123–32
building portable skills, 126–27
company sabbaticals, 130–31
downswing jobs, 131–32
education, 122–23, 125–26
"foot-in-doormanship," 124–25, 134, 135
independent business, 127–30
volunteer work, 124
in journalism, 132–36
You Ought to Patent That (Jones), 105

Zagoria, Sam, 12, 122
Zaro's House of Africa, 84–85